ATLAS OF
MIGRATION
IN EUROPE

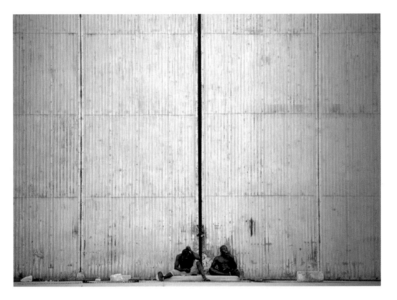

A critical geography
of migration policies

migreurop__   NewInternationalist

Atlas of Migration in Europe: A Critical Geography of Migration Policies

Published in the UK by New Internationalist Publications Ltd
55 Rectory Road
Oxford OX4 1BW, UK
newint.org

Co-ordinated by Olivier Clochard for Migreurop with the collaboration of Emmanuel Blanchard, Violaine Carrère, Alain Morice, Pierre-Arnaud Perrouty and Claire Rodier

Cartography: Olivier Clochard, Thomas Honoré and Nicolas Lambert, with the collaboration of Françoise Bahoken, Agathe Etienne, Frédéric Piantoni, David Lagarde, Nicolas Pernet, Julie Person and Laurence Pillant.

Translation of texts: Katie Booth and Alexandra Pomeon O'Neill. Migreurop is grateful for the support of the European Programme for Integration and Migration (EPIM) in making the English translation of the Atlas possible.

Translation of maps: Jasper Cooper (Migreurop); Agathe Etienne; Olivier Clochard; Thomas Honoré; David Lagarde; Nicolas Lambert; Martin Marie (migration policy analyst, Statewatch, Migreurop); Alain Pierre; Eleanor Staniforth (Migreurop).

Migreurop would like to thank Barbara Harrell-Bond for her helpful editing of the Atlas of Migration in Europe.

Printed by PBtisk s.r.o., Czech Republic, who hold environmental accreditation ISO 14001.

FSC
FSC ACCREDITED

British Library Cataloguing-in-Publication Data.
A catalogue record for this book is available from the British Library.

Library of Congress Cataloging-in-Publication Data.
A catalog record for this book is available from the Library of Congress.

ISBN 978-1-78026-083-9

Contents

Demonstration demanding the closure of the detention
centre in Madrid, Spain, November 2010.
Photo: Olmo Calvo Rodríguez

Introduction

This second edition of the Atlas on asylum and immigration policies in the European Union cannot ignore the dramatic events that have taken place at its borders, on a daily basis, throughout 2012. Each year hundreds of migrants die, through drowning or exhaustion, stranded at sea on overcrowded and ill-equipped vessels. Migrants fleeing countries in crisis or at war are unable to use legal routes, as a result of tightened surveillance of European borders, especially to the south and east. International law is often applied restrictively, or not applied at all. The beginning of the 21st century, marked by the global economic crisis, has brought little hope of improvement: policy makers, lacking solutions, promote the militarization of borders and the reinforcement of controls. This hostile climate is illustrated by mass arrests of immigrants in the streets of Athens and Rabat, as well as declarations made by political leaders, across Europe and neighbouring States, on the "dangers" presented by immigration.

For the past 10 years, the Migreurop network has been closely following this tragic demonstration of the selfish approach of European States to the movement of migrants and has regularly alerted EU bodies to violations of migrants' human rights. The fieldwork on which this publication is based has enabled us to discover, measure and comprehend the factors that have marked European asylum and immigration policies since the 1980s. For example, increasing obstacles to obtaining "Schengen" visas from consulates; tightened controls at internal and external borders and their relocation to neighbouring countries, including Libya, Turkey and Ukraine; the creation of the European agency Frontex and the gradual increase in operations aimed at intercepting "illegal" migrants; the construction of walls, as in the Spanish enclaves of Ceuta and Melilla in northern Morocco and along the Evros River in the northeast of Greece; the multiplication of means of detaining migrants; the regular organization of "charter"

flights for deportations; and the marked reduction in the exercise of the right to asylum. All these processes create ever greater obstacles to legal immigration into EU territory.

The measures taken by European States to control migratory flows do not operate independently: they are linked by various mechanisms, with detention centres playing a pivotal role. Frontex, which co-ordinates surveillance operations at the EU's external borders and organizes joint flights for deportees (euphemistically referred to as "joint returns operations"), is also in charge of establishing links between various control units. The same applies to computer networks such as the Visa Information System (Vis), the Schengen Information System (Sis) and Eurodac.

Thus, in response to a supposed "migratory risk", the European border system follows an increasingly reticular pattern, with the establishment of surveillance measures all along the routes taken by potential migrants. These developments are causing the conventional border model to be called into question. The combination of various methods of control sometimes makes us forget this, while allowing the EU to drive forward its networking logic on a large scale.

This publication is structured around four main themes:

- Migration: globalized but impeded
- Controlling international migration: towards greater protectionism?
- Detention at the heart of asylum and immigration policies
- Impact on departure and transit areas

On each theme, the Atlas brings together texts, maps, charts, graphics and photographs in an attempt to change the way borders are traditionally represented, to contribute to an understanding of the displacement and externalization of controls, to reveal the infrastructure established to serve European migration policies and to illustrate the deployment of security measures around migration, based on observations in Europe and beyond.

LEGAL FRAMEWORK

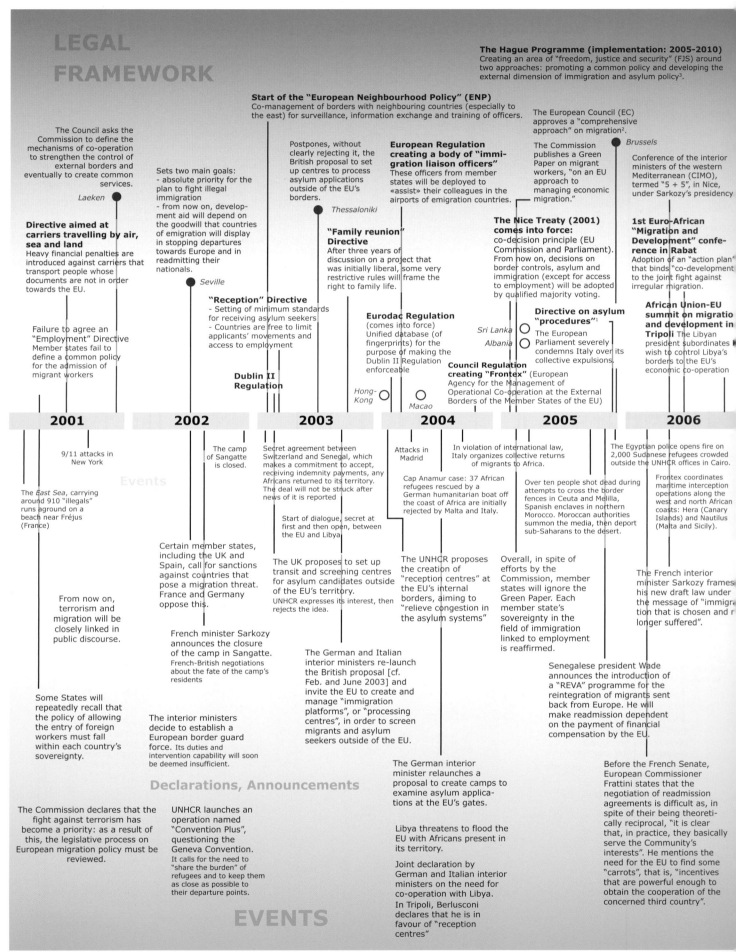

The Hague Programme (implementation: 2005-2010)
Creating an area of "freedom, justice and security" (FJS) around two approaches: promoting a common policy and developing the external dimension of immigration and asylum policy[3].

Start of the "European Neighbourhood Policy" (ENP)
Co-management of borders with neighbouring countries (especially to the east) for surveillance, information exchange and training of officers.

The European Council (EC) approves a "comprehensive approach" on migration[2].

Brussels

The Council asks the Commission to define the mechanisms of co-operation to strengthen the control of external borders and eventually to create common services.

Laeken ●

Postpones, without clearly rejecting it, the British proposal to set up centres to process asylum applications outside of the EU's borders. ●

Thessaloniki

European Regulation creating a body of "immigration liaison officers"
These officers from member states will be deployed to «assist» their colleagues in the airports of emigration countries. ┐

The Commission publishes a Green Paper on migrant workers, "on an EU approach to managing economic migration."

Conference of the interior ministers of the western Mediterranean (CIMO), termed "5 + 5", in Nice, under Sarkozy's presidency

Directive aimed at carriers travelling by air, sea and land
Heavy financial penalties are introduced against carriers that transport people whose documents are not in order towards the EU.

Sets two main goals:
- absolute priority for the plan to fight illegal immigration
- from now on, development aid will depend on the goodwill that countries of emigration will display in stopping departures towards Europe and in readmitting their nationals.
● *Seville*

"Family reunion" Directive
After three years of discussion on a project that was initially liberal, some very restrictive rules will frame the right to family life.

The Nice Treaty (2001) comes into force:
co-decision principle (EU Commission and Parliament). From now on, decisions on border controls, asylum and immigration (except for access to employment) will be adopted by qualified majority voting.

1st Euro-African "Migration and Development" conference in Rabat
Adoption of an "action plan" that binds "co-development to the joint fight against irregular migration.

Failure to agree an "Employment" Directive
Member states fail to define a common policy for the admission of migrant workers

"Reception" Directive
- Setting of minimum standards for receiving asylum seekers
- Countries are free to limit applicants' movements and access to employment

Eurodac Regulation
(comes into force)
Unified database (of fingerprints) for the purpose of making the Dublin II Regulation enforceable

Sri Lanka ○
Albania ○

Directive on asylum "procedures"[1]
The European Parliament severely condemns Italy over its collective expulsions.

African Union-EU summit on migratio and development in Tripoli The Libyan president subordinates wish to control Libya's borders to the EU's economic co-operation

Dublin II Regulation

Council Regulation creating "Frontex" (European Agency for the Management of Operational Co-operation at the External Borders of the Member States of the EU)

Hong-Kong ○   ○ *Macao*

2001 | 2002 | 2003 | 2004 | 2005 | 2006

Events

9/11 attacks in New York

The camp of Sangatte is closed.

Secret agreement between Switzerland and Senegal, which makes a commitment to accept, receiving indemnity payments, any Africans returned to its territory. The deal will not be struck after news of it is reported

Attacks in Madrid

In violation of international law, Italy organizes collective returns of migrants to Africa.

The Egyptian police opens fire on 2,000 Sudanese refugees crowded outside the UNHCR offices in Cairo.

The *East Sea*, carrying around 910 "illegals" runs aground on a beach near Fréjus (France)

Cap Anamur case: 37 African refugees rescued by a German humanitarian boat off the coast of Africa are initially rejected by Malta and Italy.

Over ten people shot dead during attempts to cross the border fences in Ceuta and Melilla, Spanish enclaves in northern Morocco. Moroccan authorities summon the media, then deport sub-Saharans to the desert.

Frontex coordinates maritime interception operations along the west and north African coasts: Hera (Canary Islands) and Nautilus (Malta and Sicily).

Start of dialogue, secret at first and then open, between the EU and Libya.

From now on, terrorism and migration will be closely linked in public discourse.

Certain member states, including the UK and Spain, call for sanctions against countries that pose a migration threat. France and Germany oppose this.

The UK proposes to set up transit and screening centres for asylum candidates outside of the EU's territory.
UNHCR expresses its interest, then rejects the idea.

The UNHCR proposes the creation of "reception centres" at the EU's internal borders, aiming to "relieve congestion in the asylum systems"

Overall, in spite of efforts by the Commission, member states will ignore the Green Paper. Each member state's sovereignty in the field of immigration linked to employment is reaffirmed.

The French interior minister Sarkozy frames his new draft law under the message of "immigra tion that is chosen and n longer suffered".

French minister Sarkozy announces the closure of the camp in Sangatte.
French-British negotiations about the fate of the camp's residents

The German and Italian interior ministers re-launch the British proposal [cf. Feb. and June 2003] and invite the EU to create and manage "immigration platforms", or "processing centres", in order to screen migrants and asylum seekers outside of the EU.

Senegalese president Wade announces the introduction of a "REVA" programme for the reintegration of migrants sent back from Europe. He will make readmission dependent on the payment of financial compensation by the EU.

Some States will repeatedly recall that the policy of allowing the entry of foreign workers must fall within each country's sovereignty.

The interior ministers decide to establish a European border guard force. Its duties and intervention capability will soon be deemed insufficient.

Declarations, Announcements

The German interior minister relaunches a proposal to create camps to examine asylum applications at the EU's gates.

Before the French Senate, European Commissioner Frattini states that the negotiation of readmission agreements is difficult as, in spite of their being theoretically reciprocal, "it is clear that, in practice, they basically serve the Community's interests". He mentions the need for the EU to find some "carrots", that is, "incentives that are powerful enough to obtain the cooperation of the concerned third country".

The Commission declares that the fight against terrorism has become a priority: as a result of this, the legislative process on European migration policy must be reviewed.

UNHCR launches an operation named "Convention Plus", questioning the Geneva Convention.
It calls for the need to "share the burden" of refugees and to keep them as close as possible to their departure points.

Libya threatens to flood the EU with Africans present in its territory.

Joint declaration by German and Italian interior ministers on the need for co-operation with Libya.
In Tripoli, Berlusconi declares that he is in favour of "reception centres"

EVENTS

---

1. (2005) States may detain applicants in special facilities. Asylum requests may not result in the right to reside in the country. Exceptional procedures are envisaged: rejection of manifestly unfounded applications, fast-track and priority procedures. Among the criteria for rejection, notions of "safe countries of origin", "first countries of asylum" and "safe third countries" are placed in the spotlight. The right to an effective appeal clashes with the fact that this does not suspend deportation.
2. (2005) Spain commits to exchange readmission agreements for the opening of its employment market with quotas for migrants from the concerned countries (Africa Plan 1). The EC approach is based on work in partnership with third countries, co-development and the fight against illegal immigration.
3. (2004) Issues related to security will be predominant. The principle that the issue of the immigration of workers falls within the competency of each member state is recalled.

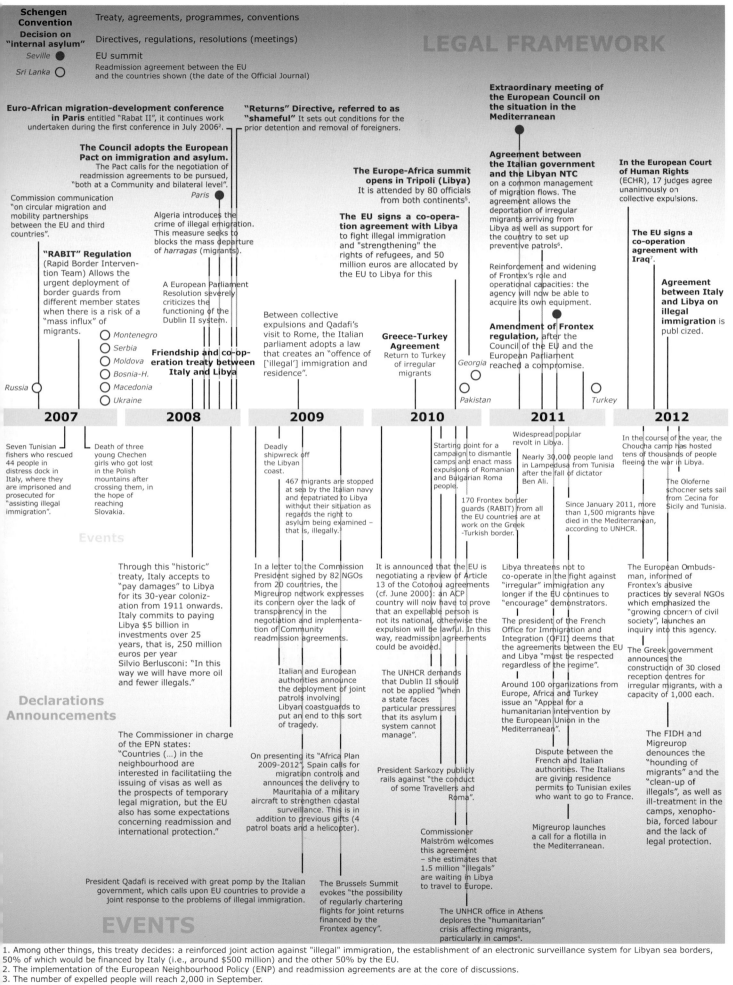

LEGEND:

Schengen Convention — Treaty, agreements, programmes, conventions

Decision on "internal asylum" — Directives, regulations, resolutions (meetings)

Seville ● — EU summit

Sri Lanka ○ — Readmission agreement between the EU and the countries shown (the date of the Official Journal)

LEGAL FRAMEWORK

Euro-African migration-development conference in Paris entitled "Rabat II", it continues work undertaken during the first conference in July 2006[2].

"Returns" Directive, referred to as "shameful" It sets out conditions for the prior detention and removal of foreigners.

Extraordinary meeting of the European Council on the situation in the Mediterranean

The Council adopts the European Pact on immigration and asylum. The Pact calls for the negotiation of readmission agreements to be pursued, "both at a Community and bilateral level".

Paris ●

Agreement between the Italian government and the Libyan NTC on a common management of migration flows. The agreement allows the deportation of irregular migrants arriving from Libya as well as support for the country to set up preventive patrols[6].

In the European Court of Human Rights (ECHR), 17 judges agree unanimously on collective expulsions.

Commission communication "on circular migration and mobility partnerships between the EU and third countries".

Algeria introduces the crime of illegal emigration. This measure seeks to blocks the mass departure of *harragas* (migrants).

The Europe-Africa summit opens in Tripoli (Libya) It is attended by 80 officials from both continents[5].

Reinforcement and widening of Frontex's role and operational capacities: the agency will now be able to acquire its own equipment.

The EU signs a co-operation agreement with Iraq[7].

"RABIT" Regulation (Rapid Border Intervention Team) Allows the urgent deployment of border guards from different member states when there is a risk of a "mass influx" of migrants.

A European Parliament Resolution severely criticizes the functioning of the Dublin II system.

The EU signs a co-operation agreement with Libya to fight illegal immigration and "strengthening" the rights of refugees, and 50 million euros are allocated by the EU to Libya for this

Amendment of Frontex regulation, after the Council of the EU and the European Parliament reached a compromise.

Agreement between Italy and Libya on illegal immigration is publicized.

○ Montenegro
○ Serbia
○ Moldova
○ Bosnia-H.
○ Macedonia
○ Ukraine

Friendship and co-operation treaty between Italy and Libya

Between collective expulsions and Qadafi's visit to Rome, the Italian parliament adopts a law that creates an "offence of ['illegal'] immigration and residence".

Greece-Turkey Agreement Return to Turkey of irregular migrants

Georgia ○

Russia ○

Pakistan ○

Turkey ○

2007 — 2008 — 2009 — 2010 — 2011 — 2012

EVENTS

Seven Tunisian fishers who rescued 44 people in distress dock in Italy, where they are imprisoned and prosecuted for "assisting illegal immigration".

Death of three young Chechen girls who got lost in the Polish mountains after crossing them, in the hope of reaching Slovakia.

Deadly shipwreck off the Libyan coast.

467 migrants are stopped at sea by the Italian navy and repatriated to Libya without their situation as regards the right to asylum being examined – that is, illegally.[3]

Starting point for a campaign to dismantle camps and enact mass expulsions of Romanian and Bulgarian Roma people.

170 Frontex border guards (RABIT) from all the EU countries are at work on the Greek-Turkish border.

Widespread popular revolt in Libya.

Nearly 30,000 people land in Lampedusa from Tunisia after the fall of dictator Ben Ali.

Since January 2011, more than 1,500 migrants have died in the Mediterranean, according to UNHCR.

In the course of the year, the Choucha camp has hosted tens of thousands of people fleeing the war in Libya.

The Oloferne schooner sets sail from Cecina for Sicily and Tunisia.

Declarations Announcements

Through this "historic" treaty, Italy accepts to "pay damages" to Libya for its 30-year colonization from 1911 onwards. Italy commits to paying Libya $5 billion in investments over 25 years, that is, 250 million euros per year. Silvio Berlusconi: "In this way we will have more oil and fewer illegals."

In a letter to the Commission President signed by 82 NGOs from 20 countries, the Migreurop network expresses its concern over the lack of transparency in the negotiation and implementation of Community readmission agreements.

It is announced that the EU is negotiating a review of Article 13 of the Cotonou agreements (cf. June 2000): an ACP country will now have to prove that an expellable person is not its national, otherwise the expulsion will be lawful. In this way, readmission agreements could be avoided.

Libya threatens not to co-operate in the fight against "irregular" immigration any longer if the EU continues to "encourage" demonstrators.

The European Ombudsman, informed of Frontex's abusive practices by several NGOs which emphasized the "growing concern of civil society", launches an inquiry into this agency.

The Commissioner in charge of the EPN states: "Countries (...) in the neighbourhood are interested in facilitatiing the issuing of visas as well as the prospects of temporary legal migration, but the EU also has some expectations concerning readmission and international protection."

Italian and European authorities announce the deployment of joint patrols involving Libyan coastguards to put an end to this sort of tragedy.

The UNHCR demands that Dublin II should not be applied "when a state faces particular pressures that its asylum system cannot manage".

The president of the French Office for Immigration and Integration (OFII) deems that the agreements between the EU and Libya "must be respected regardless of the regime".

Around 100 organizations from Europe, Africa and Turkey issue an "Appeal for a humanitarian intervention by the European Union in the Mediterranean".

The Greek government announces the construction of 30 closed reception centres for irregular migrants, with a capacity of 1,000 each.

On presenting its "Africa Plan 2009-2012", Spain calls for migration controls and announces the delivery to Mauritania of a military aircraft to strengthen coastal surveillance. This is in addition to previous gifts (4 patrol boats and a helicopter).

President Sarkozy publicly rails against "the conduct of some Travellers and Roma".

Dispute between the French and Italian authorities. The Italians are giving residence permits to Tunisian exiles who want to go to France.

The FIDH and Migreurop denounces the "hounding of migrants" and the "clean-up of illegals", as well as ill-treatment in the camps, xenophobia, forced labour and the lack of legal protection.

Commissioner Malström welcomes this agreement – she estimates that 1.5 million "illegals" are waiting in Libya to travel to Europe.

Migreurop launches a call for a flotilla in the Mediterranean.

President Qadafi is received with great pomp by the Italian government, which calls upon EU countries to provide a joint response to the problems of illegal immigration.

The Brussels Summit evokes "the possibility of regularly chartering flights for joint returns financed by the Frontex agency".

The UNHCR office in Athens deplores the "humanitarian" crisis affecting migrants, particularly in camps[4].

EVENTS

---

1. Among other things, this treaty decides: a reinforced joint action against "illegal" immigration, the establishment of an electronic surveillance system for Libyan sea borders, 50% of which would be financed by Italy (i.e., around $500 million) and the other 50% by the EU.
2. The implementation of the European Neighbourhood Policy (ENP) and readmission agreements are at the core of discussions.
3. The number of expelled people will reach 2,000 in September.
4. It notes that the Greek government claims it no longer controls the situation, neither on land, nor on the islands of the Aegean Sea.
5. Qadafi ups the stakes: he demands "at least five billion euros per year" from the EU to stop illegal immigration, otherwise "Libya will no longer act as Europe's border guard".
6. Italian decree-law extending the maximum length of detention to 18 months, in line with what is authorized by the "shameful directive".
7. Among other things, allows the readmission of Iraqis present illegally in EU and resolves to open negotiations for a readmission agreement applicable to Iraqis, third-country nationals and the stateless.

Migrants waiting for transfer from the camp on the
Italian island of Lampedusa, February 2012.
Photo: Sara Prestianni

Part 1

Migration: globalized but impeded

Linked to specific historical and largely regionalized routes, migration flows today are also a consequence and a symptom of unequal globalization. International media, telecommunication methods and the reduced costs of air travel have reduced distances and contributed to making the world smaller. But new barriers (physical, regulatory, police, military, etc.) have been erected in order to curtail the movements of today's "undesirables". In the context of globalization, based on differentials in living standards and rights between interconnected individuals and spaces ("North" and "South"), the capacity to migrate and choose one's place of residence appears powerfully subversive. Responding to a range of factors – from individual border-crossings to recommendations made by certain international organizations – this economic, social and legal segregation relies on militarized means and increasingly warlike violence.

Migrants in the world

In less than two decades, migration has become a major theme of international relations. As a result of the first Global Forum on Migration and Development, held in Brussels in July 2007, UN Member States decided to establish a "high-level dialogue" and to maintain this item on the General Assembly's permanent agenda. Their aim was to "foster co-operation and dialogue at the regional and global levels" and to "strengthen States' capacities [...] to design and implement migration policies and recommend practices that promote development".

Fear of migrants: a fatal spiral

Behind this conventional language, with its reference to hypothetical "development", there seems to hide an increasingly obsessive fear, held by rich and dominant countries, of invasion by hordes of poor people who will snatch away their prosperity. For those governing these countries, human migration, in contrast to the movement of goods and capital, is not a historical reality but a threatening problem. Across the world, border controls are tightened, to the point where any migrant is potentially "illegal". Henceforth, it is not only "our jobs" and "our social services" that are under attack, as in the common

xenophobic fantasy, but the very identity and security of the host country. Following the terrorist attacks in New York in September 2001, warlike terminology tends to amalgamate uncontrolled migrations, Islamist terrorism and various forms of criminality, including cross-border trafficking in human beings.

In June 2002, in Seville, Heads of State of the European Union (EU) made the fight against irregular immigration a priority, while underlining the desirability of "selective" immigration. Since then, Member States have opened and closed their doors as their national contexts dictate. Sometimes, the rigidity of public discourse conceals a genuine interest in the demographic, economic and social benefits brought by migrants. Thus, in the United States of America, President George W. Bush's last mandate was marked by vigorous demonstrations, including within his own party, in favour of a liberal policy towards introducing migrant labour in sectors such as agriculture and construction, while other citizens formed voluntary patrols to hunt down *Chicanos* along the Mexican border.

Throughout the world, migrants are subjected to an alternating push-pull mechanism, depending on utilitarian and

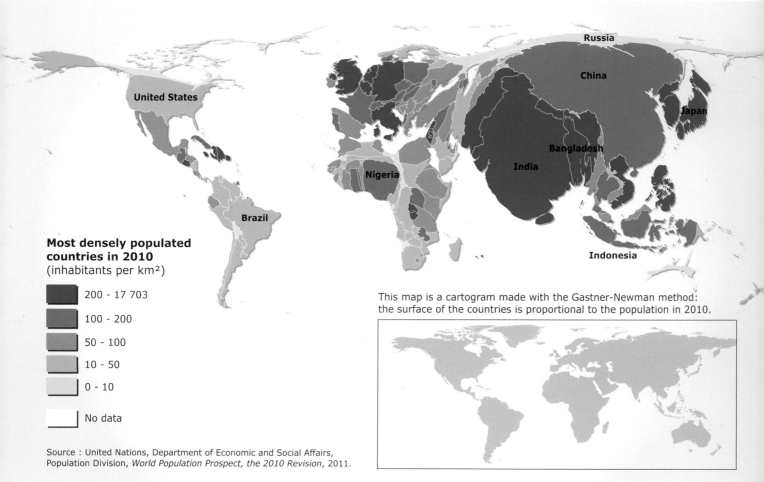

Most densely populated countries in 2010
(inhabitants per km²)

- 200 - 17 703
- 100 - 200
- 50 - 100
- 10 - 50
- 0 - 10
- No data

This map is a cartogram made with the Gastner-Newman method: the surface of the countries is proportional to the population in 2010.

Source : United Nations, Department of Economic and Social Affairs, Population Division, *World Population Prospect, the 2010 Revision*, 2011.

A third of the world's population lives in Asia

WHAT IS A MIGRANT?

There is no precise definition of the word "migrant", necessitating a cautious approach to statistics. The UN only defines the notion of "migrant worker". According to UNESCO, a migrant is a person who "leaves a country to settle in another where he or she creates social ties". Internal migration is not taken into account, despite the fact that such migration is significant in countries such as China, Brazil and the Democratic Republic of Congo (DRC), for example. The explosion of the Soviet Union created new categories of migrants.

Migration is a right recognized by various international documents, including the Universal Declaration of Human Rights of 1948, which states in Article 13 that every person is free to leave any country. However, this principle is permanently infringed, owing to States' concerns to exert sovereign rights over their borders, on entry and sometimes exit.

For a traveller to be defined as a "migrant", the combined factors of length of stay and exercising a remunerated activity in the host country are applied: children, tourists, students, even business people and young people from dominant countries working abroad in lieu of military service, are generally not considered to be "migrants". Likewise, the word reveals a significant asymmetry between rich and poor countries.

In the modern age, we can distinguish between three major types of migratory movements:

- *Historical pioneer fronts, aimed at colonizing territories deemed unexploited*, with, if necessary, the massacre, deportation or submission of local populations. Such was the case of the "New World", Australia, South Africa, various Soviet and Chinese territories, Palestine, etc. Immigrants are invited to settle and become full-fledged citizens. For the most part, this type of movement, which prolonged the Barbarian population of the planet, has come to an end;

- *Contemporary migration, driven by economic, environmental, family and/or protection factors*. These are the targets of restrictive policies introduced by prosperous countries, including the United States, the EU and the Gulf oil-producing countries. Seeking to attract workers corresponding to quantitative and qualitative needs, but reluctant to grant them the status of permanent citizens, host countries attempt to strictly condition migrants' right to residency to the validity of their employment contracts. Undocumented migrants who work on the black market are included in this contingent;

- *Massive displacements as a result of conflicts*. Dominant countries use any means to prevent such migrants from behaving like ordinary migrants or refugees. Kept at a distance in temporary camps which often become permanent, these "forced migrants" are confined to closed or semi-open areas, which are the object of substantial transfers of money and goods, (the price to be paid for the tranquillity of donor countries). International aid is coupled with a parallel economy based on trafficking and the exploitation of the most vulnerable, including children and women.

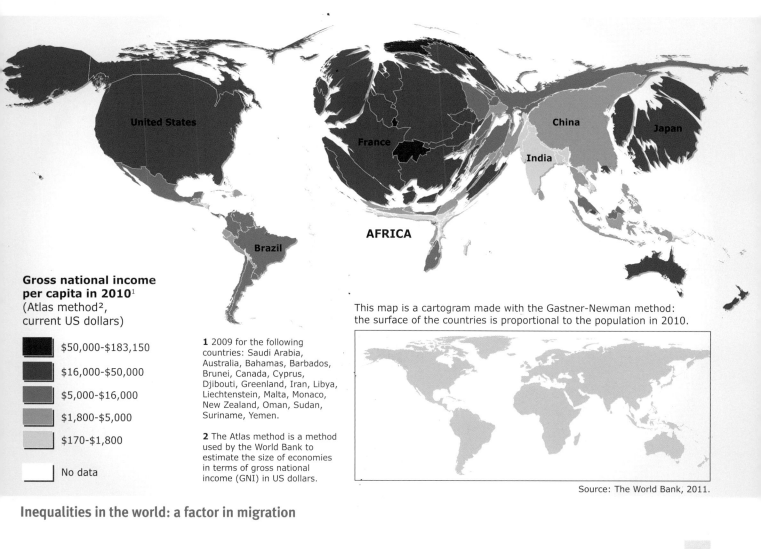

Gross national income per capita in 2010[1]
(Atlas method[2], current US dollars)

- $50,000-$183,150
- $16,000-$50,000
- $5,000-$16,000
- $1,800-$5,000
- $170-$1,800
- No data

1 2009 for the following countries: Saudi Arabia, Australia, Bahamas, Barbados, Brunei, Canada, Cyprus, Djibouti, Greenland, Iran, Libya, Liechtenstein, Malta, Monaco, New Zealand, Oman, Sudan, Suriname, Yemen.

2 The Atlas method is a method used by the World Bank to estimate the size of economies in terms of gross national income (GNI) in US dollars.

This map is a cartogram made with the Gastner-Newman method: the surface of the countries is proportional to the population in 2010.

Source: The World Bank, 2011.

Inequalities in the world: a factor in migration

shifting interests. Yet we also observe that human movements are increasingly framed by laws aimed at asserting the sovereignty of States, rather than at protecting individuals. In view of the diversity of the situations and interests at stake, developing a global and coherent approach to these issues remains wishful thinking. In practice, and taking into consideration the unequal relations between countries, calls for the co-ordinated management of migration policies lead to the creation of spaces for bilateral and multilateral haggling (which reinforces such inequalities), with migrants as bargaining chips. They also contribute to the ineffective and increasingly costly, in both financial and human terms, militarization of borders, with the support of dominant countries. In parallel, this warlike mechanism has placed the notion of "illegal migration" at the heart of political programmes, justifying an endless increase in the means used in the war against migrants.

The limits of the push-pull effect

According to a common approach, migratory flows are perceived as being driven upstream (the *push* effect) or drawn downstream (the *pull* effect).

On the one hand, countries with a high gross national income (GNI) have, by constructing barriers to entry, paradoxically reinforced their attractiveness. In certain sectors, preference for a flexible, available and cheap workforce pushes employers to recruit migrants, including undocumented migrants, who are expected to be docile. In dominated countries, these opportunities are well known, as are the possibilities (increasingly restrictive) of obtaining asylum. Migrants who are already present in a territory can act as vectors of this pull effect.

On the other hand, human movements are a reaction to any form of distress: sub-Saharan Africans prepared to face death in the desert or at sea, in order to escape their countries "without futures" and reach the doors to Europe; Central Americans embarking on perilous journeys across Mexico to reach the United States; these examples feed into images of desperate migrants seeking *El Dorado*. Wars, ethnic killings, famines and violations of human rights, the *de facto* legacy of the Cold War period and colonialism, in addition to economic deadlocks, provoke individual and collective departures. Examples include ex-Yugoslavia, Central and Eastern Africa, Iraq, Afghanistan, Ceylon, Haiti, Chechnya and Zimbabwe. In the spring of 2011, the uncertainties that followed the Tunisian revolution sparked migration towards Italy and France. Soon afterwards, Libya was the scene of the forced departure of several hundred thousand black Africans, formerly attracted to the

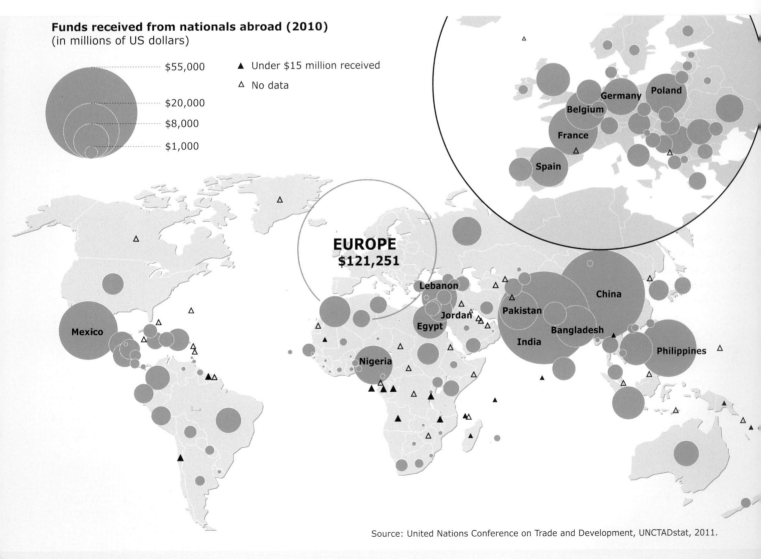

Funds received from nationals abroad (2010)
(in millions of US dollars)

$55,000
$20,000
$8,000
$1,000

▲ Under $15 million received
△ No data

Germany Poland
Belgium
France
Spain

EUROPE
$121,251

Lebanon
Jordan
Egypt
Nigeria

Pakistan
China
Bangladesh
India
Philippines

Mexico

Source: United Nations Conference on Trade and Development, UNCTADstat, 2011.

Remittances from residents overseas

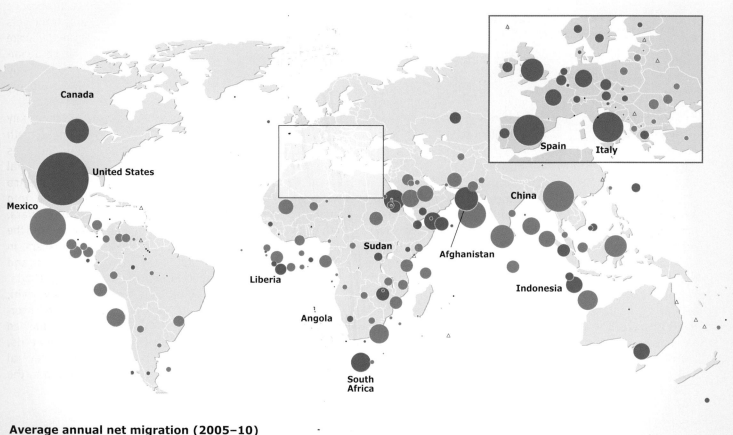

Average annual net migration (2005–10)
(annual number of immigrants minus emigrants, in thousands)

- 1,110
- 500
- 200
- 50

● Positive net migration

● Negative net migration

· Net migration close to zero

△ No data

Source : United Nations, Department of Economic and Social Affairs, *Population Division : International Migration 2009*.

Rich countries are not the only ones hosting migrants

country and suddenly driven out by the cruelties of the civil war. It should be noted that this exodus was directed towards neighbouring countries and not towards Europe.

Thus, a simple binary push-pull model hides the diversity of historical situations, causes and modalities of migration, and more generally the social and political dimensions which make it a more complex phenomenon than a mere reflection of the principle of supply and demand.

The pull effect of countries that require workers is undoubtedly a relevant factor of immigration, although it is not that simple. For example, in 2000, Germany offered 20,000 employment contracts in Information Technology to Indian nationals, but only 8,700 visas were issued and the majority were granted to Eastern Europe nationals. Yet the "misery in the world" is not itself sufficient to trigger the exile of populations to better-off countries. Accurate studies are required to explain why populations in comparable countries or groups are, at any given time, likely to emigrate or not. Numerous authoritarian States have, officially or unofficially, made the export of their citizens a resource for the import of currency, based on the transfer of money from emigrants. Examples include the Philippines, Morocco and some States or regions of Mexico and China.

According to UN data (which must be treated with caution), in 2007, out of 210 to 220 million international migrants

(i.e. approximately 3.3% of the world population), two-fifths headed towards an OECD country. Almost one half left for another poor or autocratic country, such as the Emirates or Singapore, where this workforce without rights represents up to a third of the total population. Furthermore, migratory projects can lead to the abuse of others (including the exploitation of children and pimping) and may end in disillusion (some highly qualified migrants end up begging and homeless in European capitals).

Migration in precarious conditions is increasing, resulting either in permanent wandering, or in settlement initially believed to be temporary but which becomes lasting, in particular in so-called "transit" countries, where nothing is done to provide shelter to migrants who find themselves trapped. Such is the case, for example, in Morocco, Turkey and Ukraine as "transit countries" towards Europe. Finally, migratory projects can be very flexible, depending on the obstacles confronted and the successes experienced. This is the case of the "adventurers" or "ants" who, alone or in networks, travel along migratory routes, adjusting stays and movements in response to prospects of productive and commercial activity. This variability contrasts with the strictness of visa and residency permit systems, which currently rule the planet.

Alain MORICE ◘

Exiles, refugees, displaced people, rejected applicants... Towards a world without asylum?

etween the 1930s and the 1960s, the exile of Spanish, Italian, Jewish, Hungarian and Russian refugees was the living illustration of barbarism and then of the Cold War. Compassion and solidarity were based on political commitments and intellectual certainties, confirmed by contact with the suffering of exiles. Today, in the Middle East, traces remain in the unique, almost anachronistic Palestinian victim, embodied in the interminable camps, with their one and a half million residents and their martyrs (*shahid*), but without the figure of the resistance fighter (*fedayin*), diluted by the political sacrifices of the post-Cold War era.

At that time, in order to identify refugees, mainly from Europe and the Middle East, the moral, intellectual and political dimensions preceded any institutional approach and did not depend on it. In fact, the latter was a consequence of the former when, in the middle of the 20th century, at the international level, the status of refugees and the right to asylum were inscribed in the Geneva Convention, adopted in 1951. This was just a few years after the establishment of the United Nations Relief and Works Agency for Palestinian Refugees (UNRWA) in 1948 and the same year as the Office of the United Nations High Commissioner for Refugees (UNHCR) became operational.

Thereafter, while exile continued to be an experience of moral and material displacement for individuals, associated with the loss of a place, ties and belongings, its meaning to others (host societies, governments, international organizations) was affected by the vacuum of the end of the Cold War. Over the years, the situation of these "wanderers" became more uncertain and the international category of "refugee" was progressively assimilated to a status of right-holder, increasingly difficult to obtain and subject to a multiplicity of conditions and restrictions. The refugee became a burden ("the misery of the world..."), from which the noble pain of exile was detached.

The 1980s and 1990s saw "population displacements" on a massive scale and the establishment of camps in Africa: huge ethnicized and depersonalized crowds, collectively granted the status of refugee at border crossings[1], packed into immense makeshift camps, providing protection from war but spreading epidemics. At that time, political solidarity gave way to concerns aroused by televised scenes of the movement of masses in Africa and the Orient: individuals roaming, scared; anonymous "victims" perceived as undesirable surpluses. The period was marked by the internationalization of large

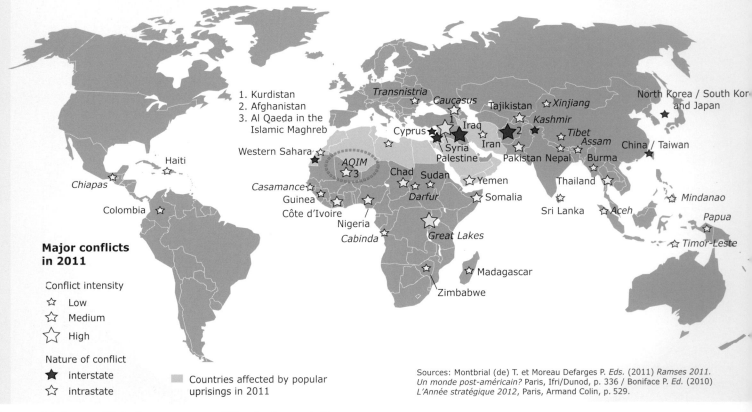

1. Kurdistan
2. Afghanistan
3. Al Qaeda in the Islamic Maghreb

Major conflicts in 2011

Conflict intensity
☆ Low
☆ Medium
☆ High

Nature of conflict
★ interstate
☆ intrastate

Countries affected by popular uprisings in 2011

Sources: Montbrial (de) T. et Moreau Defarges P. *Eds.* (2011) *Ramses 2011. Un monde post-américain?* Paris, Ifri/Dunod, p. 336 / Boniface P. *Ed.* (2010) *L'Année stratégique 2012*, Paris, Armand Colin, p. 529.

Major conflicts in 2011, year of the Arab revolutions

Asylum seekers

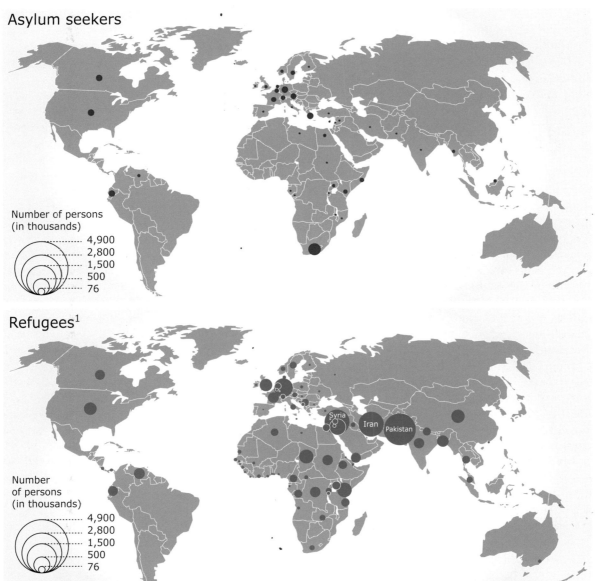

Number of persons
(in thousands)
- 4,900
- 2,800
- 1,500
- 500
- 76

Refugees[1]

Number
of persons
(in thousands)
- 4,900
- 2,800
- 1,500
- 500
- 76

1. Persons recognized as refugees according to the 1951 United Nations Convention and the 1967 New York Protocol, but also with regard to the 1969 Organization of African Unity Convention, as well as persons holding temporary protection status. Persons who find themselves outside their country of origin for reasons similar to those of refugees but who have not been able to access refugee status for practical reasons have also been taken into account.

Internally displaced people

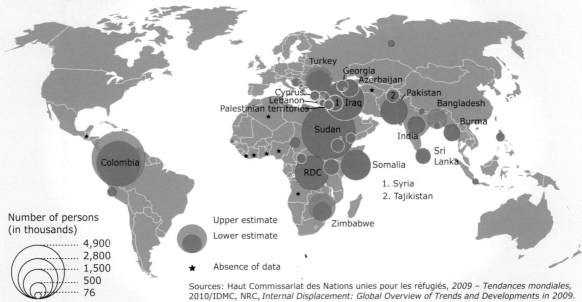

1. Syria
2. Tajikistan

Number of persons
(in thousands)
- 4,900
- 2,800
- 1,500
- 500
- 76

Upper estimate
Lower estimate

★ Absence of data

Sources: Haut Commissariat des Nations unies pour les réfugiés, *2009 – Tendances mondiales, 2010*/IDMC, NRC, *Internal Displacement: Global Overview of Trends and Developments in 2009.*

The majority of refugees live in developing countries

humanitarian NGOs and the proliferation of camps. In Africa, in most cases, conserving the status of refugee, following collective attribution at border crossings, meant accepting confinement in a camp. Thus, identification as a refugee was generally based not on a refugee card issued by the UNHCR or host State, but on a card issued by the World Food Programme (WFP), designating those entitled to the monthly or twice-weekly distribution of food rations, and with it a minimum recognition of humanity in a given time and place.

In the 2000s, Europe deconstructed what it had built in the 1950s (see below), thus revealing the arbitrariness that gave birth to universalism, and the strategic over-determination of choices consisting of speaking a universal language... or subsequently getting rid of it. At the same time, exiles experienced the opposite. Today they need this minimum recognition of common humanity, and for them the sustainable solution is this "common world", in the words of Hannah Arendt, designating the place where human beings are linked together.

Let us briefly summarize this European evolution, from the post-war years to today's war against migrants. Until the 1970s, there were numerous people who were entitled to apply for asylum owing to persecution, war or the risk of violence (potential "refugees" under the 1951 Convention), but who did not have recourse to this system, simply because it was not necessary. In Europe, migrants found recognition and a social position as migrant workers. With the economic crisis, with tensions surrounding identity and mounting nationalism in the face of globalization, and with reforms to laws on immigration, everything became more difficult for foreigners from countries in the South, in terms of employment, residency and freedom of movement. Progressively, South-North or even South-South international mobility was criminalized. Today, the universal reference to a common human identity, and no longer to a social identity as immigrant workers, is the basis of a right to international mobility: a *last resort*, so to speak, which affirms the right to flee, circulate or emigrate. This sees departure and ultimately exile as the most realistic strategy from the perspective of preserving life, if not necessarily the most desirable solution.

But, over a period of just a few years, the right to asylum was drastically reduced to almost nothing. At the beginning of the 1980s, 85% of asylum applications were accepted in Europe. By the mid-2000s more than 85% were rejected. This had the effect of discouraging potential applicants, who lost belief in European countries as host countries. On 20 June 2011, the United Nations High Commissioner for Refugees, António Guterres, declared: "The global dynamics of asylum are changing. Asylum claims in the industrialized world are much lower than a decade ago." The same day, the UNHCR announced that in 2010, "80% of the refugees in the world were hosted by developing countries". This signifies an imminent end to asylum policies, or at least, for the immediate future, a reduction in offers of asylum to numbers that are insignificant compared to the numbers in exile, with public gestures of a "humanitarian minimum" annexed to policies on deportation of undesirable aliens. The humanitarian banner henceforth explicitly serves policies on migration control. Indeed, on 11 March 2011, in Brussels, the then French President Nicolas Sarkozy, invoking the threat of a European invasion of migrants, proposed to his European counterparts that "humanitarian zones" should be created in North Africa, in order to "handle the issue of migratory flows peacefully". He thus added a compassionate tone to a policy of rejection of foreigners. The French President went on to adopt the posture of a UNHCR commissioner, evoking a project for camps for refugees, which would be "decent humanitarian zones, with schools for children" and "sanitary facilities", built "under the aegis of the UN, with financial and logistical contributions from Europe...".

The end of asylum is a brick wall, hit by those who have experienced persecution, threats, latent wars, diffuse or targeted violence (based on regional issues, gender, ethnicity, politics, etc.) and who are therefore entitled, under the Geneva Convention, to apply for and obtain asylum. The externalization of European asylum policy is the method used to implement this radical change without saying it: it transforms requests for recognition through asylum into the remote processing of undesirables. Since the end of the 1990s, its aim has been to block human migration beyond European borders, in Morocco, Senegal, Ukraine, Libya and many other "third" countries. The arbitrariness of this system represents a denial of the universal humanity which was once proclaimed a political principle. Thus, several European countries (including France) refuse to recognize the right to asylum of Iraqis exiled in Europe, but negotiate with countries in the Middle East (in return for financial aid and UNHCR collaboration) for them to recognize Iraqis as "refugees" and to host them. Buffer states, internal asylum, humanitarian and temporary, externalization: this is the vocabulary of a new processing language upset by the very idea of asylum. The rejection of refugees is one of the highly symbolic components of a larger system that calls into question freedom of movement of citizens, workers and their families from Southern countries. Such people are thereby reduced to a mass of undesirables.

In the 1990s, the issue of "internally displaced persons" (IDPs) appeared before the major international bodies, at the same time as the application of the Geneva Convention, the right to asylum and refugee status were being challenged. The number of IDPs worldwide registered in 2010 reached nearly 30 million, compared to 11 million refugees officially recognized by the UNHCR, to which must be added 4 million Palestinian refugees. After several years of negotiations, in 2006 the UNHCR became the agency in charge of the internally displaced. This did not entail the recognition of IDPs as rights-holders but constituted a mere extension of the UNHCR's mandate – the maintenance of camps and "emergency shelters" – to IDPs.

At the end of the 1990s, the concept of "internal flight or relocation" (also referred to as "internal asylum") appeared in discussions on European migration control policies, as European states and UN agencies discussed strategies for the externalization of asylum procedures. Once again, the idea was to keep asylum seekers outside European borders. The concept of internal asylum was an ideal solution because it doubly sidelines undesirables: by placing them in camps, and by maintaining them at a distance of several countries from the European borders, either in the East, or beyond the Mediterranean in North or West Africa.

Two further features affecting contemporary migration movements – especially South-North, though also South-South and, to some extent, East-West – are the increasing difficulties involved in crossing borders and the systematic use of camps. Camps are expanding and taking new forms: accommodation centres, detention centres and waiting and transit zones. Officially, the UNHCR has three options for dealing with refugees: 1) local integration; 2) resettlement in a third country; 3) repatriation. Camps are a fourth option, but are also a means of controlling migration on routes leading to Europe.

The end of the right to asylum is at the core of the criminalization of movement from one country to another, and at the strategic centre of the rejection of foreigners. It not only has a demographic impact, through the number of applications refused, but also an immediate symbolic effect through the refusal of the minimum of humanity to which each human being is entitled. This refusal applies to everyone: foreigners, police and inhabitants of host countries. This leads to the identification and sidelining of part of the world population, as "remains", "waste", "surplus", qualified merely as undesirables. It also leads to arbitrary insults and contempt, and eventually to the right to shoot, to injure or kill, which some

police feel entitled to exercise at borders. Applied to all those "without", the word *undesirable* refers to this vacuum, this roaming in time and in space. So, at the very moment when the world appears as our shared destiny, indifference becomes policy, criminalizing universal solidarity towards those who, formerly considered refugees, are today refused all rights.

Michel AGIER ○

---

1   According to the so-called *prima facie* procedure, which does not involve any prior individual checks but takes into account the displaced group. This procedure was added by the United Nations in 1967 to the initial and individualized criteria defining a "refugee" under the 1951 Geneva Convention.

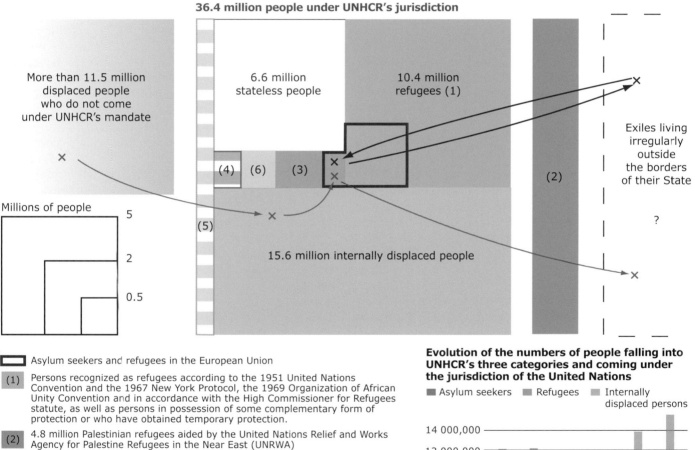

36.4 million people under UNHCR's jurisdiction

More than 11.5 million displaced people who do not come under UNHCR's mandate

6.6 million stateless people

10.4 million refugees (1)

Exiles living irregularly outside the borders of their State

Millions of people

(4) (6) (3)

(2)

?

(5)

15.6 million internally displaced people

Asylum seekers and refugees in the European Union

(1) Persons recognized as refugees according to the 1951 United Nations Convention and the 1967 New York Protocol, the 1969 Organization of African Unity Convention and in accordance with the High Commissioner for Refugees statute, as well as persons in possession of some complementary form of protection or who have obtained temporary protection.

(2) 4.8 million Palestinian refugees aided by the United Nations Relief and Works Agency for Palestine Refugees in the Near East (UNRWA)

(3) Asylum seekers   (4) Repatriated refugees

(5) Internally displaced returnees   (6) Others

Examples of people passing from one UNHCR category to another:

✕ Colombians, having been displaced in their country, emigrate towards the United States of America or Europe. Some claim asylum. When this is refused, they find themselves living 'irregularly' and risk being placed in detention.

✕ In Lampedusa, in 2011, sub-Saharan migrants fleeing the war in Libya and seeking to enter Italian territory as asylum seekers are sometimes pushed into irregularity.

Sources: United Nations High Commissioner for Refugees, 2009 – Global Trends, 2011, UNRWA.

Evolution of the numbers of people falling into UNHCR's three categories and coming under the jurisdiction of the United Nations

■ Asylum seekers   ■ Refugees   ■ Internally displaced persons

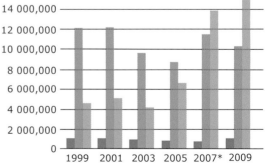

* Some methodological changes within UNHCR's statistics do not allow a complete comparison of the years 2007 and 2009 with preceding years.

Asylum seekers, refugees and displaced people in 2009: criteria established by the United Nations High Commissioner for Refugees (UNHCR)

The ecological crisis: an increasing factor in migration

Today we can no longer close our eyes to the deterioration of the environment, some of it irreversible. The news provides plenty of examples: climate change, the nuclear accident in Fukushima, earthquakes in Haiti, cyclones, damage caused by armed conflicts and large-scale infrastructure projects. These events directly affect living conditions, sometimes going as far as to endanger a population's very means of existence. They push ever-increasing numbers of people to take flight, representing the human face of this phenomenon.

Estimates of tens or even hundreds of millions of people affected by such displacement are to be treated with caution, but all recent studies agree on one point: the ecological crisis is an increasing factor in migration, which can no longer be ignored. The multiplication and intensification of these extreme hazards, the foreseeable nature of some catastrophes, as well as the role played by human activity in climate damage, are among the most alarming elements. In 2007, the Intergovernmental Panel on Climate Change (IPCC) established the link between such damage and human activity with more certainty than ever before.

Affected populations, who are often among the most vulnerable, respond to climate change and the deterioration of their environment in creative ways. They invent, adapt their behaviours and resist as best they can. For example, faced with the salinization of their arable land, the inhabitants of the Sundarbans region in Bangladesh created a substitute for their traditional activities of stock-breeding and rice-growing by installing shrimp ponds. But often such adaptation strategies are insufficient in the long term, or are simply not possible when a disaster area has become unfit for human life. In such cases, there is no choice but to leave the region to try one's luck elsewhere. The Maldives, as well as many Pacific islands, are going to be submerged, raising the issue of their future as nation-states. The same applies to Shishmaref Island in Alaska, which is subsiding as the permafrost thaws. Its inhabitants are already planning the rebuilding of their village on the mainland.

Western countries, despite having greater capacities of anticipation and reaction, are not spared ecological and climate catastrophes. This can be illustrated by the difficulties of the United States in coping with the emergency situation in New Orleans after Hurricane Katrina. In Europe, the Netherlands has for many years been exploring a means of stopping the rising sea level. According to the OECD, several mega-cities, including Kolkata and Dhaka, but also Miami and Shanghai, are exposed to the risk of flooding.

An absence of protection

Today, environmental damage and the inequalities that result from it are scarcely taken into consideration in studies or policies on migration. It was not until 1985 that a report issued by the United Nations Environment Programme (UNEP) proposed a definition of "environmental refugees" (see box below). Several typologies were presented to determine the different forms of forced displacement generated by environmental deterioration. These can be very diverse, explaining the heterogeneity and complexity of migration that ensues.

Environmental deterioration can be more or less diffuse and varies in intensity, depending on whether it is caused by gradual processes or by a one-off, sudden event. It can thus take different forms: monsoons, dry seasons, floods, etc. Damage may be temporary, but it can also be irremediable. Moreover, although environmental damage usually leads to internal migration, it can also immediately or in the long term provoke international migration. Finally, the extent to which such displacement is constrained needs examining. To what extent can the decision to leave be considered a choice? Which situations require recognition by and protection from the international community? How can environmental or climatic causes of displacement be distinguished from other interacting causes of migration?

Debates on these issues remain unresolved and those displaced receive no legal recognition or protection. Any support that is provided is usually limited to humanitarian assistance in emergency situations, which does not enable affected populations to rebuild their lives.

According to the Office of the United Nations High Commissioner for Refugees (UNHCR), most environmental migrants do not fall within its mandate, unless they can be considered as stateless persons. This may be the case for the inhabitants of small island-states, should their territory disappear completely. Indeed, the application of the Geneva Convention on refugees requires asylum seekers to have crossed a border, which is often not the case for these displaced people. Moreover, other criteria for the application of this instrument, in particular the definition of "refugee", are not currently interpreted to ensure effective protection for environmental migrants.

The Geneva Convention, like other existing legal instruments, thus appears ill-adapted to the situation of environmental migrants. But any reform of the Geneva Convention carries the risk, in the eyes of many, of threatening its very existence. In this context, what mechanisms should be implemented to guarantee the protection of these populations? Should a

ENVIRONMENTAL REFUGEES

Environmental refugees are "those people who have been forced to leave their traditional habitat, temporarily or permanently, because of a marked environmental disruption (natural and/or triggered by people) that jeopardized their existence and/or seriously affected the quality of their life". UNEP Report *Environmental Refugees*, El Hinnawi, 1985, Nairobi.

specific status for these environmental refugees be created? Should the mandate of the UNHCR be enlarged? Should regional protection mechanisms be envisaged? In any event, it will first be necessary to reach a consensus on the international legal terminology applicable to human mobility in the context of environmental deterioration and catastrophes.

Other major challenges

While it is essential to support adaptation strategies and to explore the possibility of establishing a protection mechanism, other major challenges must also be confronted.

Given the stakes in terms of equity and justice, it is necessary to explore mechanisms at the international level for providing reparation and compensation for the damage suffered. The conditions for hosting these displaced populations, and their status, remain to be determined. For example, the populations stricken by Hurricane Katrina, at first welcomed benevolently by the inhabitants of Houston, faced hostility from certain segments of the population as their stay lengthened. Furthermore, displaced populations often resettle in regions close to their place of origin, which are often subject to the same climatic problems. This can consequently increase pressure on natural resources in the host region, sometimes causing new departures or creating tensions. Finally, a massive influx towards cities raises challenges in terms of security, sanitation and precarious living conditions.

All of these issues must be considered.

An emerging realization

On 17 October 2009, the government of the Maldives organized its council of ministers underwater. A few weeks later, the initiative was followed by a council of ministers in Nepal taking place at an altitude of over 5,000 metres, in order to draw attention to the consequences of global warming in the Himalayas... These calls for help are beginning to be heard and the debate is now open within international bodies: the United Nations is working on these issues, which are also being raised within the European Union (EU). At the end of 2009, the UNHCR recognized that there may be a need for new legal instruments, while the European Parliament adopted a resolution that explicitly made reference to the necessity of setting up a protection mechanism[1]. At the beginning of 2011, the European Parliament's Committee on Foreign Affairs presented a report which set forth several proposals aimed at improving responses to this type of displacement[2]. The text was discussed in plenary in April 2011.

Several civil society organizations have also attempted to put the issue on the agenda. In France, a group of French academics, acting independently, produced a draft of what could be a future convention on the protection of environmentally displaced populations.

Awareness of the challenges posed by environmental and climate migration is thus slowly increasing but the consequences of such forced displacement remain for the most part ill-identified. Much remains to be done to ensure that debates on these issues lead to the adoption of concrete measures, especially since it will first be necessary to reconsider our own models of development.

Chloé ALTWEGG BOUSSAC ◘

1 European Parliament Resolution of 25/11/2009 on the EU strategy for the Copenhagen Conference on Climate Change.
2 Report of the European Parliament Committee on Foreign Affairs, 22 March 2011, on migration flows arising from instability.

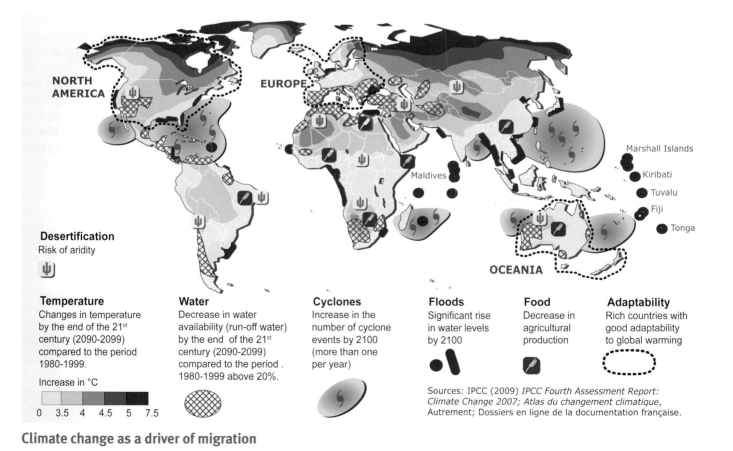

Desertification
Risk of aridity

Temperature	Water	Cyclones	Floods	Food	Adaptability
Changes in temperature by the end of the 21st century (2090-2099) compared to the period 1980-1999.	Decrease in water availability (run-off water) by the end of the 21st century (2090-2099) compared to the period 1980-1999 above 20%.	Increase in the number of cyclone events by 2100 (more than one per year)	Significant rise in water levels by 2100	Decrease in agricultural production	Rich countries with good adaptability to global warming
Increase in °C					

0 3.5 4 4.5 5 7.5

Sources: IPCC (2009) *IPCC Fourth Assessment Report: Climate Change 2007; Atlas du changement climatique*, Autrement; Dossiers en ligne de la documentation française.

Climate change as a driver of migration

TEMPTING WALLS

At the beginning of 2011, Greece announced the construction of a wall along its border with Turkey. In the United States, in the run-up to the 2012 presidential elections, debate focused on immigration and borders. No border is spared: following the election promise to build a reinforced barrier at the southern border with Mexico, the possibility of building a selective barrier along the Canadian border is now openly being mentioned. The number of walls has tripled since the end of the Cold War. Today, they scar 48 borders and stretch over 30,000 kilometres, taking the form of fences with stone foundations, topped with barbed wire, covered in sensors, punctuated with watch posts, infrared cameras, lighting devices, the whole coupled with a genuine legal arsenal (criminalization of emigration, restrictions on the right to asylum, multiplication of increasingly complex residence permits and visas, etc.).

However, a study of these walls leads to two key conclusions. On the one hand, walls have a disastrous impact on the environment: they alter ecosystems (as noted in 2003 by a team from the University of Beijing, who discovered that the flora on either side of the Great Wall underwent genetically differentiated evolutions); they have an impact on animal migration (for example, the migration of bears and leopards in Kashmir); and

they endanger biodiversity (as demonstrated in an American study published by Diversity and Distributions in 2011).

On the other hand, and most importantly, history demonstrates that, in general, walls do not stop people crossing. Examples include the Roman Fossatum Africae in North Africa, the Great Wall in China, the Maginot Line, the wall between the United States and Mexico and the wall between Israel and Egypt. Rather, they reveal the weakness of a State distressed by an imagined threat (irregular migrants, traffickers, possibly terrorists). Worse, unable to stem flows, they divert them. The impact on migrants is thus immediate: they become more vulnerable to smugglers and to the hazards of less familiar ground, all the more so since walls stimulate underground economies and parallel flows, making them more difficult to control. Sometimes they achieve the opposite effect to that intended, as in the United States where the wall with Mexico has made irregular workers more likely to settle for the long term, whereas previously many went back and forth following a seasonal migration cycle. Under the cloak of security, walls are built to reassure public opinion and keep undesirables outside a territory that is proclaimed as a sanctuary.

Élisabeth Vallet

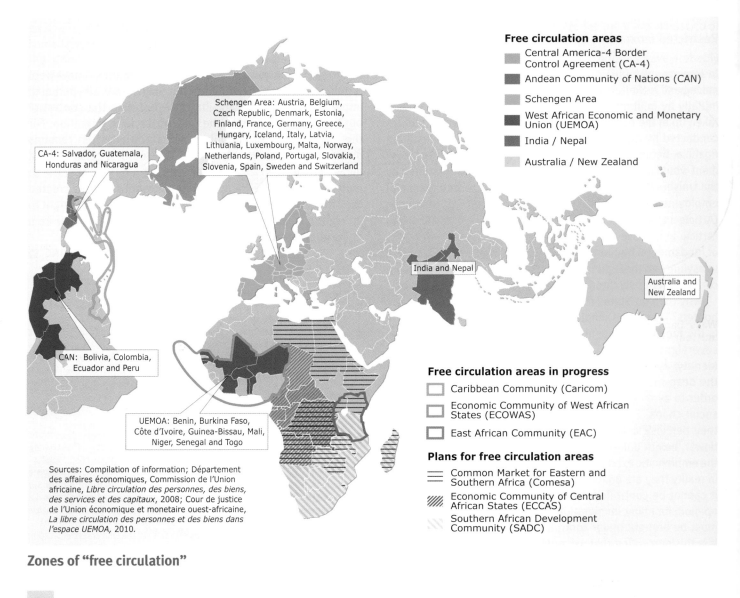

CA-4: Salvador, Guatemala, Honduras and Nicaragua

Schengen Area: Austria, Belgium, Czech Republic, Denmark, Estonia, Finland, France, Germany, Greece, Hungary, Iceland, Italy, Latvia, Lithuania, Luxembourg, Malta, Norway, Netherlands, Poland, Portugal, Slovakia, Slovenia, Spain, Sweden and Switzerland

India and Nepal

Australia and New Zealand

CAN: Bolivia, Colombia, Ecuador and Peru

UEMOA: Benin, Burkina Faso, Côte d'Ivoire, Guinea-Bissau, Mali, Niger, Senegal and Togo

Free circulation areas
- Central America-4 Border Control Agreement (CA-4)
- Andean Community of Nations (CAN)
- Schengen Area
- West African Economic and Monetary Union (UEMOA)
- India / Nepal
- Australia / New Zealand

Free circulation areas in progress
- Caribbean Community (Caricom)
- Economic Community of West African States (ECOWAS)
- East African Community (EAC)

Plans for free circulation areas
- Common Market for Eastern and Southern Africa (Comesa)
- Economic Community of Central African States (ECCAS)
- Southern African Development Community (SADC)

Sources: Compilation of information; Département des affaires économiques, Commission de l'Union africaine, *Libre circulation des personnes, des biens, des services et des capitaux*, 2008; Cour de justice de l'Union économique et monetaire ouest-africaine, *La libre circulation des personnes et des biens dans l'espace UEMOA*, 2010.

Zones of "free circulation"

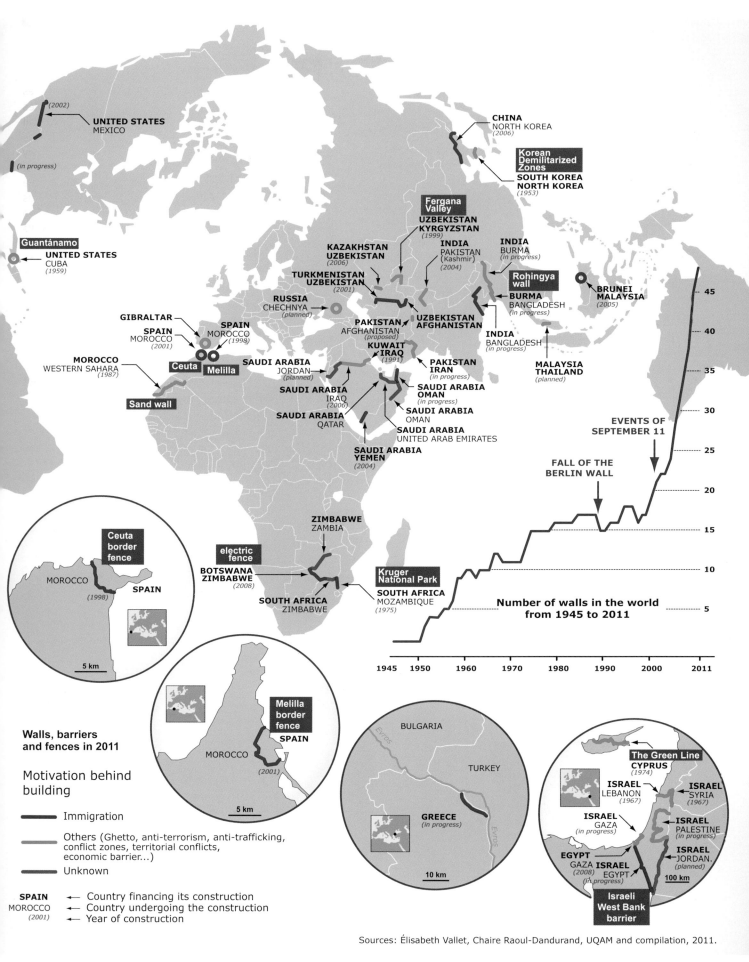

(2002)

UNITED STATES
MEXICO

(in progress)

Guantánamo
UNITED STATES
CUBA
(1959)

CHINA
NORTH KOREA
(2006)

Korean Demilitarized Zones
SOUTH KOREA
NORTH KOREA
(1953)

Fergana Valley
UZBEKISTAN
KYRGYZSTAN
(1999)

INDIA
PAKISTAN
(Kashmir)
(2004)

INDIA
BURMA
(in progress)

KAZAKHSTAN
UZBEKISTAN
(2006)

TURKMENISTAN
UZBEKISTAN
(2001)

RUSSIA
CHECHNYA
(planned)

PAKISTAN
AFGHANISTAN
(proposed)

UZBEKISTAN
AFGHANISTAN

Rohingya wall
BURMA
BANGLADESH
(in progress)

INDIA
BANGLADESH
(in progress)

BRUNEI
MALAYSIA
(2005)

GIBRALTAR

SPAIN
MOROCCO
(2001)

SPAIN
MOROCCO
(1998)

MOROCCO
WESTERN SAHARA
(1987)

Ceuta   **Melilla**

Sand wall

KUWAIT
IRAQ
(1991)

SAUDI ARABIA
JORDAN
(planned)

SAUDI ARABIA
IRAQ
(2006)

SAUDI ARABIA
QATAR

SAUDI ARABIA
YEMEN
(2004)

PAKISTAN
IRAN
(in progress)

SAUDI ARABIA
OMAN
(in progress)

SAUDI ARABIA
OMAN

SAUDI ARABIA
UNITED ARAB EMIRATES

MALAYSIA
THAILAND
(planned)

45
40
35
30
25

EVENTS OF SEPTEMBER 11

FALL OF THE BERLIN WALL

20
15

ZIMBABWE
ZAMBIA

electric fence
BOTSWANA
ZIMBABWE
(2008)

SOUTH AFRICA
ZIMBABWE

Kruger National Park
SOUTH AFRICA
MOZAMBIQUE
(1975)

10

Number of walls in the world from 1945 to 2011

5

1945 1950   1960   1970   1980   1990   2000   2011

Ceuta border fence
MOROCCO
SPAIN
(1998)

5 km

Melilla border fence
MOROCCO
SPAIN
(2001)

5 km

Walls, barriers and fences in 2011

Motivation behind building

━━━ Immigration

━━━ Others (Ghetto, anti-terrorism, anti-trafficking, conflict zones, territorial conflicts, economic barrier...)

━━━ Unknown

SPAIN ← Country financing its construction
MOROCCO ← Country undergoing the construction
(2001) ← Year of construction

BULGARIA
Evros
TURKEY
GREECE
(in progress)
Evros

10 km

The Green Line
CYPRUS
(1974)

ISRAEL
LEBANON
(1967)

ISRAEL
SYRIA
(1967)

ISRAEL
GAZA
(in progress)

ISRAEL
PALESTINE
(in progress)

ISRAEL
JORDAN.
(planned)

EGYPT
GAZA
(2008)

ISRAEL
EGYPT
(in progress)

100 km

Israeli West Bank barrier

Sources: Élisabeth Vallet, Chaire Raoul-Dandurand, UQAM and compilation, 2011.

More and more walls in a "world of open borders"

Unaccompanied migrant children in Europe

According to the United Nations Committee on the Rights of the Child, unaccompanied minors who arrive in the European Union, mainly from Asia and North and West Africa, are children temporarily or permanently deprived of their family environment. As such, they are entitled to special protection and assistance from the State where they find themselves[1].

In most European States, such populations are dealt with under laws on migration and asylum, rather than child protection laws. Under European law, there has been little attention paid to this specific population: only one legal instrument (and that not binding) deals specifically with this group (a resolution of the Council adopted on 26 June 1997). Other directives and regulations merely adapt to unaccompanied minors the restrictive standards that apply to asylum seekers and adult migrants. Recently, the Action Plan on Unaccompanied Minors (2010-2014) adopted by the European Commission proposed a comprehensive strategy for the first time. It provides for the simultaneous application of preventive measures in countries of departure and protection measures in countries of arrival.

In the first part of this Action Plan, the Commission places the standards established by the United Nations Convention on the Rights of the Child "at the heart of any action concerning unaccompanied minors". The Commission outlines a common EU-wide approach to the migration of unaccompanied minors, which respects the rights of the child, in particular the principle of the child's best interests. With this declaration as a starting point, the Action Plan sets out three strands for action: prevention of this type of migration; regional protection programmes; reception and identification of durable solutions. The present analysis centres on prevention actions and the identification of durable solutions.

According to the Action Plan, the prevention of unsafe migration and trafficking of children is the first stage in "effectively deal[ing] with the issue of unaccompanied minors". The Plan sets out four main axes of intervention: first, tying the issue of migration of unaccompanied minors to development co-operation, to enable children "to grow up in their countries of origin with good prospects of personal development and decent standards of living". This worthy objective is difficult to achieve in practice: it would require not only the total revision of existing development co-operation policies but also putting an end to the imbalances in commercial and political relations between countries in the North and South. Neither European institutions nor Member States are ready to take such steps.

The second and third axes concern children themselves and those who are in contact with them: the Commission proposes implementing awareness-raising campaigns aimed

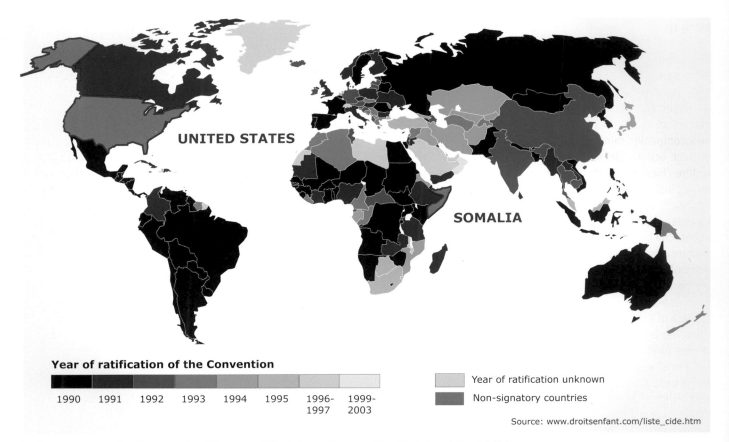

Year of ratification of the Convention

| 1990 | 1991 | 1992 | 1993 | 1994 | 1995 | 1996-1997 | 1999-2003 |

Year of ratification unknown

Non-signatory countries

Source: www.droitsenfant.com/liste_cide.htm

Only two countries have not ratified the UN Convention on the Rights of the Child

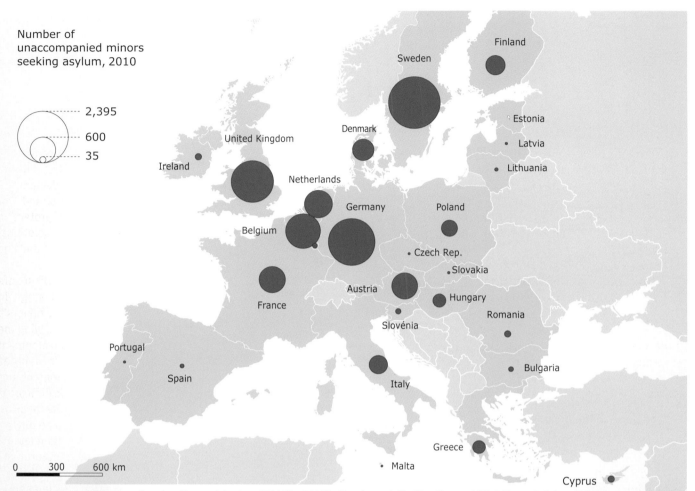

Number of
unaccompanied minors
seeking asylum, 2010

2,395
600
35

Sources: *Annual Report on Immigration and Asylum* (2010); BAMF –*Bundesamt für Migration und Flüchtlinge*, Belgium country assessment, *Separated Children in Europe Programme*, STC-UNHCR; Service des tutelles – Ministère fédéral de Justice; Agence Fedasif; Comisión de Derechos Humanos de Naciones Unidas, *Boletin Oficial de las Cortes Generales*; Comatito Minori Stranieri, Ministero del Lavoro, della Salutee della politiche sociali; *Home Office Statistical Bulletins*.

More than 10,000 unaccompanied minors seeking asylum

at improving identification and protection of potential victims of human trafficking and to inform children and families of the risks associated with irregular migration. Finally, the Plan proposes continuing to promote the development of child protection systems and funding projects aimed at protecting unaccompanied minors in their countries of origin.

Such actions aimed at preventing migration and protecting children have already been implemented in several countries of origin, including Morocco, sometimes with European support[2]. However, according to some experts, the results achieved by these projects are often very limited. While some positive impact can be observed in improvements to the daily lives of the children directly concerned, the preventive and security-based aims of the projects tend to pervert the potential benefits. Furthermore, the bald transfer of a European protection model into contexts in which children have different needs, as well as the lack of sufficiently qualified professionals, tends to limit the effectiveness of the measures set out in the Action Plan.

The final section of the Action Plan deals with "durable solutions" which should be based on an individual assessment of the best interests of the child. The three solutions proposed are: return and reintegration in the country of origin; granting legal status to unaccompanied minors, entitling them to reside permanently in the country of arrival; and resettlement in a third country.

The Action Plan expresses a preference for the first of these solutions, considering that, "in many cases, the best interest of the child is to be reunited with his/her family and to grow up in his/her own social and cultural environment". The text goes on to state that return is one of the options, that the best interests of the child must always be a primary consideration at the time of making a decision and that voluntary departure must be prioritized (which implies tolerance towards forced return). The Commission also makes reference to the "Return" Directive, adopted on 16 December 2008, in particular Article 10 on the return and removal of unaccompanied minors, specifying that measures aimed at complying with provisions applied under the Directive are eligible under the European Return Fund.

The preference accorded by the Commission to the return of unaccompanied minors as the best solution appears to contradict the principle of the best interests of the child, which is also proclaimed. An examination of existing statistics and studies reveals that policies on repatriation of unaccompanied minors have been ineffective, both in quantitative terms (the numbers of minors repatriated are very low compared to the numbers that remain, in conditions of varying adequacy) and qualitative terms. In respect of the latter, in addition to the violations of human rights which occur during most return procedures (in particular when family reunification does not

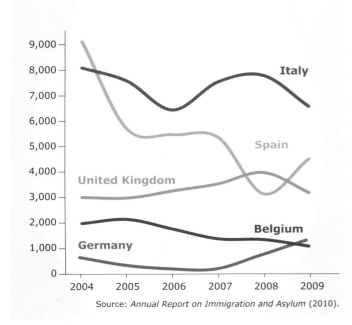

Source: *Annual Report on Immigration and Asylum* (2010).

Changes in the number of unaccompanied minors, 2004-09

take place), several studies have underlined that a significant percentage of minors who are returned to their countries of origin emigrate once again[3].

With the exception of asylum cases, the Commission leaves to national legislators the issue of granting durable legal status to enable unaccompanied minors "who cannot be returned" to reside in the host country. This provision confirms the priority accorded by the Commission to the solution of return. Furthermore, the document does not address the key question of prolonging a residency permit once a minor reaches the age of majority.

Finally, resettlement in a third country is briefly evaluated

as a possible option when there are no other durable solutions available.

In conclusion, the Action Plan 2010-2014 constitutes the European Union's first step towards the establishment of specific policies and legal measures governing the phenomenon of migration of unaccompanied minors. Fundamental aspects, including the conditions of access to territories and protection systems, as well as ensuring that the best interests of the child are taken into account, are sidelined. However, the Action Plan represents a step forward compared to pre-existing EU regulations: the limits of existing norms are recognized and, for the first time, the notion of a durable solution based on the best interests of the child is evoked. Nevertheless, improvements in protection measures appear to be conditional on the control and limitation of migratory flows, which is the real priority of EU Member States. This is particularly obvious in the Conclusions of the EU Council, adopted on 3 June 2010, which underline the importance of envisaging "practical measures to facilitate the return of the high number of unaccompanied minors who do not require international protection, while recognizing that the best interest for many of them may be their reunion with their families and development in their own social and cultural environment".

Daniel SENOVILLA HERNÁNDEZ ▣

---

1 General Comment no. 6 (2005), Treatment of unaccompanied and separated children outside their country of origin, UN Committee on the Rights of the Child, CRC/GC/2005/6, 1 September 2005, para. 39.

2 Examples include the SALEM project (Solidarité avec les enfants du Maroc) implemented by the IOM and financed by the Italian Ministry of Foreign Affairs, (in French) www.un.org.ma/IMG/pdf/OIM_5_fr.pdf; and the project "Pourquoi je veux émigrer?" ("Why do I want to emigrate?"), implemented by the Moroccan organization, Tanmia, with the support of the Italian Co-operation Agency and the United Nations Development Programme, see (in French) www.tanmia.ma/emigrer

3 See, for example, (in Italian) "I minori albanesi non accompagnati. Una ricerca coordinata fra Italia e Albania", Servizio Sociale Internazionale, sezione italiana e Istituto Psicoanalitico per la Ricerche Sociali, 2001.

Labour migration: communitizing precariousness

Labour immigration is conspicuously absent from the process which is supposed to lead to the establishment of an EU migration policy: it was absent at the beginning and, 13 years after the entry into force of the Treaty of Amsterdam in 1999 and the Summit (European Council) of Tampere which defined its application, no positive objectives have been agreed in this domain. From directives to regulations, it was intended that the then 12 Member States adopt common standards on the right to asylum, controlling the movement of persons at the borders and the integration of foreigners. But policies on the introduction and settlement of migrants for participation in national labour markets were removed from the scope of communitization and left to the discretion of each government. The word "labour" is absent from the Tampere "final conclusions", which simply recall the "need for consistent control of external borders" in order to "tackle illegal immigration at its source".

Two years later, the 2001 terrorist attacks in New York confirmed the EU's position. However, even before the Seville Council of 2002 gave absolute priority to the fight against illegal immigration, numerous other voices insisted that Europe needed to prepare itself to resume the importation of workers: a UN report estimated that the European economy would require 70 million foreigners in the first half of the century. At the same time, States remained cautious and as each in turn confronted the failure of policies on integration of immigrants and their families and were pushed to embark on increasingly xenophobic electoral programmes, each of their leaders sought to maintain control of their own migration flows at the point of entry.

Thus, following Tampere and marked by the setting of "minimum regulations for controlled immigration", communitization adopted a scissor movement. On the one hand, there was agreement to reinforce the most restrictive provisions that were most unfavourable to foreigners. The aims were drastically to limit asylum, to reinforce the hunting down of "illegal migrants" and to enjoin minorities not to draw attention to themselves. On the other hand, it was tacitly agreed that as they were common policies, labour immigration remained within the competence of national governments. This does not prevent States, in the name of the Schengen principles, from keeping each other under surveillance, or

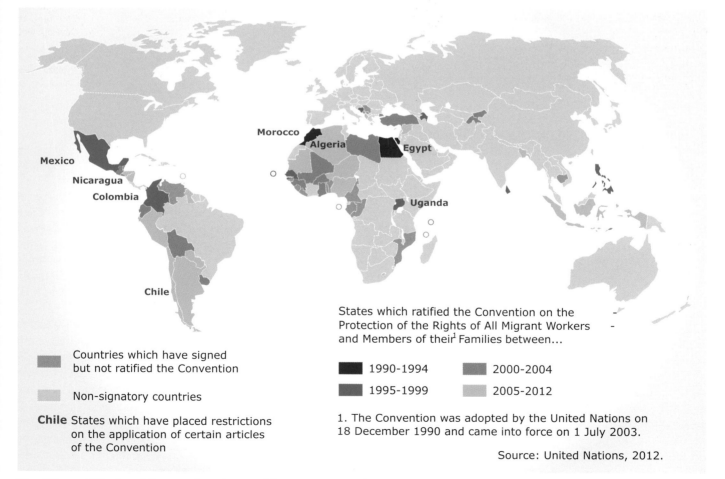

States which ratified the Convention on the Protection of the Rights of All Migrant Workers and Members of their[1] Families between...

Countries which have signed but not ratified the Convention

Non-signatory countries

Chile States which have placed restrictions on the application of certain articles of the Convention

- 1990-1994
- 1995-1999
- 2000-2004
- 2005-2012

1. The Convention was adopted by the United Nations on 18 December 1990 and came into force on 1 July 2003.

Source: United Nations, 2012.

The Migrant Workers' Convention: ignored by most countries

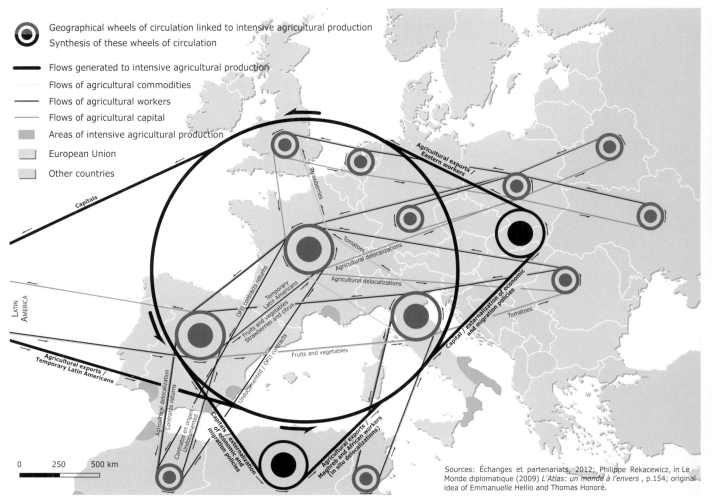

Geographical wheels of circulation linked to intensive agricultural production

Synthesis of these wheels of circulation

Flows generated to intensive agricultural production

Flows of agricultural commodities

Flows of agricultural workers

Flows of agricultural capital

Areas of intensive agricultural production

European Union

Other countries

Sources: Échanges et partenariats, 2012; Philippe Rekacewicz, in Le Monde diplomatique (2009) *L'Atlas: un monde à l'envers* , p.154; original idea of Emmanuelle Hellio and Thomas Honoré.

This map shows the financial flows and the circulation of workers and goods generated by areas of agricultural production that need a large workforce (fruits and vegetables in greenhouses, citrus for exportation). Increasing competition between international production areas forces agricultural firms to mobilize specific resources: large amounts of capital, natural resources (land, water, sun) and cheap labour. That is why such zones of production relocate to the south and east, reproducing in Europe the "Californian model" described in John Steinbeck's novel *The Grapes of Wrath* (1939). Growers staying in Europe use immigrant workers to remain competitive. Those foreign farmworkers are weakened by the lack of a residence permit ("undocumented workers"), or a special legal status with limited rights (OFII contracts, *contratos in origen*). These legal casualizations allow some areas to stand international competition by creating an obedient, flexible and cheap workforce. This gives producers the opportunity to enjoy an "*in situ* delocalization", according to an expression used by Emmanuel Terray in 1999. This map was drawn from specific cases (Andalusian greenhouses, southern Italy, French department of Bouches-du-Rhône, Morocco). It is not exhaustive but tries to give some benchmarks to think about the consequences of agricultural globalization. For this specific industry, it summarizes the deregulation and flexibilization of labour that shape the routes and the living conditions of foreign labourers. It announces, as Alain Morice predicted for other sectors, the end of the immigrant worker and the generalization of a "circular migrant workforce" whose installation is not permitted.

Seasonal workers within the gears of globalization

even reprimanding each other when it appears that, here or there, the EU external borders are porous to flows of people seeking work. This constant mutual suspicion echoes the common suspicion towards foreigners, suspected of wanting to "steal" jobs from nationals. It is reinforced by the decision, adopted in Amsterdam, to incorporate asylum issues into migration, thereby consolidating notions of "fake refugees" and "economic refugees", and providing ideological support to justify their expulsion from European territory.

In principle, the issue of labour migration, left out of community policy, remains a leitmotif in each country: the reasons for exile are diverse but, whether or not migrants are in a regular situation, they need to work. Considered undemanding, they make the fortune of some economic sectors, including agriculture, construction and services. Faced with a phenomenon that their governments do not control, the 27 Member States have different traditions, sensibilities and needs in relation to foreign workers. The role played by bilateral relations with third countries, which are sometimes still marked by a set of obligations inherited from colonial times, must also be taken into account. If we also consider that labour

needs are unpredictable and variable during periods of alternate growth and recession, we understand why these States fail to agree on a common line and simply define a set of obstacles to entry and residence within the Union. Such obstacles are designed to remind potential migrants, who are sometimes tolerated and can always be deported, of the precariousness of their situation. An opportunistic system is thus developed, in a context of permanent tension between EU countries and between the EU and emigration or so-called "transit" countries.

At the Hague Summit in November 2004, Member States asked the Commission to make proposals for an effective EU policy. In January 2005, it published a *Green Paper on an EU approach to managing economic migration*, intended to open a broad debate on the issue. The document is marked by efforts not to provoke negative reactions from any government. It contains a sort of catalogue of options in terms of selection, mobility, skills, status, etc. for foreign labour. It launches the proposal (which of course remains optional) of a "green card", modelled on the American green card. It puts emphasis on two significant restrictions: it asserts the legitimacy of the principle of "community preference" in the context of employment and emphasizes the ultimate sovereignty of each State.

In December 2005, the Commission published a *Policy Plan on Legal Migration, including admission procedures capable of responding promptly to fluctuating demands for migrant labour in the labour market.* The Plan recalls this principle of sovereignty, takes note of "important differences in the approaches to be followed and in the expected end result" and incidentally mentions the need to "reduce the informal economy, a clear 'pull factor' for illegal immigration, as well as a catalyst for exploitation".

Various common measures on immigration were subsequently proposed, the majority of which were still in draft form in 2012:

1. A general framework directive, the so-called "single permit" directive, defining the rights of foreign workers present in the official labour market and paving the way for expulsion in the event of lack or nullity of an employment contract. In parallel, a "sanctions directive" (effectively adopted in June 2009) provides for the repression of employers of "illegal immigrants". In fact it targets so-called "ethnic" employers.
2. A directive concerning highly qualified workers (the "European blue-card" directive, effectively adopted on 25 May 2009), which is characterized by restrictions on time and place.
3. A directive concerning seasonal workers. A "temporary"

document combining a residency and work permit, valid for several months each year, requires such migrants to retain their residency in their country of origin (as of June 2012, a draft dating back to July 2010 was still being considered).
4. A directive concerning persons transferred within their companies (submitted for debate on the same date as the "seasonal workers" directive), designed to facilitate temporary mobility within multinationals.
5. A directive concerning remunerated trainees.

In return, some fundamental rights of foreigners and the principle of equality of treatment with nationals are recalled. However, there are many exceptions in the 2005 Plan. It should also be noted that the EU has never ratified the 1990 International Convention on the Protection of the Rights of All Migrant Workers and Members of their Families.

Beyond the various specific categories, this illusion of a programme of communitization is marked by one common concern (the only one which receives unanimous support): limiting, as far as possible, the status of long-term resident (which is regulated by a 2003 directive) and institutionalizing the legal precariousness of migrants by deterring the slightest attempt to settle permanently. This is an illustration of the application of the principle of "circular migration", which has its origins in the same document and presupposes "partnerships" with third countries, without any clear benefit for the

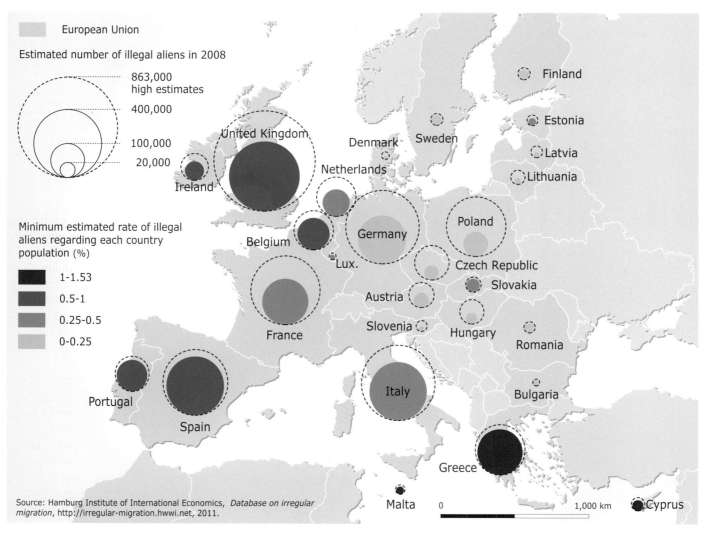

Source: Hamburg Institute of International Economics, *Database on irregular migration,* http://irregular-migration.hwwi.net, 2011.

Illegal aliens in Europe: counting the uncountable

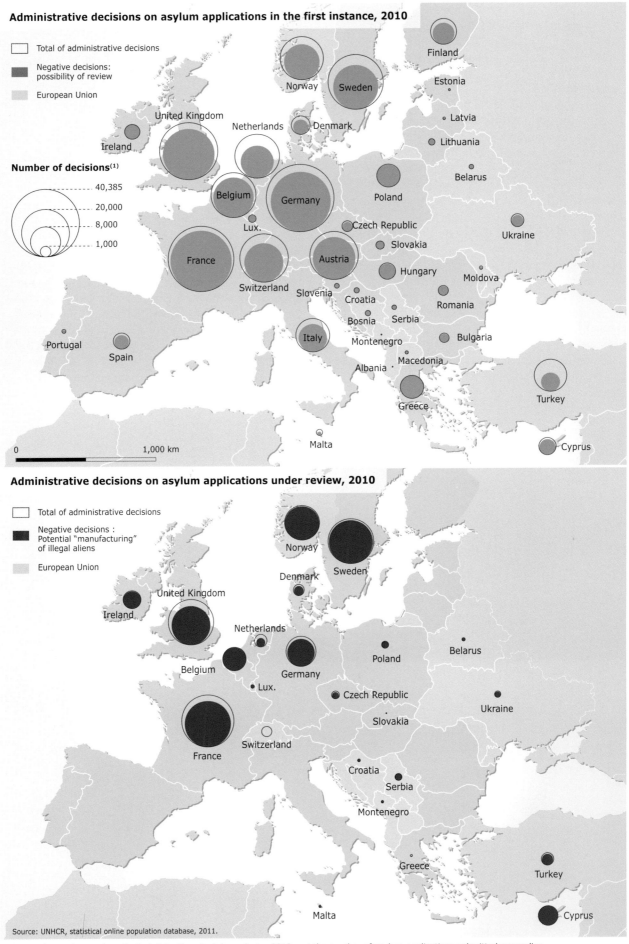

Administrative decisions on asylum applications in the first instance, 2010

Total of administrative decisions

Negative decisions:
possibility of review

European Union

Number of decisions[1]

40,385
20,000
8,000
1,000

Finland
Estonia
Norway   Sweden
Latvia
United Kingdom   Lithuania
Netherlands   Denmark
Ireland   Belarus
Belgium   Poland
Germany
Lux.   Czech Republic   Ukraine
France   Slovakia
Austria   Hungary
Switzerland   Moldova
Slovenia   Croatia   Romania
Bosnia   Serbia
Portugal   Montenegro   Bulgaria
Spain   Italy   Macedonia
Albania
Greece   Turkey
0   1,000 km   Malta   Cyprus

Administrative decisions on asylum applications under review, 2010

Total of administrative decisions

Negative decisions :
Potential "manufacturing"
of illegal aliens

European Union

Norway   Sweden
Denmark
Ireland   United Kingdom
Netherlands
Belgium   Belarus
Germany   Poland
Lux.
Czech Republic
Ukraine
Slovakia
France   Switzerland
Croatia
Serbia
Montenegro
Greece   Turkey
Malta   Cyprus

Source: UNHCR, statistical online population database, 2011.

[1] Data shows the number of **administrative decisions** during 2010, not the number of asylum applications submitted or pending

A restrictive interpetation of the Geneva Convention: "the illegal aliens factory"

latter. Logically, these provisions are coupled with commitments to "support" the "return" of migrants (or even to provoke them under the guise of a hypothetical voluntary initiative).

The overall community policy thus conceived and applied to various categories of migrant workers, crushes their projects, social existence and integration. In summary, it rejects migrant workers, while attracting them as and when necessary. The EU requires a simple workforce, without burdening itself with the people that form it, and places a Sword of Damocles above their heads. States proclaim in unison: "They should come when and where we want, with the skills and in the quantity we want, and for the time period that we have set, but they should not claim the right to stay!" Thus, the EU considers that it can, in a single gesture, resolve the difficult problems of integration of non-native populations, while promoting effective control of its borders.

This trend has begun to align the destiny of future workers with that of seasonal workers, undocumented or even undeclared migrants and more generally "flexible" employees, whose jobs are characterized by uncertainty, in full accordance with the decline in labour law protection. In practice, its implementation is unlikely but it carries with it the predictable prospect of increased human suffering. On the horizon is the return of the most primitive forms of piece work, which would signal the end of the migrant worker, and of the refugee in its wake.

Alain MORICE ▢

Guardia Civil patrol at the frontier of Melilla, Spain's
enclave in Morocco, in March 2012.
Photo: Sara Prestianni

Part 2

Controlling international migration: towards greater protectionism?

Paradoxically, the increase in international mobility over the last 20 years has been accompanied by multiplying controls on migration. While in certain parts of the world borders are blurred to facilitate trade (European Union, NAFTA, Mercosur, ECOWAS, etc.), elsewhere walls are erected to prevent the movement of people... or rather to channel such movement. Increased border surveillance has not demonstrated its effectiveness in contributing to the stated objective of deterring so-called illegal immigration. But it contributes to a certain globalized order, over which wealthy countries seek to retain control.

The Schengen system: highly problematic freedom of movement

"Henceforth, nearly 400 million Europeans will be able to fully enjoy one of the freedoms they most cherish: freedom of movement." With these words, pronounced on the eve of the integration of nine new Member States to the Schengen system in December 2007, José Barroso, President of the European Commission, probably expressed the shared aspiration of a majority of Europeans. But in the enlarged European Union, the same rules do not apply to everybody.

Varying degrees of mobility

In 1985, five of the six Member States of the European Economic Community (Germany, the Benelux countries and France) signed an agreement in Schengen aimed at enabling free movement of goods and persons across the internal borders of the signatory countries. It was a means for several states, acting as test cases, to come closer to the objective which would be fixed by the Single Act of 1986: every citizen of the future European Union (EU) should have the right to travel, work and live in any other Member State, without suffering discrimination on the basis of his or her nationality. The Schengen Convention of 1990 progressively applies these provisions to other EU States.

The gradual approach to establishing the Schengen system was supposed to respond to a problem faced by its instigators: how to abolish internal borders without losing control of the movement of non-European foreigners, all the while guaranteeing the "security" of the EU's external borders. It should be noted that of the Convention's 126 articles, only one deals with freedom of movement. The others are devoted to measures to be taken against the "security deficit", which is supposed to result from the opening of borders. The Convention provides for cases in which border controls can be re-established, the installation of a band of 20 kilometres along the "free" borders in which controls remain authorized, and the Schengen Information System (SIS), which is a vast computerized database maintaining data on wanted or other undesirable persons and stolen property. The obsessive nature of the fight against illegal immigration and terrorism since the Seville Summit of June 2002 and the establishment of the Dublin II Regulation have contributed to generalizing surveillance of the movements of non-EU

1. For each legislative measure relating to "Schengen" migration policy, Denmark, the United Kingdom and Ireland are permitted to choose whether or not to participate. Iceland, Norway and Switzerland, which are not members of the European Union, participate in the measures taken in this area.

European Union (EU) expansions

- 1957-1973
- 1981-1986
- 1995
- 2004-2007
- — External borders of the Schengen Area[1]
- ••• Occasional reinstatement of controls on internal borders in 2011
- Country recognized as a candidate for EU membership
- Country which has applied for membership, but is not yet recognized as a candidate by the EU
- Berlin • Large European airport

The "Schengenization" of Europe

Source: European Union homepage.

0   300   600 km

nationals and systematizing rules for granting a "Schengen visa" to non-residents.

The Schengen system was "communitized" by the Amsterdam Treaty in 1997 and has since been destined to apply to all EU territory, but although all new members of the EU are obliged to adhere to the so-called "Schengen experience", with the consequent burdens, full adhesion is not automatic and new arrivals must establish their credentials. It took almost four years for nine of the ten countries that benefited from EU enlargement in 2004 to be considered apt to have their internal border controls lifted, once they had been able to justify that their external border controls were sufficiently tight. In 2012, Bulgaria and Romania, the most recent entries to the EU after those of 2007, were still not considered secure enough to be fully integrated into the Schengen system.

The Schengen system, conceived to facilitate movement, in reality maintains thousands of intangible borders which create a hierarchy of internal mobility according to status (European citizen, foreign resident, visitor etc.) Controls in border areas and across the whole territory remain necessities in this misleading system of "free" movement: far from disappearing, police cooperation between EU Member States has become a major EU objective, with each State wary of the potential laxity of its neighbour.

A two-tiered approach to European citizenship: the Roma population

The fear of having to confront a massive displacement of new European citizens is shared by several European countries. It emerged in 1986 with the entry of Spain and Portugal, then in 2004 with the integration of eight new countries from Central and Eastern Europe. Today, systems have been put in place by national authorities that *de facto* maintain Roma people in vulnerable conditions and justify their expulsion. Thus, although most of them are Romanian or Bulgarian nationals, and therefore European citizens, they do not have the same rights or legal status. In nine EU countries, including France, it is very difficult for them to work legally due to administrative obstacles. Yet the resulting lack of resources is exploited by the authorities of these countries which issue removal orders, sometimes *en masse*, with the objective of driving them out of the territory. This is particularly the case in France. Since 30 July 2010, when former President Sarkozy delivered a speech in Grenoble announcing a vast campaign to dismantle illegal camps, targeted on the basis of their occupants' origin, Roma have been branded with two labels: that of the illegal immigrant who is deported to reassure public opinion, and that of a notoriously delinquent population that rebels against

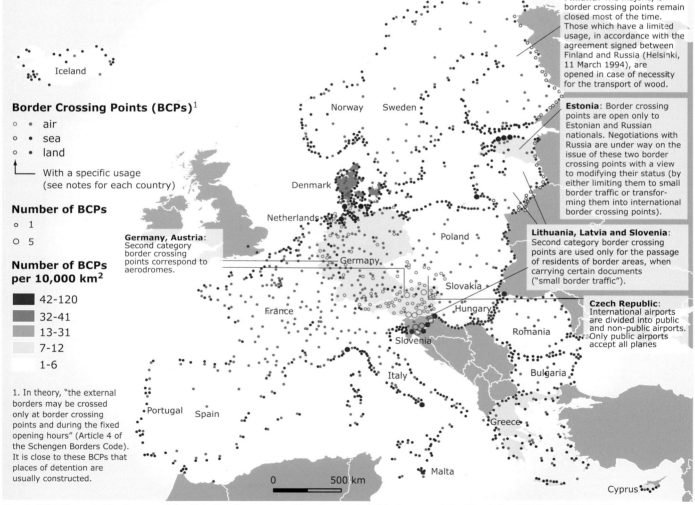

Source: Official Journal of the European Union (list of border crossing points referred to in Article 2, paragraph 8, of Regulation (EC) No. 562/2006 of the European Parliament and of the Council establishing a Community Code on the rules governing the movement of persons across borders (Schengen Borders Code), 28 December 2007.

The punctuation of the Schengen Area's external borders

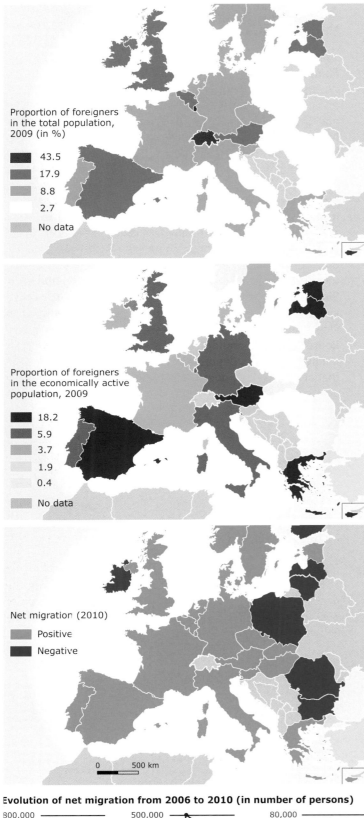

Evolution of net migration from 2006 to 2010 (in number of persons)

Spain

Italy

Ireland

Source: Eurostat, 2011.

The foreign population in Europe

integration.

Expressed for the first time at the highest level of State, this rejection of the Roma (in this case confusing migrants originating from Romania and Bulgaria and French "travellers"), while not new, gave an official ethnically motivated character to government action. The Grenoble speech sparked strong reactions from the public, a polemic between the European Commission and Paris, but also xenophobic actions and police hunts.

Today, Roma are treated as guinea pigs on whom authorities test new policies aimed at excluding undesirables, whether foreign or not. In France, several provisions of the Law on immigration, adopted on 16 June 2011, are aimed at enabling the administration to call into question an EU citizen's right to stay for a maximum of three months, if he or she becomes an "unreasonable burden on the social security system" or if he or she constitutes, by his or her behaviour, a "threat... to a fundamental interest of French society"[1]. In order to carry out forced returns, local authorities issue orders, which are often poorly reasoned and are based on a standard model that does not take individual circumstances into account. In numerous cases, the names of those concerned are filled in by hand on a standard document, sometimes with empty boxes. Under the Law on internal security, adopted on 14 March 2011, new public order offences are defined, including "aggressive begging", "abuse of the right to short-stay", and "illicit establishment of a group on property publicly or privately owned with a view to erecting dwellings, carrying serious threats to public hygiene, security or peace". We can therefore consider that these measures do not only target the estimated 15,000 to 20,000 Roma from Eastern Europe present on French territory.

Towards the end of the Schengen system?

Today, the surrender by Member States of their prerogatives over internal border controls in the Schengen Area, for the benefit of the community, is once again a central focus.

Chapter 2 of Section III of the Schengen Borders Code enables national authorities to reintroduce border controls, exceptionally and temporarily, in the case of a serious threat to public policy and internal security. This safeguard clause has been used on 26 occasions at the time of significant sporting events or meetings between heads of government. However, some Member States would like to extend the application of this provision to the arrival of significant numbers of third-country nationals on their territory, considering them as a threat to stability.

Following the "Arab Spring" of 2011, many Tunisians took to the sea in an attempt to reach Europe. Italy, having tried for several months to return these migrants, whom they considered undesirable, attempted to discharge this "burden" by granting a temporary residence permit on "humanitarian grounds". The permit was valid for three months and could be renewed, thus enabling its holder to travel in the Schengen Area. Strong tensions between France and Italy revealed the potential for discord in the Schengen zone. Indeed, France decided to reinstitute controls at the border between France and Italy in order

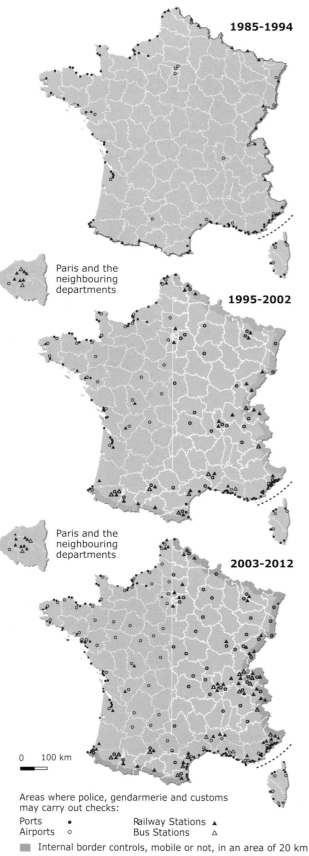

1985-1994

Paris and the
neighbouring
departments

1995-2002

Paris and the
neighbouring
departments

2003-2012

0   100 km

Areas where police, gendarmerie and customs
may carry out checks:

Ports   •   Railway Stations ▲
Airports   ○   Bus Stations   △

▨ Internal border controls, mobile or not, in an area of 20 km

Following the arrival of many Tunisians in spring 2011, the
Member States agreed at the Council for Justice and Home
Affairs (Brussels, 7 and 8 June 2012) the possibility to decide
unilaterally the temporary reintroduction of internal border
controls in exceptional circumstances.

Source: J.O no. 113, 16 May 2003 and no. 72, 25 March 1995.

**Since Schengen, border controls have always been
maintained, as the example of France shows**

to prevent these persons entering its territory, on the pretext of a readmission agreement signed by the two countries in 1997. An observation mission conducted by French NGOs in April 2011 revealed that the controls introduced by the French authorities were illegal, since there was no evidence of a threat to public order.

France thereby reignited the latent conflict between Brussels and several Member States prepared to call one of the bases of European integration into question. In June 2012, the Justice and Internal Affairs Council agreed on the principle of reforming Schengen to give Member States the possibility of temporarily reintroducing national border controls in cases of uncontrollable migratory pressures at one of their external borders. A compromise text has to be negotiated with the European Parliament, which in 2011 showed its anger at having been excluded from the process of evaluating and revising the Schengen Borders Code of 2006.

If this text is adopted, it will afford the possibility of temporarily re-establishing controls in two "limited" cases: first, that of "foreseeable events" such as sporting or political demonstrations; and second, that of "urgent situations", such as terrorist attacks. A third case is, however, foreseen, still limited in theory, which demonstrates that the Tunisian episode in 2011 will have highlighted the limits of the common space of "freedom, security and justice", laid down in Amsterdam in 1997. In this proposition, the Commission can, beyond the control of the European Parliament, "recommend to one or several Member States that they reintroduce controls on all their internal borders or on specific sections of them". This would be for a six-month duration, renewable up to two years, if public order or internal security is threatened (a sudden invasion of migrants is implied). The initiative has been approved by the French government.

This last clause has provoked a lively response from diverse groups of parliamentarians, some of whom consider that the Council has declared war on the European Parliament, while others judge that European interior ministers have "put the head of freedom of circulation on the block". Thus, as of September 2012, the question of internal borders within the Schengen Area was not yet settled.

Lola SCHULMANN and Alexandre LE CLÈVE ▣

---

1   French laws cited in this text are unofficial translations.

Implications of European visa policies

Since 2001, a European Regulation has set out the list of countries from which nationals require a visa to cross the external borders of EU Member States. Presented as the price to be paid for the free movement of citizens within the Schengen Area, the European visa policy is characterized by an administrative and security-based approach to border management, based on the notion of "migratory risk".

Increased European co-operation beyond borders

European consulates abroad have become the first point of control, before the border police and customs. In the context of strengthened border controls, the Schengen visa enables states to prevent the travel of foreign nationals labelled undesirable, by keeping them outside. A common consular instruction adopted in December 2002 provides that "local consular co-operation... [covers] the evaluation of migratory risk", adding that it is aimed at "detecting candidates for immigration who seek to enter and settle in the territory of contracting parties, under the cover of tourist, student, business and family visit visas". This strategy, intended to ensure the surveillance of potential travellers before their departure, is implemented in a climate of permanent suspicion. Consular services have the capacity to define criteria for the issuance of visas, which often vary from one place to another.

One of the conditions imposed on Eastern European countries, when they were candidates for membership of the European Union (EU) in 2004 and 2007, was to put an end to the practice of partially opening borders to nationals of neighbouring countries. Since 2003, Belarusian, Russian, Ukrainian and Moldovan nationals have required a visa to enter the EU. In 2007, the introduction of the Schengen visa scheme caused the number of entries of nationals from these countries to reduce dramatically. As an example, between 2007 and 2008, the number of Schengen visas granted to Belarusians decreased by 73% in Poland, by 52% in Lithuania and by 34% in Latvia.

The Community Code on Visas provides for the harmonization of procedures; in reality, in addition to the standard documents (forms, passport, letter of invitation), each consulate may require additional items. Nationals from Ukraine, for example, must provide more documents than

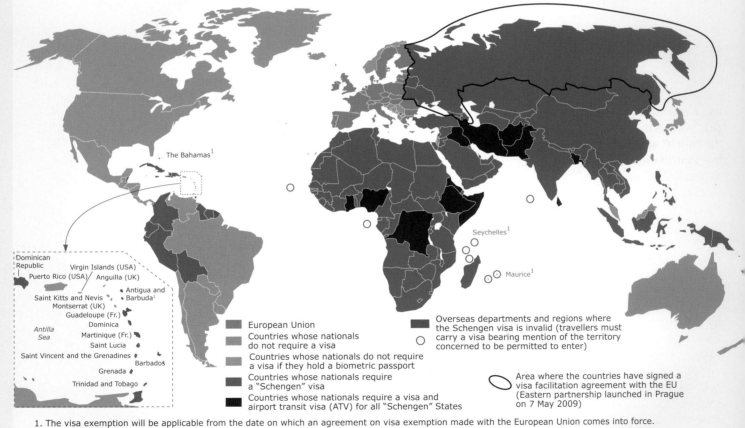

The Bahamas[1]

Seychelles[1]

Maurice[1]

Dominican Republic
Virgin Islands (USA)
Puerto Rico (USA)
Anguilla (UK)
Antigua and Barbuda[1]
Saint Kitts and Nevis
Montserrat (UK)
Guadeloupe (Fr.)
Antilla Sea
Dominica
Martinique (Fr.)
Saint Lucia
Saint Vincent and the Grenadines
Barbados
Grenada
Trinidad and Tobago

European Union
Countries whose nationals do not require a visa
Countries whose nationals do not require a visa if they hold a biometric passport
Countries whose nationals require a "Schengen" visa
Countries whose nationals require a visa and airport transit visa (ATV) for all "Schengen" States

Overseas departments and regions where the Schengen visa is invalid (travellers must carry a visa bearing mention of the territory concerned to be permitted to enter)

Area where the countries have signed a visa facilitation agreement with the EU (Eastern partnership launched in Prague on 7 May 2009)

1. The visa exemption will be applicable from the date on which an agreement on visa exemption made with the European Union comes into force.

Sources: Regulation (EC) no. 539/2001 of the Council of 15 March 2001 (version consolidated on 19 December 2009), Regulation (EC) no. 810/2009 of the European Parliament and of the Council on 13 July 2009 establishing a Community Code on visas, Decision 2007/340/EC of the Council of 19 April 2007 concerning the conclusion of an agreement intended to facilitate the granting of short-stay visas between the European Union and the Russian Federation.

European visa policies

those from Belarus, who wait half the time to get a Schengen visa. Administration fees paid at the time of the application add to the cost of obtaining a visa. While rates for short-term visas are set within the framework of the EU, those of long-term visas are set freely by each Member State. The impression of impunity prevailing in many consulates encourages fraud and corruption, increasing the cost of a visa application. Applicants are sometimes encouraged to purchase fake documents or to pay an intermediary. Paradoxically, while the fight against corruption is imposed as a requirement in negotiations on the liberalizing of visas, EU restrictions increase the need to resort to informal networks.

The consular system is particularly opaque. Until 2011, no grounds for the refusal of visas were given and applicants were not informed about ways of challenging consular decisions, leading to misunderstandings and a sense of arbitrariness among those whose applications were denied. Since the establishment of the Community Code on Visas, Member States are required to provide grounds for any refusal and to indicate legal remedies and time limits for appealing decisions.

Visa versus "migratory risk"

Visa exemptions are set within the framework of Schengen co-operation and apply to nationals from countries without any "migratory risk". The criteria are linked to the efforts made by a country to co-operate with the EU in the fight against irregular immigration. The category of countries enjoying Schengen visa exemptions contains a majority of "developed" countries and some countries said to be "emerging". Those without such exemptions include African countries, most of Asia and some of the Americas. The list of countries considered to be sources of "migratory risk" reveals the anxieties of European states, a fear of the "other" and distrust towards countries in crisis and the poorest countries.

The introduction of visa facilitation regimes, or their abolition, can serve as a bargaining chip in negotiations with third countries. Within the framework of the Eastern partnership launched in Prague on 7 May 2009, the EU offered six states (Armenia, Azerbaijan, Belarus, Georgia, Moldova and Ukraine) the prospect of future abolition of the visa requirement and granted 600 million euros in return for efforts to curb emigration.

Successive developments to the principle established by Schengen put an end to the project of an open Europe, which prevailed at its inception. The establishment of a common visa policy sped up the development of technology to manage populations and increased the contrast between countries subjected to a visa requirement and those exempted. It should also be noted that, although some foreign nationals are allowed to enter the Schengen Area without visas, this does not exempt them from having to meet other legal requirements. Their stay must be limited to a maximum of three months and they are required to provide

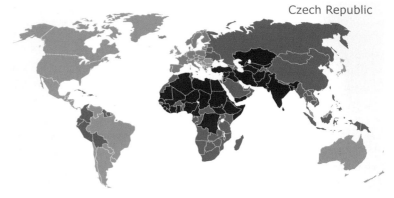

Czech Republic

Since 2009, Morocco has been removed from the list of countries whose nationals require an ATV.

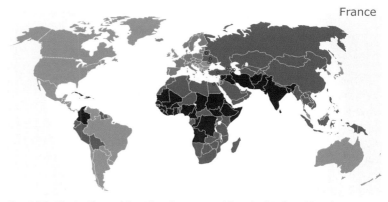

France

Since 2009, Albania, Libya and Egypt have been removed from the list of countries whose nationals require an ATV.

○ Russians require an ATV when they are transiting France and originate from an airport located in Armenia, Azerbaijan, Georgia, Ukraine, Belarus, Moldova, Turkey or Egypt. This measure came into force in 2008 but has latterly been banned by the Council of State.

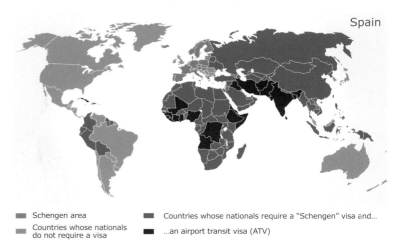

Spain

■ Schengen area
■ Countries whose nationals do not require a visa
■ Countries whose nationals require a "Schengen" visa and...
■ ...an airport transit visa (ATV)

Number of third countries targeted by ATVs by member state

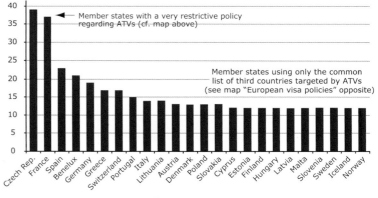

Source: Foreign Office (Belgium): www.dofi.fgov.be (consulted in January 2012).

The use of the ATV (airport transit visa) in fighting "clandestine" immigration varies between Member States

documentary evidence on the purpose and conditions of stay, or to demonstrate adequate financial means.

Visa exemption versus readmission agreement

In return for visa facilitation agreements, the EU asks third states to sign readmission agreements. These agreements enable Member States to deport not only nationals from signatory countries, but also any migrant who passed through their territory. Russia is the first country with which, in 2003, the EU negotiated this type of agreement. The following year, Ukraine was offered an accelerated application process (10 days), the reduction of visa expenses and the introduction of further categories of people eligible for a multiple entry visa. A visa facilitation agreement was adopted by the European Council on 29 November 2007, the implementation of which was subjected to the entry into force, on the same date,

of a readmission agreement. In 2008, the same took place with Moldova and the Balkan countries (with the exception of Kosovo).

Readmission, one of the main elements of EU external relations in the area of migration, has thus become a condition for visa facilitation. In spite of the risks entailed for the fundamental rights of those deported, the terms of such agreements are rarely made public. The economic interests of Member States take precedence.

In November 2007, the European Commission proposed that the visa facilitation process be based on "roadmaps" defining the conditions to be met by states aspiring to conclude a visa liberalization agreement. Macedonia, Montenegro and Serbia were the first to follow the "roadmaps". They had to introduce new biometric passports, increase border controls and resources allocated to fighting corruption, and strengthen co-operation with Frontex. Ukraine and Moldova were the next

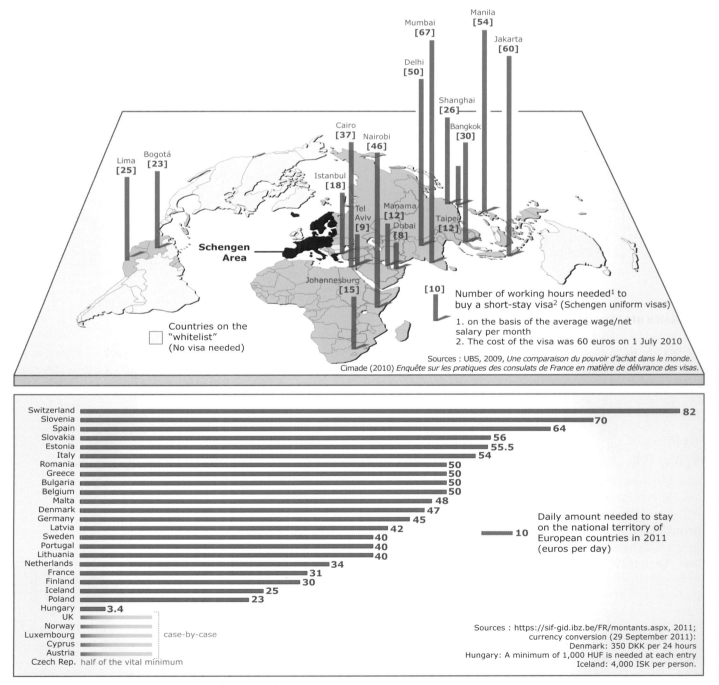

Sources : UBS, 2009, *Une comparaison du pouvoir d'achat dans le monde.*
Cimade (2010) *Enquête sur les pratiques des consulats de France en matière de délivrance des visas.*

Number of working hours needed[1] to buy a short-stay visa[2] (Schengen uniform visas)

1. on the basis of the average wage/net salary per month
2. The cost of the visa was 60 euros on 1 July 2010

Countries on the "whitelist" (No visa needed)

Daily amount needed to stay on the national territory of European countries in 2011 (euros per day)

Sources : https://sif-gid.ibz.be/FR/montants.aspx, 2011; currency conversion (29 September 2011): Denmark: 350 DKK per 24 hours Hungary: A minimum of 1,000 HUF is needed at each entry Iceland: 4,000 ISK per person.

The cost of visas to Europe is not the same for everyone

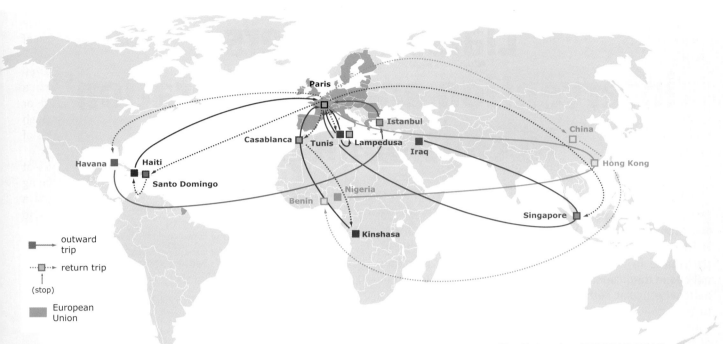

outward
trip

return trip

(stop)

European
Union

Javier, CUBAN (2009)

Javier, Cuban, fled from his country following six months' imprisonment in 2008 because of his anti-government activism. Arriving in Turkey, he was arrested and locked in a centre for irregular migrants from November 2008 to June 2009. He arrived from Istanbul at Roissy airport, near Paris, on 1 July 2009 and six days later the Ministry of the Interior denied his asylum request. On 17 July 2009 he was sent back to Havana.

**Khaled, Morad, Nourdin,
TUNISIAN (2011)**

Khaled, Morad and Nourdin left their country on 1 March 2011 after the fall of the Tunisian regime. At France's Roissy airport, their request for refuge was denied. They were sent back to Tunis on 13 March where they were handed over to the Tunisian authorities and are subjected to violent treatment. Khaled reached Roissy for the second time on 24 March and was released four days later. Morad, meanwhile, tried to reach Lampedusa (Italy) by boat.

Edithe, CONGOLESE (2010)

Edithe, from the Democratic Republic of the Congo, arrived at Orly airport near Paris on 9 October 2010. Her request for refuge was denied a few days later. Because she had transited via Morocco, she was sent back to Casablanca on 17 October 2010. She was held in the airport there for three weeks before being deported to Kinshasa, where she was imprisoned.

Sylvette, HAITIAN (2010)

Sylvette arrived from Haiti on 24 February 2010 at Roissy airport. She fled her country after the devastating earthquake of 12 January 2010. Her asylum request was considered unfounded, and was refused by the Ministry of the Interior. The Ministry also refused to grant her right of entry to France on humanitarian grounds. She was deported to Santo Domingo in the Dominican Republic, which she had transited through. She was immediately sent to prison and then to Haiti.

Christopher, NIGERIAN (2010)

Threatened for being opposed to the genital mutilation of his daughter, Christopher left Nigeria to join his wife and children, asylum-seekers in Germany. He travelled via Hong Kong to Roissy airport where he was arrested on 1 December 2010. He filed an asylum request, but was refused by the Ministry of the Interior. He was expelled to China on 10 December 2010. In order to avoid being sent back to Nigeria by the Chinese authorities, he purchased a ticket to Benin.

Karim et Diana, IRAQI (2010)

Karim arrived at Roissy airport near Paris on 3 September 2010 with his wife and their two children. They wanted to go to Sweden to join their families and to ask for consular protection. They were told they would be deported to Singapore, their last point of transit. After refusing to board the plane 11 times in 16 days, the family was finally unable to resist and on 20 September were deported to Singapore.

Source: Information gathered by Laure Blondel, Anafé, 2011.

The police are pleased to welcome you...

countries to be offered the prospect of a visa-liberalization agreement and are now subjected to continuous evaluation of operations to regulate the flow of migrants passing through their territories on their way to the EU.

Airport transit visas: a weapon for refusing asylum requests

The airport transit visa (ATV) regime is defined, according to consular instructions adopted in 2003, as "entitl[ing] aliens who are required to have such a visa to pass through the international transit area of airports without actually entering the national territory of the country concerned, during a stop-over or transfer between two stages of an international flight". Since the 1990s, without such a visa, nationals from countries subjected to this requirement are forbidden to make a stop-over when they pass through airports in a state within the Schengen Area.

Obtaining an ATV is complicated: for example, the visa issued for the outward journey is not valid for the return. Often, those who have entered an airport without an ATV are not aware that they have infringed the rules on residence within

the Schengen Area. They are entered on "black lists" for having stayed illegally in Schengen territory, which deprives them of the possibility of returning in the future.

Following the arrival of Chechen asylum seekers at Roissy Airport in Paris, between December 2007 and January 2008, France set up the ATV for "Russian nationals coming from an airport situated in Ukraine, Belarus, Moldova, Turkey or Egypt". Since Chechens hold Russian nationality, this measure was clearly aimed at blocking their entry. It led to a decrease in the number of asylum applications from Chechnya. This method was condemned a few months later by the *Conseil d' Etat*, which considered that the ATV requirement could not be determined according to the airport of origin of the persons concerned. But the court approved the principle of transit visas, on the basis that they respond to "public order needs to prevent the abuse of transit, on the occasion of a stop-over or change of plane, with the sole aim of entering France". This mechanism thus allows European governments to impede the entry of numerous persons to Europe, though they are often in urgent need of international protection and cannot wait months to obtain a visa.

Paulina NIKIEL

people leaving their countries of origin, some of whom suffer constant violence.

At the political level, experts organize courses, in Europe and elsewhere, to advise and train foreign police officers. They are intended to foster co-operation between third countries and European States and to facilitate exchanges between the various police services. As a French manager said, they aim to "oil the wheels". These contacts are all the more important in that they enable European authorities to get through to the authorities of a third country more easily when the latter are reluctant to accept a readmission. In 2007, French officers intervened to facilitate the execution of 4,358 deportation orders with police escorts.

Ad hoc missions can be deployed during "migration crises", as shown by the intervention of Spanish delegations in Mauritania and Senegal in 2006, when more than 30,000 migrants disembarked in the Canary Islands. This was also the case in the spring of 2011, following the arrival in Europe of Tunisian migrants; Italian and French representatives were sent to Tunisia to meet the authorities.

According to a Spanish liaison officer, these European civil servants constitute intermediaries to enable "fast communication". Within the EU, their objective is to make contacts to solve problems related to the application of the Dublin Regulation as rapidly as possible (see page 61). Beyond the EU, they participate in organizing joint operations by Member States, such as the collective deportations conducted by several EU countries and the Frontex agency. "Immigration" liaison officers and the agency are indeed co-operating ever more closely. The scope of the officers' actions is therefore destined to expand, whether with regard to gathering data on illegal immigration, or risk analysis with a view to deploying new means to control the EU's external borders.

Sara CASELLA-COLOMBEAU and Olivier CLOCHARD ○

---

1 EU Council Regulation (EC) No. 377/2004 of 19 February 2004 on the creation of an "immigration" liaison officers network.
2 Bigo Didier, *Polices en réseaux: L'expérience européenne*. Presses de Sciences Po, 1996, p. 32.

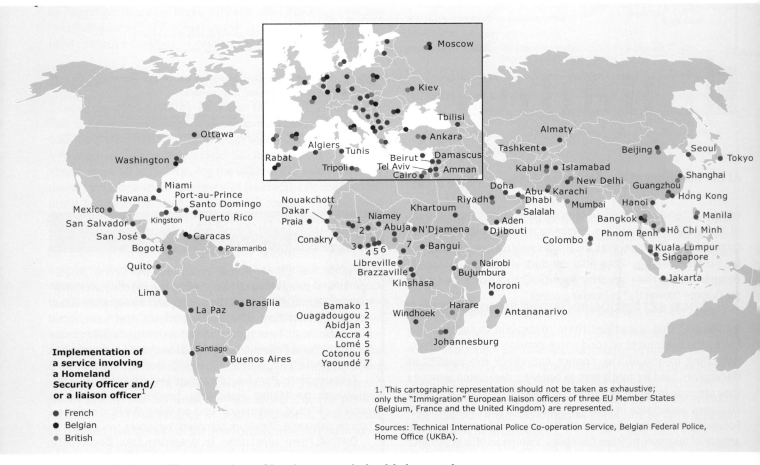

Implementation of
a service involving
a Homeland
Security Officer and/
or a liaison officer[1]

● French
● Belgian
● British

1. This cartographic representation should not be taken as exhaustive; only the "Immigration" European liaison officers of three EU Member States (Belgium, France and the United Kingdom) are represented.

Sources: Technical International Police Co-operation Service, Belgian Federal Police, Home Office (UKBA).

European Liaison Officers: a view of border controls in third countries

INSERTING TRANSPORT COMPANIES IN THE CONTROL CHAIN

Transport and freight companies' responsibilities in the management of foreigners/people without documents has existed for some time for air freight. The responsibilities were introduced later for sea, road and rail transport. But it was particularly on the application of the Schengen agreements that European Union countries forced all transportation companies to collaborate over migration controls. So, the directive of 28 June 2001 asks Member States to take "the necessary measures to impose on transport companies that are not able to ensure the return of a foreign national

who has been refused entry, the obligation to immediately find the best method of redirection and to support the costs of accommodating and then returning the national to the country in question" (Article 3). The directive indicates a minimum of 3,000 euros and a maximum of 5,000 euros. "Independently of the number of people transported" (Article 4), a fine of not less than 500,000 euros can also be charged to the transport companies, but this last clause has never been applied to our knowledge. To avoid incurring financial penalties, companies have established controls that are as efficient as those of the border agencies.

The Belgian network of immigration liaison officers

Source: Belgian Federal Police, 2009

Source: Home Office (UKBA), 2009

■ Countries where immigration liaison officers operate permanently*

■ In the United Kingdom, the liaison officers are responsible for identifying foreigners in "illegal situations" from three states (Afghanistan, China, Pakistan). Their aim is to facilitate the deportation of foreigners to their country of origin**.

* The British device also supports the establishment of different missions. In each country, one liaison officer is present, except those where the number is indicated in brackets. In the European Union, Spain, France and Italy each has two British liaison officers.
** From January 2006 to January 2007, 12 charter flights went from London to Afghanistan. There were also 2 charter flights to Kurdistan and 55 to Eastern Europe.

The UK Border Agency in the world

The European Neighbourhood Policy and migration: the cases of Moldova and Ukraine

In elaborating a common migration policy, the European Union (EU) addresses the way in which non-member states deal with this issue. Established in 2003, the European Neighbourhood Policy (ENP) is the central instrument of the EU's relations with bordering countries. Its stated objective is to "create a common area of stability, security and prosperity". The ENP involves bilateral relations with each partner, which are translated into individualized "action plans" intended to take account of the specificities of the countries concerned. The ENP is based on the principle of "shared responsibility": the financial "carrot" constitutes the main lever. If progress matches predictions, financial support to the partner country is renewed, otherwise funds are reduced or cut. Since 2009, migration and border control are essential components of the Eastern Partnership of the ENP.

Moldova: a Mobility Partnership pilot country

Moldova, as a beneficiary of the ENP, was one of the first States to sign an action plan. The country is strongly affected by emigration. This aspect is barely taken into account; the primary focus of the ENP is the management of migratory flows into the EU and the strengthening of border controls, although the number of migrants entering Moldova remains low.

Under the 2005 Action Plan, migration and asylum occupied a central place. Its aims included: controlling migratory movements and preparing the reform of Moldovan laws to align them with European and international standards; supporting the development of bodies responsible for asylum and refugees; concluding a readmission agreement between the EU and the Republic of Moldova, and encouraging the latter to conclude similar agreements with the main countries of origin of migrants entering or transiting through the country; supporting the development of an "efficient" border control system and facilitating cross-border co-operation with Moldova's neighbours and EU Member States. This action plan was renewed in 2008.

The impact of the action plan was mainly on the legislative and institutional framework of migration control. Agreements with the EU to make visa and readmission procedures less stringent entered into force in 2008. Moldova adopted a National Programme of Action on Migration and Asylum in 2006, an Action Plan on Tackling Human Trafficking in 2007 and promulgated a law on the entry and residency of foreigners in 2010. A body of border guards trained and equipped by the EU was formed to combat cross-border activities. The EU Border Assistance Mission for Moldova and Ukraine (EUBAM), established at the end of 2005 to align standards on border control with those of the EU, was renewed three times to remain in place until 2015. Asylum issues remain on the back burner, despite amendments made to the law on refugees in 2003. It can be assumed that the EU seeks to equip Moldova with the operational capacity to enable it ultimately to take responsibility for selecting refugees so as to restrict their entry into Member States. It should be noted that the 2008 readmission agreement does not provide for specific protection measures for asylum seekers and refugees.

In 2008, Moldova was also the first country to sign a Mobility Partnership agreement with the EU, elaborated within the framework of the ENP and the EU's Global Approach to Migration and Mobility (GAMM). The GAMM was adopted in 2005 and revised in 2011. It is defined as the "overarching framework of EU external migration policy, complementary to other, broader, objectives that are served by EU foreign policy and development co-operation". The EU/Moldova Mobility Partnership constitutes a test of a common EU external migration policy, which aims to expand the EU's fields of action in emigration countries with a view to improving the management of migratory flows. It has three components: promoting legal migration; developing the link between migration and development; and fighting illegal immigration. Within this framework, 25 projects were selected and funded by 15 EU member States, NGOs and European agencies. The difficulties confronted in implementing the Partnership reveal the gap between the stated aims (to respond to the concerns of both parties) and the reality: Moldovan local actors have little room for manoeuvre to ensure that the system responds to their needs. The Partnership is above all a mechanism for the benefit of EU interests.

Ukraine: Migration control under the influence of the ENP

Ukraine is a country of significant emigration and one of the main countries of transit for migrants seeking to enter the EU. Its character as a transit country led to the adoption of an Action Plan on Justice and Internal Affairs (JIA) between Ukraine and the EU in 2001. This Plan was then integrated into the Ukraine/EU Action Plan drafted within the framework of the ENP. As was the case with Moldova, migration and borders were priority issues in negotiations, with a view to enhancing controls. The movement of Ukrainian workers within the Schengen Area was dealt with only as an ancillary issue.

Since the beginning of the 2000s, collaboration between the EU and Ukraine has focused on three areas. First, the joint negotiation of agreements on the movement of persons, which in October 2006 led to the signature of a visa facilitation agreement and bilateral readmission agreements between

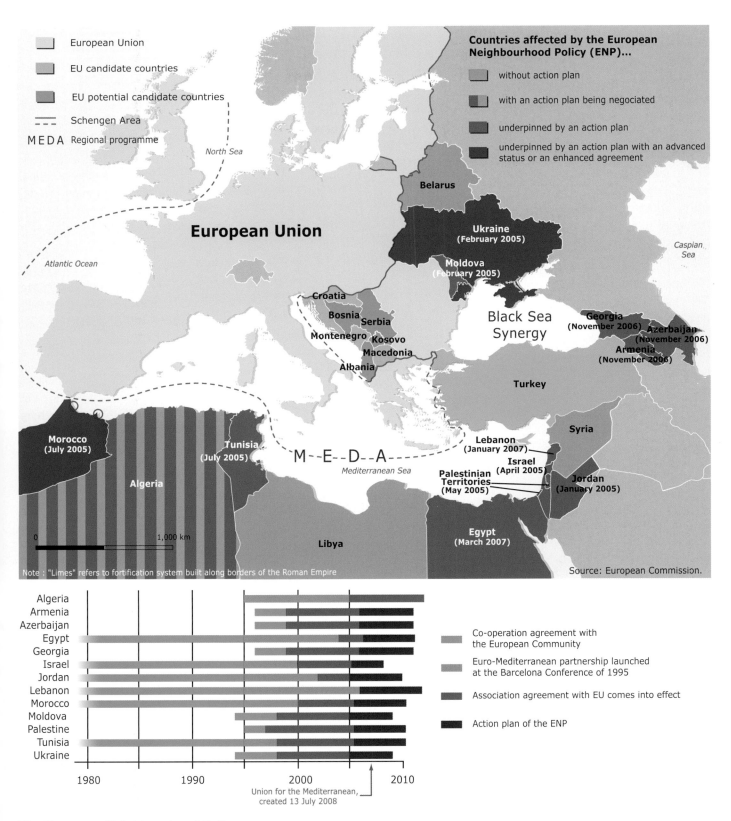

Countries affected by the European Neighbourhood Policy (ENP)...

- without action plan
- with an action plan being negociated
- underpinned by an action plan
- underpinned by an action plan with an advanced status or an enhanced agreement

- European Union
- EU candidate countries
- EU potential candidate countries
- Schengen Area

MEDA Regional programme

North Sea

Atlantic Ocean

European Union

Belarus

Ukraine (February 2005)

Moldova (February 2005)

Caspian Sea

Croatia

Bosnia Serbia

Montenegro Kosovo

Macedonia

Albania

Black Sea Synergy

Georgia (November 2006)

Azerbaijan (November 2006)

Armenia (November 2006)

Turkey

Syria

Morocco (July 2005)

Tunisia (July 2005)

M-E-D-A

Mediterranean Sea

Algeria

Lebanon (January 2007)

Israel (April 2005)

Palestinian Territories (May 2005)

Jordan (January 2005)

0   1,000 km

Libya

Egypt (March 2007)

Note : "Limes" refers to fortification system built along borders of the Roman Empire

Source: European Commission.

Algeria
Armenia
Azerbaijan
Egypt
Georgia
Israel
Jordan
Lebanon
Morocco
Moldova
Palestine
Tunisia
Ukraine

1980   1990   2000   2010

Union for the Mediterranean, created 13 July 2008

- Co-operation agreement with the European Community
- Euro-Mediterranean partnership launched at the Barcelona Conference of 1995
- Association agreement with EU comes into effect
- Action plan of the ENP

The European Neighbourhood Policy

Ukraine and 12 EU Member States. At the same time, Ukraine was encouraged to conclude readmission agreements with Russia and Belarus. Second, collaboration centres on Ukrainian border surveillance, which is mainly conducted within the framework of EUBAM. The EU supports Ukraine to reinforce infrastructure and controls at borders, to reorganize surveillance bodies and services (establishment of a State Border Guard Service) and to improve professionalism. Finally, Ukraine ratified international agreements on refugees and human

trafficking, adopted new laws on refugees (in 2001 and 2011), a law on immigration (in 2001) and the law on the status of foreigners and stateless people of 1994 was amended several times up until 2011.

The protection of foreigners and, more particularly, asylum seekers and statutory refugees, remains the poor relation of this collaboration. Although the European Commission welcomed the opening of several retention centres and temporary accommodation centres for asylum seekers in the

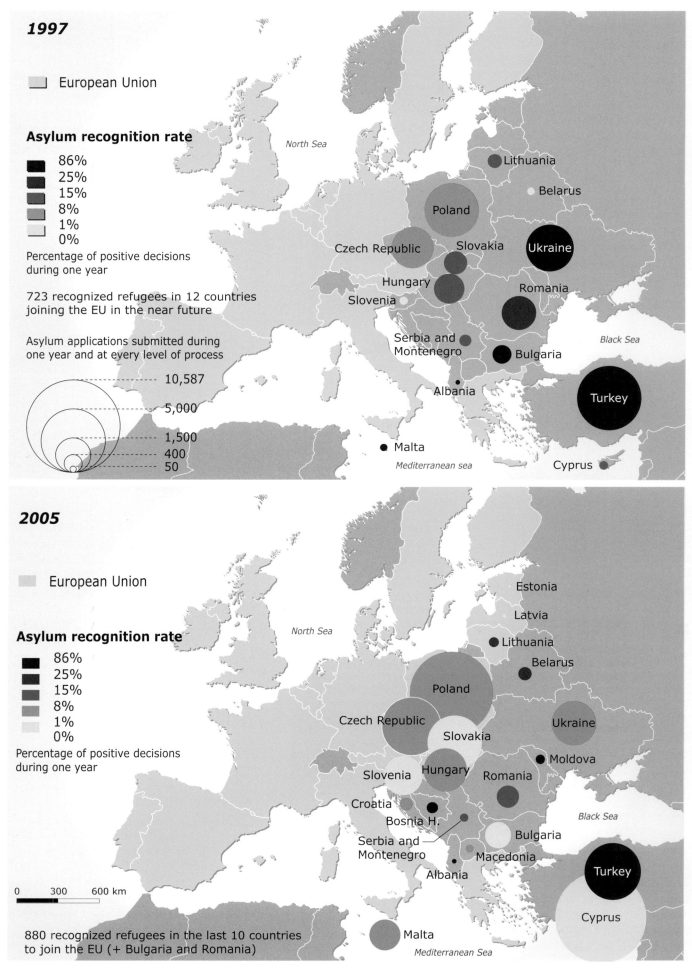

1997

European Union

Asylum recognition rate
- 86%
- 25%
- 15%
- 8%
- 1%
- 0%

Percentage of positive decisions during one year

723 recognized refugees in 12 countries joining the EU in the near future

Asylum applications submitted during one year and at every level of process

- 10,587
- 5,000
- 1,500
- 400
- 50

2005

European Union

Asylum recognition rate
- 86%
- 25%
- 15%
- 8%
- 1%
- 0%

Percentage of positive decisions during one year

0   300   600 km

880 recognized refugees in the last 10 countries to join the EU (+ Bulgaria and Romania)

Central and Eastern Europe: more asylum applications

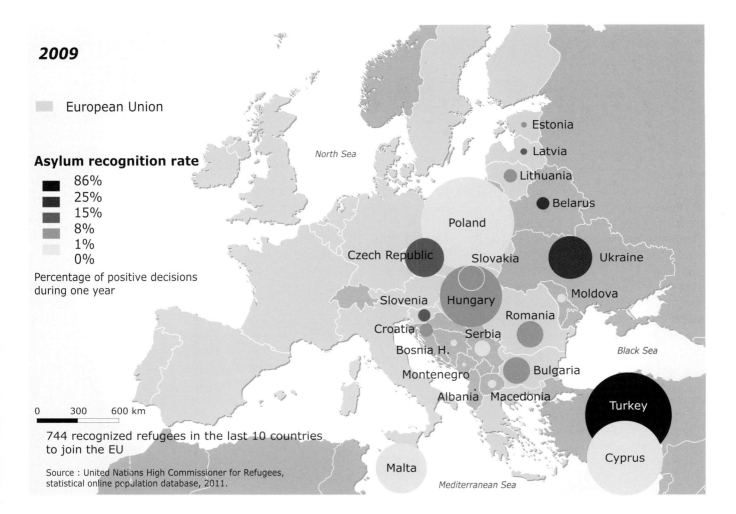

2009

European Union

Asylum recognition rate

86%
25%
15%
8%
1%
0%

Percentage of positive decisions
during one year

0   300   600 km

744 recognized refugees in the last 10 countries
to join the EU

Source : United Nations High Commissioner for Refugees,
statistical online population database, 2011.

mid-2000s, it is aware of the deficiencies in Ukrainian laws and concerned by the ill-treatment inflicted on refugees and asylum seekers – in particular frequent instances of refoulement at the borders. These concerns do not prevent the EU continuing negotiations with Ukraine for enhanced migration control and border management.

Migration and asylum under the ENP

The promotion of free movement of persons, goods, services and capital is supposed to be one of the ENP's principal objectives. Mobility is presented as a key element of reinforcing stability and security.

However, the security approach remains very much in place. The ENP is also intended to support neighbouring States to fight illegal migration, implement return policies and conclude readmission agreements. These areas of intervention became increasingly important in the mid-2000s, developing into a core objective. After 2005, the ENP frameworks deviated significantly from the founding project: a repressive and security-oriented approach to the movement of individuals was developed. This approach can be broken down as follows: fighting "migration pressure from third countries"; combating "trafficking in human beings and terrorism"; border management; police and judicial cooperation; and the conclusion of readmission agreements. The issue of the movement of workers has been excluded from the scope of future action plans, although it had been included in association and cooperation agreements concluded prior to the ENP. Irregular migration, human trafficking and terrorism are presented as major challenges to be faced by State

Parties. The security rhetoric is to be accompanied by concrete measures and increased flexibility on one side is inconceivable without "effective action" on the other. Border management lies at the heart of the ENP project: it "is likely to be a priority in most Action Plans as it is only by working together that the EU and its neighbours can manage common borders more efficiently in order to facilitate legitimate movements".

The new European Neighbourhood Policy which the EU is trying to put in place following the Arab Revolutions of 2011 signals a slight shift in policy. Legal migration is given greater emphasis, under the terminology of "mobility", which in reality refers to temporary labour in Member States by nationals from members of the ENP. An explicitly utilitarian approach to mobility is adopted, underlying the need to fill demographic gaps in the EU. But the main focus of this "mutually beneficial approach" remains "capacity-building on border management, asylum and effective law-enforcement co-operation".

As shown by the examples of Moldova and Ukraine, action plans concluded by the EU with neighbouring States can have a strong impact on the latter's migration and asylum policies. They are rendered more "European", focusing on repression, despite the fact that these issues are marginal in the context of the political and social concerns of many of these States. These developments are all the more concerning in that they constitute the counterpart of EU financial aid. Yet the failure of negotiations with Senegal and Ghana aimed at establishing Mobility Partnerships demonstrates that the power balance does not always lean in favour of the EU.

Bénédicte MICHALON ▶

Frontex: at the margins of Europe and the law

The creation of Frontex (European Agency for the Management of Operational Co-operation at the External Borders of the Member States of the European Union, with its headquarters in Warsaw), in 2005, arose from a compromise between advocates of an enhanced role for the EU in controlling migration and Member States anxious to retain their sovereignty. The agency is intended to transcend the choice between specialized centres scattered across the EU and the creation of a European body of border guards. The Board of Directors (BD) is composed of a representative of each Member State and two representatives of the Commission.

Increasing autonomy and resources

Frontex's financial autonomy is supposedly ensured by allocations from the EU budget and Schengen Member States. In practice, in order to organize an operation, the BD approves a proposal, then calls for equipment and personnel to be made available by Member States from their national border guards, since the agency does not have its own resources.

All Member States contribute to Frontex's budget, but only those strategically positioned at the external borders of the EU use its services. Supposed expertise (see below) in identifying migratory "high-risk" areas, on the basis of data gathered on migration in Member States, is the only means to legitimate operations in the eyes of all European countries.

Frontex sees its lack of resources and dependence on Member States as limiting its development. There are therefore attempts to introduce mechanisms to oblige states to participate. A new Regulation, adopted in October 2011, confirmed the importance of the "Rabit" (Rapid Border Intervention Teams) Regulation, adopted in July 2007, which provided that in the event of "a mass influx" of migrants, an operational plan should be defined by the Executive Director of Frontex, then discussed with the Member State concerned, and finally approved by participating countries.

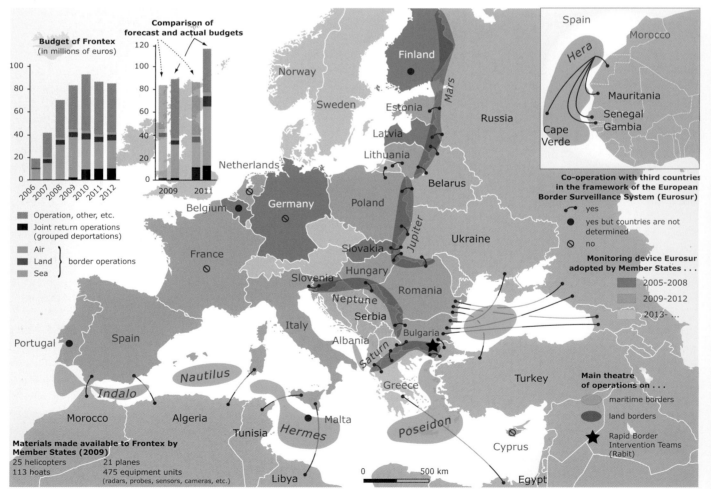

Data: Annual reports of Frontex; European Commission, *Impact Assessment accompanying the Proposal for a Regulation of the European Parliament and of the Council establishing the European Border Surveillance System (Eurosur)*, Commission staff working paper, COM (2011) 873 final.

Monitoring operations of the Frontex agency

The 2011 Regulation applies this procedure to all operations, removing the distinction between Rabit teams and standard teams; all become "European Border guard teams". The new Regulation also introduces measures aimed at forcing states to commit to long-term contributions. Reserves of European border guards and equipment are thus constituted each year and Frontex also has the capacity to acquire its own equipment.

Specific operations for each border category

Until 2010, Frontex maritime operations were concerned with the Canary Islands, Lampedusa, Malta and the Aegean Sea. Since 2011, they have been concentrated on Greece and the Strait of Sicily, in European territorial waters, international waters and those of third countries. Each new maritime operation pushes migrants to embark upon other, increasingly dangerous routes to reach Europe.

Airport operations often target various EU international terminals simultaneously, in order to control migrants according to their origin or nationality, adding a discriminatory character to controls. Transfers of experienced agents between states lead to the sharing of information on migratory routes, "smugglers", etc, and of techniques, under the guise of "efficiency", at the risk of undermining fundamental rights.

Land operations are aimed at monitoring the harmonization of controls at the eastern border of the EU and at reinforcing controls at the Greek-Turkish border.

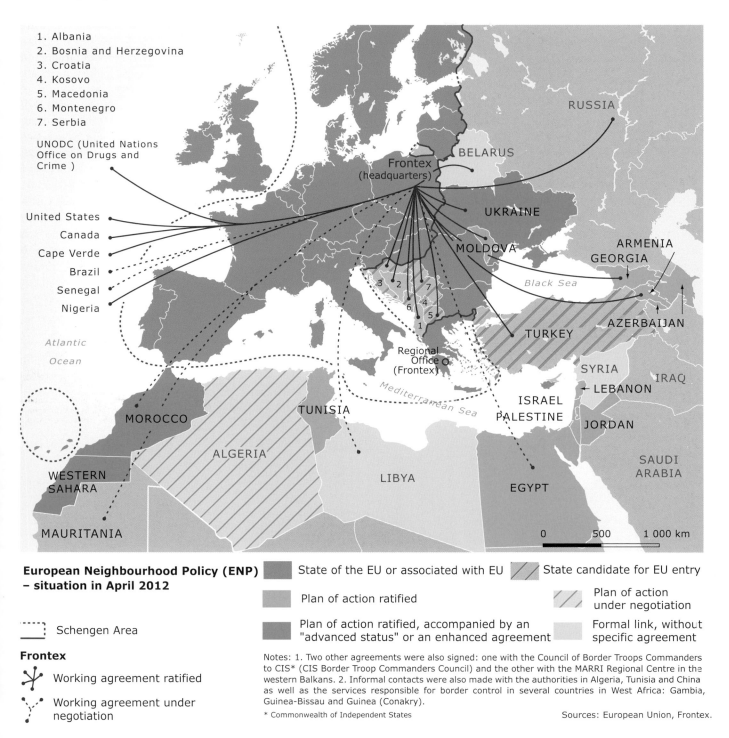

European Neighbourhood Policy (ENP) – situation in April 2012

Notes: 1. Two other agreements were also signed: one with the Council of Border Troops Commanders to CIS* (CIS Border Troop Commanders Council) and the other with the MARRI Regional Centre in the western Balkans. 2. Informal contacts were also made with the authorities in Algeria, Tunisia and China as well as the services responsible for border control in several countries in West Africa: Gambia, Guinea-Bissau and Guinea (Conakry).

* Commonwealth of Independent States

Sources: European Union, Frontex.

Outside the European Union, Frontex deploys its web

Who takes responsibility for Frontex's human rights violations?

Numerous bodies, including Human Rights Watch and the European Parliament, have denounced human rights violations committed during Frontex operations. But the sense of impunity enjoyed by the agency has increased with the dilution of responsibilities resulting from its development. How to distinguish between the responsibility of Frontex, that of national agents and that of states? Furthermore, many activities take place outside European territory, which raises the issue of the extraterritorial application of EU norms on human rights. The legal vacuum, which makes democratic control difficult, was partially filled by a decision of the European Court of Human Rights (ECHR) on 23 February 2012, condemning Italy for having returned a boat of migrants to Libya in 2009.

Refoulement and fighting "illegal emigration". The aim of maritime operations in the territorial seas of a third country is to intercept boats of migrants and to send them back to the countries of departure. Yet there is legal basis for sending them back only if the boat is in distress. In other cases, sending them back is a violation of Article 13 of the Universal Declaration of Human Rights (UDHR), which provides that, "everyone has the right to leave any country, including his own", except in the event of the suspected commission of an international crime (e.g. terrorism, drug trafficking) which should lead to criminal charges. The same applies to the interception of boats on the high seas, before they have entered European waters, when they cannot be considered to be in an irregular situation. The practice of immediate return to countries of departure also goes against the principle of non-refoulement, since operations do not take into account the possible presence of refugees on board. The agency's reports on its activities highlight statistics (numbers of interceptions, expulsions, identifications of

"smugglers", etc.), without any transparency on the potential numbers of asylum seekers. Thus, Frontex's activities beyond EU borders constitute continuous and structural violations of international law.

Co-operation with third countries and externalization of controls. Frontex has developed privileged relations with states of departure, to which EU agents provide support to prevent emigration. Agreements have been signed with 14 States and eight others are being negotiated, without any oversight by civil society. Thus, democratic control is hindered *ex ante* but also *ex post*. The agency justifies the exceptional character of such agreements and the lack of approval by the EU Parliament, by their "technical" nature. They are concluded either on the basis of a clause in an agreement concluded between respective national services (for example, between the Spanish and Senegalese border guards in the case of "Operation Hera"), or directly between the agency and the services of the State concerned. The 2011 Regulation provides for the possibility of sending liaison officers to these countries to intervene directly in border control and/or to provide expertise.

Management of personal data. Frontex gathers and shares data on migrants and their movements (costs, documents used, ways of crossing a particular border, etc.) either by sending specialized agents, or via national agents. The data is used to elaborate a "risk analysis" which determines the place and type of operations. The new Regulation provides for data gathering, which was previously undertaken without legal basis. Data is collected and made available on an inter-state "information and co-ordination network" and can be transmitted to Europol.

Joint expulsion operations. Several Members of the European Parliament have protested against the activities of Frontex in the area of forced repatriation. The adoption, in December 2008, of the so-called EU "Return" Directive, which defines the conditions under which a migrant in an irregular situation

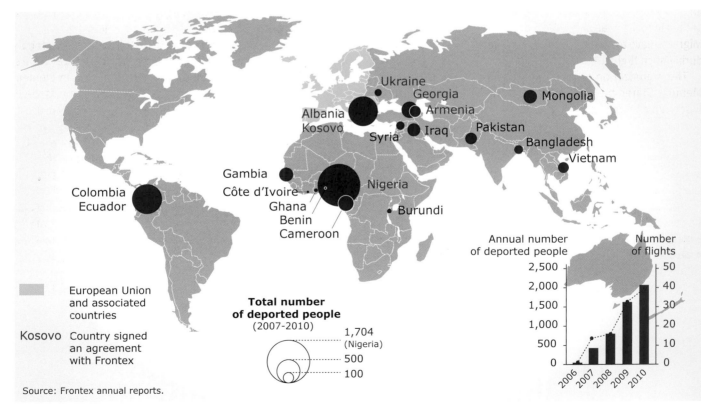

European Union and associated countries

Kosovo   Country signed an agreement with Frontex

Total number of deported people
(2007-2010)

1,704 (Nigeria)
500
100

Annual number of deported people

Number of flights

Source: Frontex annual reports.

Frontex charters

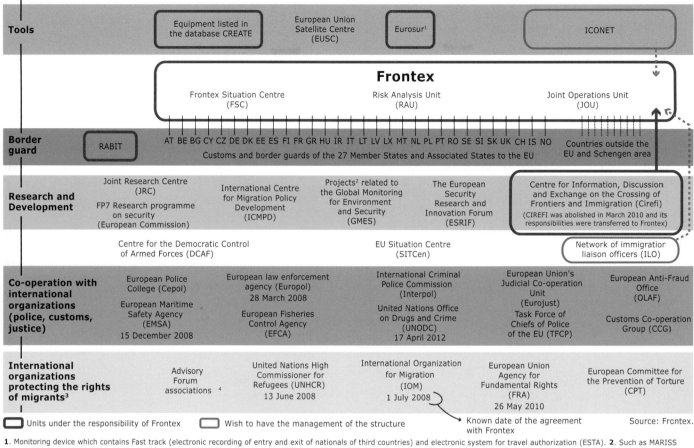

Tools		Equipment listed in the database CREATE		European Union Satellite Centre (EUSC)	Eurosur[1]		ICONET	

Frontex

	Frontex Situation Centre (FSC)	Risk Analysis Unit (RAU)	Joint Operations Unit (JOU)

Border guard	RABIT	AT BE BG CY CZ DE DK EE ES FI FR GR HU IR IT LT LV LX MT NL PL PT RO SE SI SK UK CH IS NO	Countries outside the EU and Schengen area
		Customs and border guards of the 27 Member States and Associated States to the EU	

Research and Development	Joint Research Centre (JRC) FP7 Research programme on security (European Commission)	International Centre for Migration Policy Development (ICMPD)	Projects[2] related to the Global Monitoring for Environment and Security (GMES)	The European Security Research and Innovation Forum (ESRIF)	Centre for Information, Discussion and Exchange on the Crossing of Frontiers and Immigration (Cirefi) (CIREFI was abolished in March 2010 and its responsibilities were transferred to Frontex)
	Centre for the Democratic Control of Armed Forces (DCAF)		EU Situation Centre (SITCen)		Network of immigration liaison officers (ILO)

Co-operation with international organizations (police, customs, justice)	European Police College (Cepol) European Maritime Safety Agency (EMSA) 15 December 2008	European law enforcement agency (Europol) 28 March 2008 European Fisheries Control Agency (EFCA)	International Criminal Police Commission (Interpol) United Nations Office on Drugs and Crime (UNODC) 17 April 2012	European Union's Judicial Co-operation Unit (Eurojust) Task Force of Chiefs of Police of the EU (TFCP)	European Anti-Fraud Office (OLAF) Customs Co-operation Group (CCG)

International organizations protecting the rights of migrants[3]	Advisory Forum associations [4]	United Nations High Commissioner for Refugees (UNHCR) 13 June 2008	International Organization for Migration (IOM) 1 July 2008	European Union Agency for Fundamental Rights (FRA) 26 May 2010	European Committee for the Prevention of Torture (CPT)

Units under the responsibility of Frontex ☐ Wish to have the management of the structure → Known date of the agreement with Frontex Source: Frontex.

1. Monitoring device which contains Fast track (electronic recording of entry and exit of nationals of third countries) and electronic system for travel authorization (ESTA). 2. Such as MARISS (maritime picture through the integration of satellite products) and LIMES. 3. But intended only to train EU border guards officers or present as an observer in some operations. 4. Amnesty International European Institutions Office, Caritas Europa, Churches' Commission for Migrants in Europe, Council of Europe, European Asylum Support Office, European Council for Refugees and Exiles (ECRE), European Union Agency for Fundamental Rights (FRA), International Catholic Migration Commission, International Commission of Jurists, International Organization for Migration (OIM), Jesuit Refugee Service (JRS), Organization for Security and Co-operation in Europe, Platform for International Co-operation on Undocumented Migrants (PICUM), Red Cross EU Office, United Nations High Commissioner for Refugees (UNHCR).

Who works with Frontex?

may be subjected to expulsion, increased the autonomy of the agency in this field. The new Regulation confirms its role in organizing joint charter flights and in financing such operations. Migrants have reported inhuman treatment and acts of violence during such flights.

The organization of joint expulsion operations by several Member States has become one of the key elements of the European external border control policy. The agency has been conducting such operations since 2006, either combined with joint interception operations, or dedicated to the expulsion of nationals from a specific country. In such cases, Frontex assumes a co-ordination role between the different states concerned.

Guaranteeing respect for human rights? Between surveillance and rescue, the agency has always played on the ambiguity of its missions, presenting migrants as victims to be protected against trafficking, and affirming its capacity to offer a "fair" response to the "migratory crisis". Frontex has reacted to criticisms by developing, as of 2007, co-operation with the

UNHCR to train its agents on refugee law and, as of 2010, with the European Union Agency for Fundamental Rights (FRA) for training and the development of "good practices".

Since it was amended in 2011, the Regulation supposedly provides for increased recognition of fundamental rights, notably by including respect for human rights as an element of the next evaluation of the agency, by introducing a "code of conduct" for deportation flights and by creating the positions of data protection officer and fundamental rights officer. There are no provisions concerning the independence of the evaluation, participation of civil society or remedies available in the event of violation of the code. The concrete implementation of these measures therefore gives rise to uncertainties. The European Ombudsman, an independent agency which investigates "complaints about maladministration in the institutions and bodies of the EU" opened an inquiry on 13 March 2012 into "how Frontex implements its fundamental rights obligations".

Sara Casella COLOMBEAU ◘

Libya: an outpost of externalized migration controls

I n 2008, a "Friendship Treaty" was signed between Muammar Qadafi, as Libyan Head of State, and Silvio Berlusconi, as Italian Prime Minister. Officially, it was intended to pay off the colonial debt (Libya was under Italian control between 1911 and 1951); by way of compensation, Rome committed to

paying $200 million per year for 25 years (a total of five billion euros) to its former colony. As a side issue, the arrangement proved highly profitable for Italy. On the one hand, the majority of payments were to be made in the form of investments in infrastructure projects in Libya, enabling Italian businesses

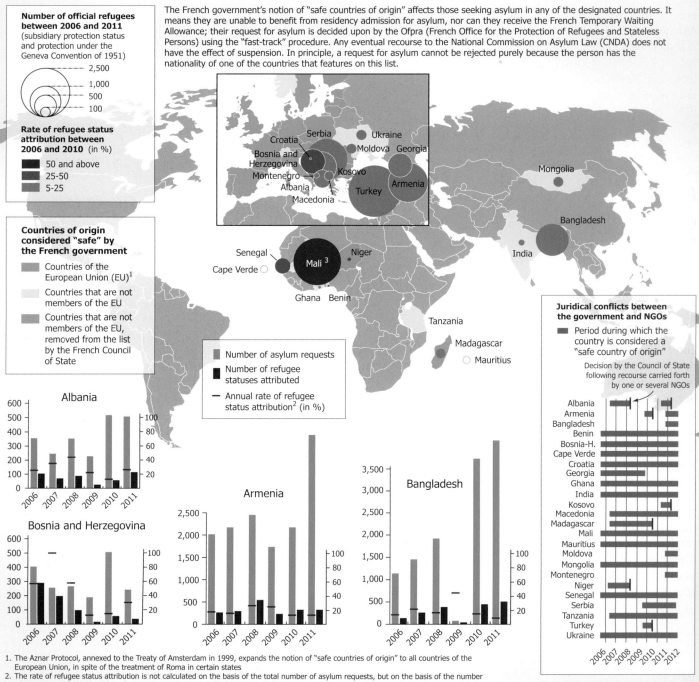

Number of official refugees between 2006 and 2011
(subsidiary protection status and protection under the Geneva Convention of 1951)

— 2,500
— 1,000
— 500
— 100

Rate of refugee status attribution between 2006 and 2010 (in %)

■ 50 and above
■ 25-50
■ 5-25

Countries of origin considered "safe" by the French government

■ Countries of the European Union (EU)[1]

■ Countries that are not members of the EU

■ Countries that are not members of the EU, removed from the list by the French Council of State

The French government's notion of "safe countries of origin" affects those seeking asylum in any of the designated countries. It means they are unable to benefit from residency admission for asylum, nor can they receive the French Temporary Waiting Allowance; their request for asylum is decided upon by the Ofpra (French Office for the Protection of Refugees and Stateless Persons) using the "fast-track" procedure. Any eventual recourse to the National Commission on Asylum Law (CNDA) does not have the effect of suspension. In principle, a request for asylum cannot be rejected purely because the person has the nationality of one of the countries that features on this list.

Croatia Serbia Ukraine
Bosnia and Herzegovina Moldova Georgia
Montenegro Kosovo
Albania Turkey Armenia
Macedonia

Mongolia

Bangladesh

Senegal Niger
Cape Verde Mali[3] India

Ghana Benin

Tanzania

Madagascar
○ Mauritius

Juridical conflicts between the government and NGOs

■ Period during which the country is considered a "safe country of origin"

Decision by the Council of State following recourse carried forth by one or several NGOs

■ Number of asylum requests
■ Number of refugee statuses attributed
— Annual rate of refugee status attribution[2] (in %)

Albania
Armenia
Bangladesh
Benin
Bosnia-H.
Cape Verde
Croatia
Georgia
Ghana
India
Kosovo
Macedonia
Madagascar
Mali
Mauritius
Moldova
Mongolia
Montenegro
Niger
Senegal
Serbia
Tanzania
Turkey
Ukraine

2006 2007 2008 2009 2010 2011 2012

Albania

600 — 100
500 — 80
400 — 60
300 —
200 — 40
100 — 20
0

2006 2007 2008 2009 2010 2011

Bosnia and Herzegovina

600 — 100
500 — 80
400 —
300 — 60
200 — 40
100 — 20
0

2006 2007 2008 2009 2010 2011

Armenia

2,500 —
2,000 — 100
1,500 — 80
1,000 — 60
500 — 40
— 20
0

2006 2007 2008 2009 2010 2011

Bangladesh

3,500 —
3,000 —
2,500 —
2,000 — 100
1,500 — 80
— 60
1,000 — 40
500 — 20
0

2006 2007 2008 2009 2010 2011

1. The Aznar Protocol, annexed to the Treaty of Amsterdam in 1999, expands the notion of "safe countries of origin" to all countries of the European Union, in spite of the treatment of Roma in certain states
2. The rate of refugee status attribution is not calculated on the basis of the total number of asylum requests, but on the basis of the number of decisions taken by the Ofpra during one year
3. The notion of "safe country of origin" is only valid for men

Source: Ofpra (French Office for the Protection of Refugees and Stateless Persons)

Countries that just aren't so safe...

to recover the funds provided by the government. The agreement provided in particular for the construction of a motorway along the 1,700 km coastline, in respect of which the majority of tenders were awarded to Italian companies. On the other hand, the Treaty required Libya to co-operate in the fight against irregular immigration led by Italy. Since the beginning of the 2000s, the Sicilian coast has been very exposed to arrivals of migrants in boats. As a result of increasingly strict controls, rendering it more and more difficult first to cross the Strait of Gibraltar and then to take the route to the west via Mauritania and the Canary Islands, Libya has become one of the main points of entry at the southern European border for Africans who are fleeing their countries of origin in search of protection or a better life. For Italy, and more generally for the European Union, Libya's geographical position made it a necessary partner in the fight against irregular immigration. But Muammar Qadafi was a shrewd and demanding negotiator, forcing European leaders to adapt strategies, methods and discourse in their relations with this formidable neighbour.

Countries of origin considered safe by the Maltese government
- Countries of the European Union [1]
- Countries that are not members of the European Union

1. See the note to the map opposite titled "Countries that just aren't so safe..."

Source: Intrand C. (2007) *The conditions in centres for third country national (detention camps, open centres as well as transit centres and transit zones) with a particular focus on provisions and facilities for persons with special needs in the 25 EU member states. Visit report to Malta*, p. 9 (available online).

Safe countries of origin according to Malta

Migrants as bargaining chips

In 2011, prior to the fall of the dictator, the Libyan regime was all the more fearsome to foreigners. Whether in transit, in some cases for long periods, or workers attracted by the opportunities offered by this underpopulated, oil-rich country, migrants suffered the effects of Qadafi's unpredictable diplomacy. Over several years, such diplomacy went from the pan-African project, under which the "King of African Kings", as he liked to be called, established regional power, to collaboration with Europeans, after the reintegration of Libya into the international community. Economic sanctions, lifted in 2004, had until then, in principle, prevented economic relations with a State qualified as "terrorist" following several deadly attacks against Western interests at the end of the 1980s. Migrants were hostages to such fluctuations, sometimes being encouraged to settle in the name of solidarity with "African brothers", and at other times hunted down and deported *en masse*. In April 2005, the European Parliament declared that it was "concerned at the treatment and deplorable living conditions of people held in camps in Libya, as well as by the recent massive repatriations of foreigners from Libya to their countries of origin in conditions guaranteeing neither their dignity nor their survival". A year later, in one of the first publications on the situation of foreigners in Libya, Human Rights Watch described the reigning climate of hostility towards persons of sub-Saharan African origin, who were victims of racism, harassment, extortion, physical attacks and police violence. The report exposed conditions of overcrowding and ill-treatment in detention centres. Underlining that the rights of refugees were being violated, the report concluded "Libya is not a safe country for migrants, asylum seekers and refugees". These observations, which were confirmed by numerous migrants' testimonies and independent mission reports, did not prevent European governments, and particularly Italy, wanting to make Libya one of the main vectors of their migration policies in the South.

Italy as the "trailblazer"

The 2008 Treaty between Italy and Libya was the result of discussions that lasted several years, increasing in intensity after sanctions were lifted. In 2000, the two countries had signed an agreement on fighting terrorism, organized crime, drug trafficking and illegal migration. Under a second operational agreement concluded in 2003, Italy, under Silvio Berlusconi, undertook: to provide Libya with support for police training; to finance a charter flight programme to return migrants who were in an irregular situation in Libya to their countries of origin; to provide assistance for rescue at sea; and to finance the construction of a detention centre in northern Libya. In 2004, after the adoption of a third agreement which was never made public, the first massive wave of deportations from the island of Lampedusa (more than 1,000 people in six days) took place, and negotiations began on the establishment of mixed (Italian and Libyan) sea, air and land patrols aimed at surveying 2,000 km of Libyan coast and 4,000 km of borders separating Libya from its neighbours. Negotiations also concerned the funding by Italy of the construction of several detention centres to hold migrants coming from Central Africa, as well as a programme for the repatriation of migrants residing illegally in Libya: almost 6,000 people, mainly from Egypt, Ghana and Nigeria, were returned from Libya to their countries of origin on charter flights at the end of 2004 [1].

The arrival of a leftwing coalition in Italian government did not call into question the links between the two countries, which mixed economic interests and the fight against illegal immigration. A short time after taking office, the new head of the Italian government, Romano Prodi, announced that he had spoken to Qadafi about the problems of irregular immigration, in particular Libyan participation in joint operations to control maritime borders, as the first of three "reception centres" for

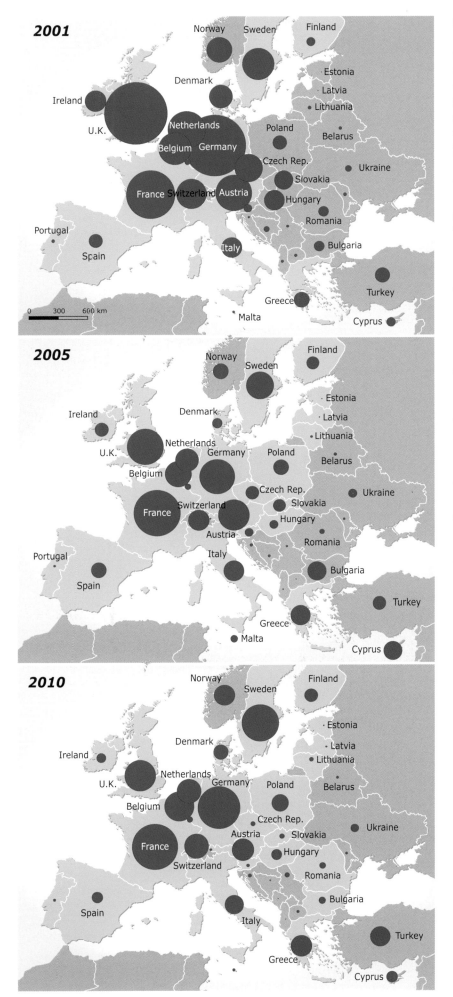

0 300 600 km

migrants that Italy had undertaken to build in Libya opened. The urgency can be explained by the Libyan authorities' powers of persuasion: they regularly "turned on the taps", relaxing coastal border controls to allow boats of migrants to leave for Sicily. This means of applying pressure was combined with barely veiled threats: at the end of 2006, a few weeks before a Euro-African Summit on migration, the Libyan Head of State declared: "[The Europeans] must compensate us for having exploited and pillaged our minerals and riches. For Africans to stay at home, we demand 10 billion dollars per year from Europe".

EU/Libya: a dangerous alliance

The message was addressed beyond Italy at European Union level. Since 2002, the EU has made the protection of its borders a priority, in particular maritime borders. The establishment of the Frontex agency in 2004 was the operational symbol of this orientation (see page 52). At the political level, the EU's external relations constitute a powerful lever to encourage third countries, as "producers" of migrants or – as in the case of Libya – transit points, to co-operate in this area. The Neighbourhood Policy, launched in 2004, is an effective tool to obtain commitments to fight irregular migration, in exchange for – mainly financial – support (see page 48). But the EU had little leverage in negotiations with Libya, which was unwilling to commit to an official partnership with Europe. Libya was not a member of the

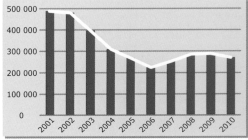

European Union

Number of requests for asylum recorded over the duration of one year

91,600
50,000
20,000
5,000
500

Evolution of the number of requests for asylum recorded in Europe

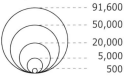

Sources: United Nations High Commissioner for Refugees, Asylum Levels and Trends in Industrialized Countries 2010; Asylum Levels and Trends in Industrialized Countries 2005.

Fewer asylum seekers in European countries since 2001

Barcelona process (which is aimed at establishing political dialogue between EU Member States and 10 countries to the south of the Mediterranean) and remained outside of the EU Neighbourhood Policy. The EU thus had no formal basis on which to initiate collaboration on migration issues with a country known for ill-treatment of migrants and, more generally, for violations of human rights. Furthermore, Libya had not ratified the 1951 Geneva Convention on the status of refugees. Yet, as of 2005, an EU/Libya Action Plan was on the table to organize the strengthening of controls at the Libyan maritime borders, the training of Libyan civil servants on asylum issues,

the renovation of detention centres and dialogue with the main countries of origin of migrants present in Libya. In 2007, a memorandum concluded with the European Commissioner for External Relations and the Neighbourhood Policy provided for the establishment of a satellite control system on the southern Libyan border, for a sum of 300 million euros.

Distancing as a migration policy

These two axes of co-operation (preventing migrants from leaving Libya for Europe, then preventing them from entering

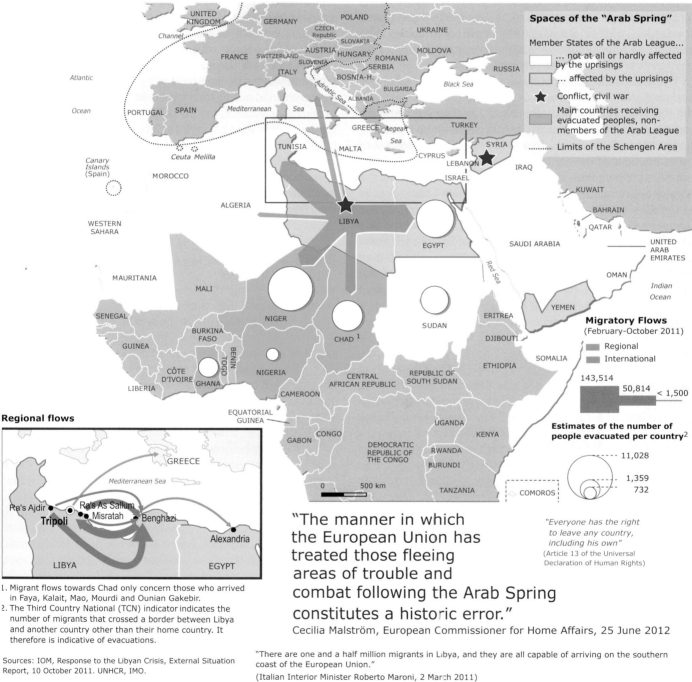

1. Migrant flows towards Chad only concern those who arrived in Faya, Kalait, Mao, Mourdi and Ounian Gakebir.
2. The Third Country National (TCN) indicator indicates the number of migrants that crossed a border between Libya and another country other than their home country. It therefore is indicative of evacuations.

Sources: IOM, Response to the Libyan Crisis, External Situation Report, 10 October 2011. UNHCR, IMO.

"The manner in which the European Union has treated those fleeing areas of trouble and combat following the Arab Spring constitutes a historic error."
Cecilia Malström, European Commissioner for Home Affairs, 25 June 2012

"Everyone has the right to leave any country, including his own"
(Article 13 of the Universal Declaration of Human Rights)

"There are one and a half million migrants in Libya, and they are all capable of arriving on the southern coast of the European Union."
(Italian Interior Minister Roberto Maroni, 2 March 2011)

"We are perfectly aware that such tragedies can bring about consequences in terms of uncontrollable migratory flows and acts of terrorism. In such an event, the whole of Europe would be at the frontline."
(French President Nicolas Sarkozy, 27 February 2011)

"Letting people enter who can only feed themselves by their own means, who can't demonstrate that they have their own resources to get by, would only give way to criminal activity, and as the minister in charge of security I cannot authorize it."
(Austrian Interior Minister Maria Fekter, 11 April 2011)

The Libyan Revolution: an exodus that barely touched the European Union

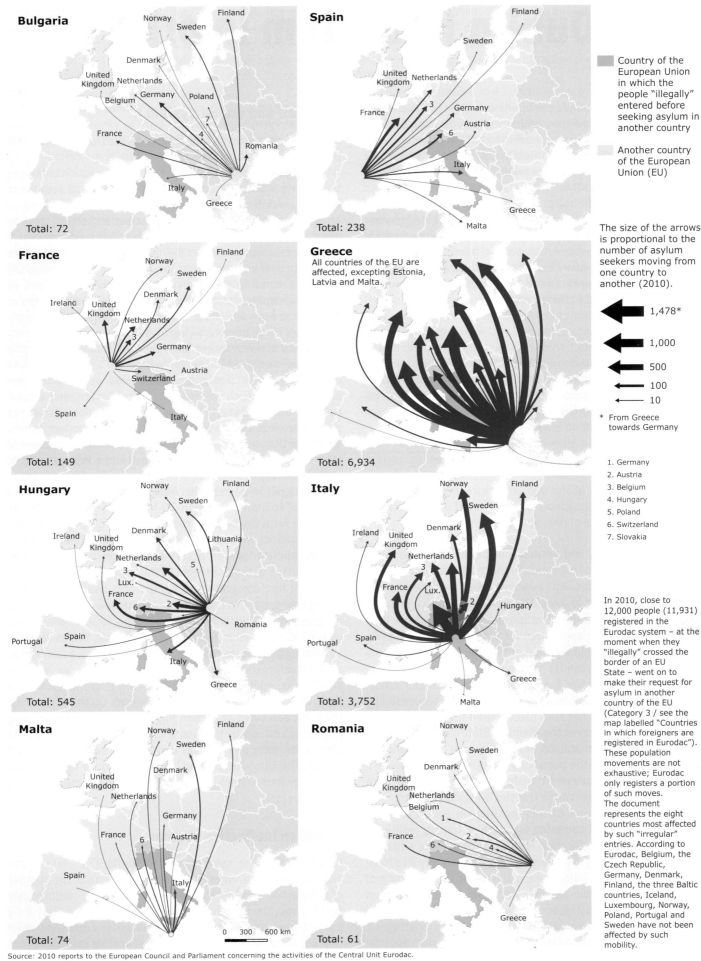

Bulgaria

Total: 72

Spain

Total: 238

France

Total: 149

Greece
All countries of the EU are affected, excepting Estonia, Latvia and Malta.

Total: 6,934

Hungary

Total: 545

Italy

Total: 3,752

Malta

Total: 74

Romania

Total: 61

Country of the European Union in which the people "illegally" entered before seeking asylum in another country

Another country of the European Union (EU)

The size of the arrows is proportional to the number of asylum seekers moving from one country to another (2010).

1,478*

1,000

500

100

10

* From Greece towards Germany

1. Germany
2. Austria
3. Belgium
4. Hungary
5. Poland
6. Switzerland
7. Slovakia

In 2010, close to 12,000 people (11,931) registered in the Eurodac system – at the moment when they "illegally" crossed the border of an EU State – went on to make their request for asylum in another country of the EU (Category 3 / see the map labelled "Countries in which foreigners are registered in Eurodac"). These population movements are not exhaustive; Eurodac only registers a portion of such moves. The document represents the eight countries most affected by such "irregular" entries. According to Eurodac, Belgium, the Czech Republic, Germany, Denmark, Finland, the three Baltic countries, Iceland, Luxembourg, Norway, Poland, Portugal and Sweden have not been affected by such mobility.

0   300   600 km

Source: 2010 reports to the European Council and Parliament concerning the activities of the Central Unit Eurodac.

The wanderings of the "Dublinites" – 1

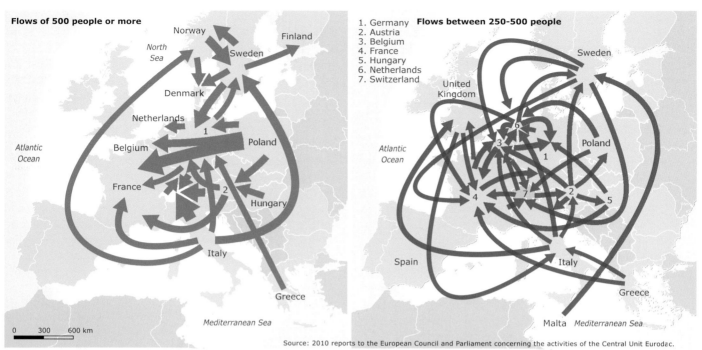

Flows of 500 people or more

Flows between 250-500 people

1. Germany
2. Austria
3. Belgium
4. France
5. Hungary
6. Netherlands
7. Switzerland

Source: 2010 reports to the European Council and Parliament concerning the activities of the Central Unit Eurodac.

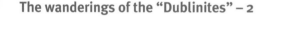

The size of the arrows is proportional to the number of asylum seekers moving from one country to another (2010).

2,081*   1,000   500   * from Poland to France

Only the flows greater than or equal to 250 are represented upon these two maps, equalling 36,228 people from a total of 57,575 claimants who – having sought asylum in one country – move to another state of the EU, for any number of reasons (refusal of claim, poor living conditions, seeking support of a parent or friend, etc.)

The wanderings of the "Dublinites" – 2

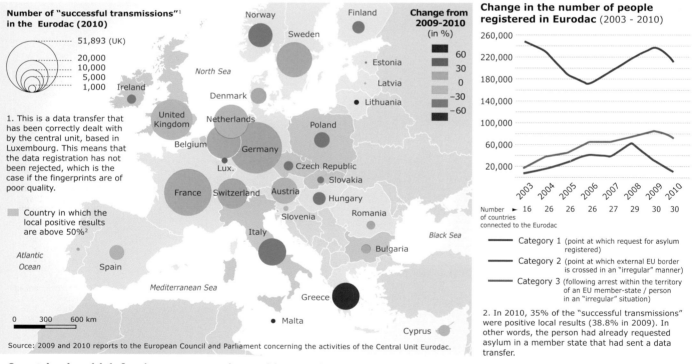

Number of "successful transmissions"[1] in the Eurodac (2010)

51,893 (UK)
20,000
10,000
5,000
1,000

1. This is a data transfer that has been correctly dealt with by the central unit, based in Luxembourg. This means that the data registration has not been rejected, which is the case if the fingerprints are of poor quality.

Country in which the local positive results are above 50%[2]

Change from 2009-2010 (in %)

60
30
0
-30
-60

• Estonia
• Latvia
● Lithuania

Change in the number of people registered in Eurodac (2003 - 2010)

	2003	2004	2005	2006	2007	2008	2009	2010
Number of countries connected to the Eurodac	16	26	26	26	27	29	30	30

—— Category 1 (point at which request for asylum registered)

—— Category 2 (point at which external EU border is crossed in an "irregular" manner)

—— Category 3 (following arrest within the territory of an EU member-state / person in an "irregular" situation)

2. In 2010, 35% of the "successful transmissions" were positive local results (38.8% in 2009). In other words, the person had already requested asylum in a member state that had sent a data transfer.

Source: 2009 and 2010 reports to the European Council and Parliament concerning the activities of the Central Unit Eurodac.

Countries in which foreigners are registered in Eurodac

Reform impossible?

The thunderbolt created by the 2011 judgment of the ECHR shook the Dublin II system, but States do not seem ready to accept all the consequences.

A resolution adopted by the European Parliament, on 2 September 2008, severely criticized the Dublin II system and called on the European Commission to "bring forward proposals for burden-sharing mechanisms which could be put in place in order to help alleviate the disproportionate load which could fall on certain Member States". The resolution also called for improved application of criteria on family reunification, additional guarantees in terms of information provided to asylum seekers and the establishment of an appeal mechanism with suspensive effect. Proposals for reform to the Dublin Regulation, presented by the European Commission in

December 2008 and adopted by the European Parliament in May 2009, were along the same lines. They included provisions on the temporary suspension of the regulation in cases in which States are faced with very high numbers of applications and introduced the possibility of filing an appeal with suspensive effect.

States, including France and Germany[1], seem to have more or less buried these proposals, abandoning these new provisions in favour of programmes for the "resettlement" of beneficiaries of international protection in countries like Malta[2]. But these adjustments do not change the main cause of dysfunction of the system – namely the principle that responsibility for the examination of an asylum application falls on the State of first arrival in EU territory. In fact, there is already a mechanism which enables the reception of persons to be shared between Member States, under the principle of solidarity, in cases of mass arrivals of asylum seekers at a border: the EU Directive on temporary protection. It is significant that this mechanism has never been implemented, despite the significant arrivals of Iraqi, Somali, Eritrean and Chechen asylum seekers, whose fears are recognized by all, that marked the beginning of the 2000s. The revolutions across the Mediterranean and the siege mentalities of the French and Italian governments did not favour its application.

Ignoring this tool, Member States preferred the Dublin II system, the symbol of a European asylum policy which tends to prioritize restrictive and deterrent measures in order to avoid hosting asylum seekers, encouraging the States that are most exposed to asylum applications to make their laws and practices tougher. Thus, in 2009, Italy concluded an agreement with Libya to prohibit the departure of boat people. As a result, the number of asylum applications fell by half. Favouring jingoism over solidarity towards asylum seekers and refugees, which should prevail in a political space shaped by numerous international human rights commitments, the application of the Dublin II Regulation presents significant risks to the right to asylum, but also to other rights protected by the European Convention on Human Rights, such as the right not to be subjected to inhuman or degrading treatment (including by being returned to a country which does not respect human rights) and the right not to be subjected to collective expulsion.

Gérard SADIK ◘

---

1 Joint contribution of France and Germany to the European Conference on Asylum, 13-14 September 2010.
2 France received almost 200 persons, in two waves of official arrivals in June 2009 and June 2010.

Biometric databases and border controls

Over the last decade, the use of biometrics has come to play an ever-more important role in EU migration policy. There are three chief European Union databases that currently do or will in future utilize biometric information (e.g. scans of fingerprints; irises; retinas; facial and palm structure; etc.) for the purposes of border control. These are Eurodac, the Visa Information System (VIS), and the second-generation Schengen Information System (SIS II).

A number of other schemes also require the collection and retention of biometric data: all EU Member States' passports; EU residence permits; and planned future border control mechanisms such as an Entry/Exit System (EES) and a Registered Travellers Programme (RTP). This overview discusses Eurodac; VIS; SIS II; and briefly examines the EES and the RTP and some of the proposed relationships between the different systems.

Eurodac

Eurodac is made up of a central database (hosted by the European Commission) that contains digital fingerprint scans collected by EU Member States' border officials, and the fingerprint scanners and computers connected to that database. The system was established by Council Regulation (EC) No. 2725/2000 and began functioning in 2003. It allows fingerprints to be used for the purposes of establishing whether an asylum applicant in one Member State has ever applied for asylum in another Member State, or whether a migrant entered EU territory irregularly.

There are three categories of record contained in Eurodac:

- Category 1: Fingerprints from all individuals aged 14 years or over who have made applications for asylum in the Member States;
- Category 2: Fingerprints of persons who were apprehended when crossing a Member State's external border irregularly;
- Category 3: Persons who were found illegally present on the territory of a Member State (in case the competent authorities consider it necessary to check a potential prior asylum application).

As of 31 December 2010, the Central Unit database contained a total of 1,704,690 records: 1,666,536 in category 1; 38,153 in category 2; and 60,696 in category 3.

The use of biometrics in the EU's asylum system has had some horrific human consequences. There have been numerous documented instances over the years of individuals mutilating their fingerprints in order to prevent them being matched to Eurodac records. This frequently involves individuals placing their fingers on a burning hob. Alternative methods include using knives, razors, glue or acid.

The second-generation Schengen Information System (SIS II)

The Schengen Information System comprises a central EU database and at least 500,000 computer terminals in the Member States – an increase of over 300% on the 2003 figure of 125,000 terminals, and of over 1,600% on the 1995 figure of 30,000. The SIS was established by the 1990 Schengen Convention and came into use in 1995. It gives authorities access to information about a variety of persons and objects, including third-country nationals to whom access to the Schengen Area should be denied.

The immigration-related aspects of SIS II are contained in Regulation (EC) No. 1987/2006. One significant change is that SIS II introduces biometric information, namely photographs and fingerprints. This will initially be used to confirm individuals' identity on the basis of searches made using alphanumeric information. However, "as soon as [it] becomes technically possible, fingerprints may also be used to identify a third-country national on the basis of his biometric identifier." This will permit both one-to-many searches (in which individual identifiers are compared to some or all the biometric information in the database) and one-to-one searches (in which biometric information will be compared to that contained in a specific record).

One-to-many searches increase the chances of finding inaccurate "matches". Biometrics, despite their high degree of accuracy, are not infallible. As noted by Steve Peers of the organization Statewatch, the European Parliament had to "compromise fundamentally on the initial objective of permitting the use of biometric data only for verification of identity, and never permitting it for one-to-many searches".

Between 1997 and 2010, the number of "hits" (successful searches) in the SIS on the basis of Article 96 (persons refused entry into the Schengen area) totalled 253,460, or 40.56% of the total number of hits. As of 1 January 2011, there were 716,797 Article 96 records, out of a total of 35,698,802 records. SIS II was initially supposed to enter into operation in 2006. It is currently expected that it will become operational in 2013 and is intended to have a capacity of between 70 and 100 million records.

The Visa Information System (VIS)

The VIS was devised, according to Regulation No. 767/2008 of the Council of the European Union, with the intention of: "[I]mproving the implementation of the common visa policy, consular co-operation and consultation between central visa authorities (...) in order to facilitate the visa application procedure, prevent 'visa shopping', to facilitate the fight against

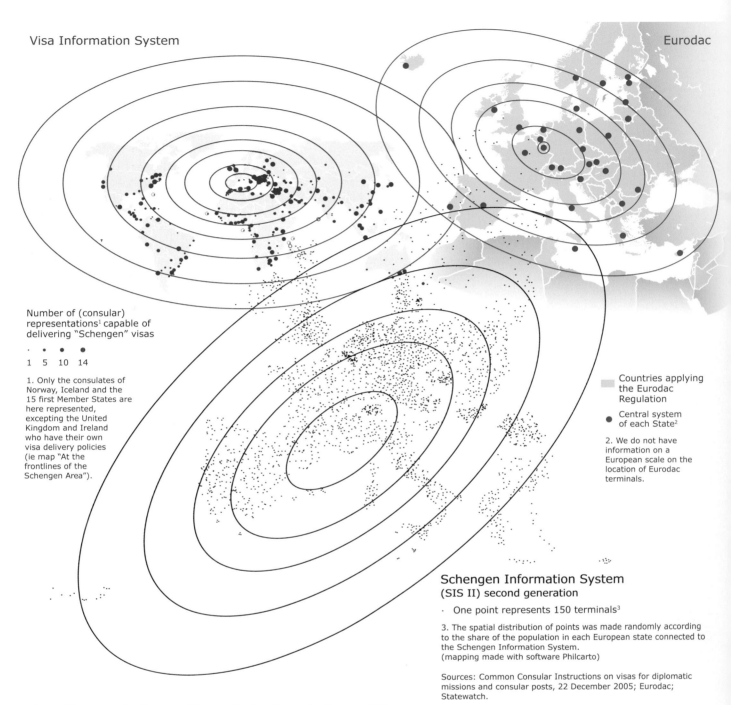

Visa Information System

Eurodac

Number of (consular)
representations[1] capable of
delivering "Schengen" visas

· • ● ●
1 5 10 14

1. Only the consulates of
Norway, Iceland and the
15 first Member States are
here represented,
excepting the United
Kingdom and Ireland
who have their own
visa delivery policies
(ie map "At the
frontlines of the
Schengen Area").

Countries applying
the Eurodac
Regulation

● Central system
of each State[2]

2. We do not have
information on a
European scale on the
location of Eurodac
terminals.

Schengen Information System
(SIS II) second generation

· One point represents 150 terminals[3]

3. The spatial distribution of points was made randomly according
to the share of the population in each European state connected to
the Schengen Information System.
(mapping made with software Philcarto)

Sources: Common Consular Instructions on visas for diplomatic
missions and consular posts, 22 December 2005; Eurodac;
Statewatch.

Who will create the largest biometric database in the world?

fraud and to facilitate checks at external border crossing points
and within the territory of the Member States".

The system will also assist authorities in determining the
state responsible for examining an asylum application, and it
is foreseen that the system will increase the level of deportations from the EU. A Communication adopted by the European
Commission in October 2011 provides that "the biometric data
of all visa holders will be registered in the VIS (...) any undocumented visa holder (...) can be more easily identified, increasing
the possibilities for return".

Since 2004, the VIS has been represented by the Council
of the European Union as "consist[ing] of a central IT system
and of a communication infrastructure that links this central
system to national systems". Eventually, all EU Member States'
consulates in non-EU countries will be connected by the system
to every external border crossing point in the Schengen Area.

The first region to be subjected to the new system is North
Africa, where EU Member States' consulates have been using
the VIS since October 2011. This will be followed by the Middle
East, then the Gulf region, with all Schengen states' consular
posts worldwide to be connected to the VIS by 2013.

The biometric information requirement of visa applicants will
be a digital photograph and ten fingerprints. Children under 12
or those unable to provide finger scans are excluded. The system
is capable of holding up to 70 million records and, when it is fully
operational, will be the largest biometric database in the world.

In late 2012, it was intended that Eurodac, SIS II and VIS
would come under the management of the new EU Agency
for the Operational Management for Large-Scale IT Systems,
which will also be able to undertake, with the permission of
the European Commission, research and pilot projects into new
systems.

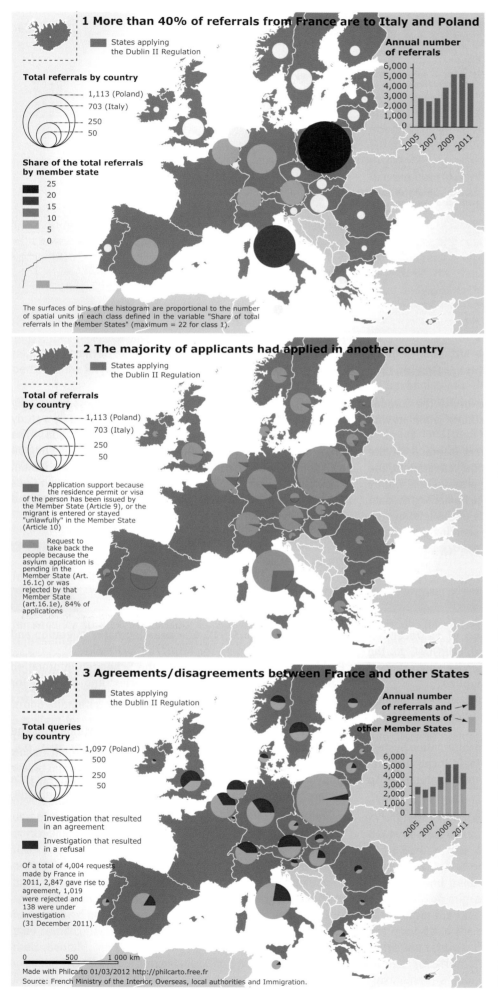

1 More than 40% of referrals from France are to Italy and Poland

States applying the Dublin II Regulation

Total referrals by country
- 1,113 (Poland)
- 703 (Italy)
- 250
- 50

Annual number of referrals

Share of the total referrals by member state
- 25
- 20
- 15
- 10
- 5
- 0

The surfaces of bins of the histogram are proportional to the number of spatial units in each class defined in the variable "Share of total referrals in the Member States" (maximum = 22 for class 1).

2 The majority of applicants had applied in another country

States applying the Dublin II Regulation

Total of referrals by country
- 1,113 (Poland)
- 703 (Italy)
- 250
- 50

Application support because the residence permit or visa of the person has been issued by the Member State (Article 9), or the migrant is entered or stayed "unlawfully" in the Member State (Article 10)

Request to take back the people because the asylum application is pending in the Member State (Art. 16.1c) or was rejected by that Member State (art.16.1e), 84% of applications

3 Agreements/disagreements between France and other States

States applying the Dublin II Regulation

Total queries by country
- 1,097 (Poland)
- 500
- 250
- 50

Annual number of referrals and agreements of other Member States

Investigation that resulted in an agreement

Investigation that resulted in a refusal

Of a total of 4,004 requests made by France in 2011, 2,847 gave rise to agreement, 1,019 were rejected and 138 were under investigation (31 December 2011).

0   500   1 000 km

Made with Philcarto 01/03/2012 http://philcarto.free.fr
Source: French Ministry of the Interior, Overseas, local authorities and Immigration.

Future systems

The biometric technologies underlying the VIS are seen as "a prerequisite" for the implementation of certain future systems that make up what is referred to by the Commission in its Communication of October 2011 as the "smart borders" initiative.

This will consist of an EU-wide Entry/Exit System (EES) and a Registered Travellers Programme (RTP). The EES will record the location and time of an individual's entry into and exit from the EU in a central database, allowing Member States' authorities to detect "overstayers" more easily, thus increasing the potential for deportation. There seems to be significant enthusiasm to base this on biometric data – "preferably e-passport and/or fingerprints", according to a note from the Presidency of the Council presented at a conference on innovation in border management at the beginning of 2012.

The RTP will allow the 'pre-screening' of individuals wishing to travel to the EU, with their biometrics used to facilitate easy access at border crossings. The Commission foresees that this system will "as far as possible (...) make use of new technologies such as Automated Border Control systems", which would be used for EU citizens as well. In the case of third-country nationals, the RTP would allow "low-risk" travellers (i.e. businesspeople or wealthy tourists) to access EU territory more easily than those deemed to constitute a greater "threat", demonstrating a shift from national to class-based discrimination.

Recent developments would suggest that there will be "a central architecture for both the EES and the RTP, since according to the Presidency of the Council, this "appeared to be the most cost-effective option, and to give the best basis for the necessary synergy and interoperability with other EU systems".

The drive for greater "synergy" and "interoperability" between national and EU IT systems has

The application of the Dublin II regulations in France (continued overleaf)

GDF-Suez (see the map below), which was one of the first partners of the penal administration in France. Since 2011, this group also manages services (cleaning, catering, etc.) in two centres in Gradisca d'Isonzo in Italy. According to the organization Melting Pot, the company won a call for tenders launched by the Italian government, with a bid putting the cost at 34 euros per detainee, per day, compared to the 42 euros per day cost of the previous contractor.

In the United Kingdom, much of the management of migrant detention is sub-contracted to private companies. Among these, we find the company G4S, one of the largest private sector employers worldwide, which also provides escorts for the repatriation by plane of migrants subject to deportation orders. Another provider is the group GEO, one of the leaders in the sector in the United States. Its net profits in the UK multiplied by five between 2000 and 2012, in large part as a result of its investment in the detention of migrants.

When structures are partly or entirely managed by private companies, with the main objective of maximizing profits and not fulfilling a mission to provide a public service, the costs of operation constitute a limit on the quality of migrants' living conditions. For example, almost 10 years after the Austrian government transferred the management of an open centre in Traiskirchen to a private German company, European Homecare, in February 2003, no further improvements had been made to the former imperial barracks. Hygiene and security conditions had deteriorated, in particular as its reception capacity is exceeded on a regular basis. In 2008, in its annual report, the organization Cimade noted that in France, the Ministry of Justice no longer provides services in the detention centre at Lyon airport. Since 2007, the company Exprimm, a subsidiary of Bouygues (see map), which won the contract, sub-contracts cleaning to the company Onet and catering to the company Avenance. Yet "the sub-contractors have drastically reduced

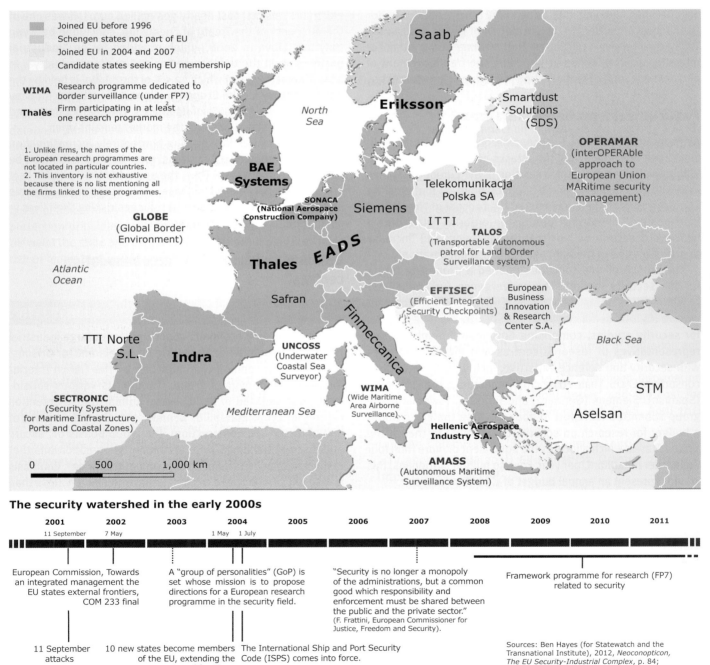

The security watershed in the early 2000s

2001	2002	2003	2004	2005	2006	2007	2008	2009	2010	2011
11 September	7 May		1 May 1 July							

European Commission, Towards an integrated management the EU states external frontiers, COM 233 final

A "group of personalities" (GoP) is set whose mission is to propose directions for a European research programme in the security field.

"Security is no longer a monopoly of the administrations, but a common good which responsibility and enforcement must be shared between the public and the private sector." (F. Frattini, European Commissioner for Justice, Freedom and Security).

Framework programme for research (FP7) related to security

11 September attacks

10 new states become members of the EU, extending the external frontiers.

The International Ship and Port Security Code (ISPS) comes into force.

Sources: Ben Hayes (for Statewatch and the Transnational Institute), 2012, *Neoconopticon, The EU Security-Industrial Complex*, p. 84; Statewatch.

The main players in the border surveillance market

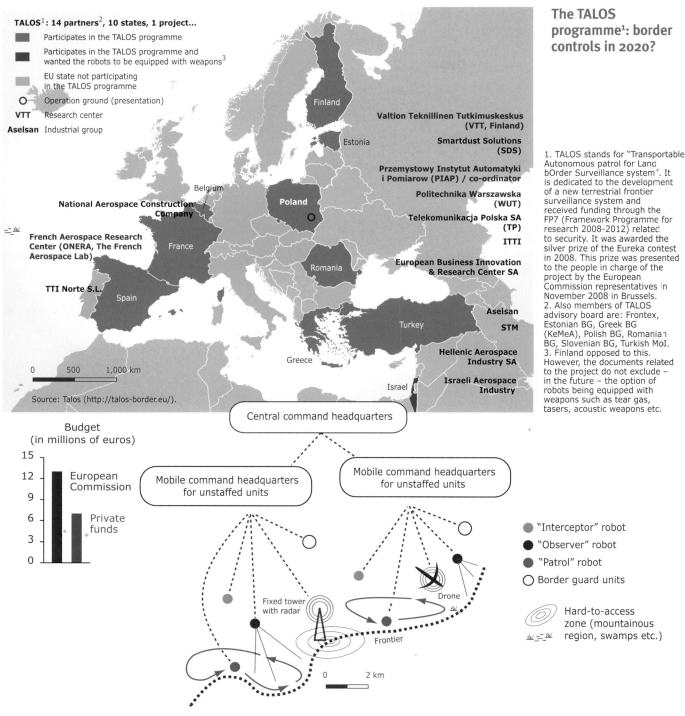

The TALOS programme[1]: border controls in 2020?

TALOS[1]: 14 partners[2], 10 states, 1 project...

Participates in the TALOS programme

Participates in the TALOS programme and wanted the robots to be equipped with weapons[3]

EU state not participating in the TALOS programme

O　Operation ground (presentation)

VTT　Research center

Aselsan　Industrial group

Valtion Teknillinen Tutkimuskeskus (VTT, Finland)
Smartdust Solutions (SDS)
Przemystowy Instytut Automatyki i Pomiarow (PIAP) / co-ordinator
Politechnika Warszawska (WUT)
Telekomunikacja Polska SA (TP)
ITTI
European Business Innovation & Research Center SA
Aselsan
STM
Hellenic Aerospace Industry SA
Israeli Aerospace Industry

National Aerospace Construction Company
French Aerospace Research Center (ONERA, The French Aerospace Lab)
TTI Norte S.L.

Finland / Estonia / Belgium / Poland / France / Romania / Spain / Turkey / Greece / Israel

Source: Talos (http://talos-border.eu/).

0　500　1,000 km

1. TALOS stands for "Transportable Autonomous patrol for Land bOrder Surveillance system". It is dedicated to the development of a new terrestrial frontier surveillance system and received funding through the FP7 (Framework Programme for research 2008-2012) related to security. It was awarded the silver prize of the Eureka contest in 2008. This prize was presented to the people in charge of the project by the European Commission representatives in November 2008 in Brussels.
2. Also members of TALOS advisory board are: Frontex, Estonian BG, Greek BG (KeMeA), Polish BG, Romanian BG, Slovenian BG, Turkish MoI.
3. Finland opposed to this. However, the documents related to the project do not exclude – in the future – the option of robots being equipped with weapons such as tear gas, tasers, acoustic weapons etc.

Budget (in millions of euros)

European Commission / Private funds

Central command headquarters
Mobile command headquarters for unstaffed units
Mobile command headquarters for unstaffed units

"Interceptor" robot
"Observer" robot
"Patrol" robot
Border guard units
Hard-to-access zone (mountainous region, swamps etc.)

Fixed tower with radar
Drone
Frontier
0　2 km

the number of staff. Of the 12 women who provided catering services, only 4 are left... and their working conditions are significantly worse".

A market of the future

The growing privatization of the management of administrative detention of migrants in many countries, where it used to be the responsibility of public authorities, applies an industrial approach which resembles that applied to the prison system, with the construction of detention centres by private companies which are subsequently rented to the State. Beyond the issue of detention, the commodification of the "management of migratory flows" raises many questions, in particular with regard to the final objective of migration controls, which weigh heavily on the

EU's budget for research in the area of advanced technology. In a context dominated by a race for profits, we can legitimately raise concerns over the spiralling application of security technology to the surveillance of borders: while it should constitute a tool serving policy, under the pressure of large companies making money, it could become the driving force.

Olivier CLOCHARD and Claire RODIER

1　Statewatch and Transnational Institute (2009), *NeoConopticon, The EU-security complex*.
2　Communication of the European Commission, *The development of a common policy on illegal immigration, smuggling and trafficking of human beings, external borders and the return of illegal residents*, COM(2003) 0323 final, 3 June 2003.
3　Rodier C. (2012), *Xénophobie business. A quoi servent les contrôles migratoires?*, La Découverte.

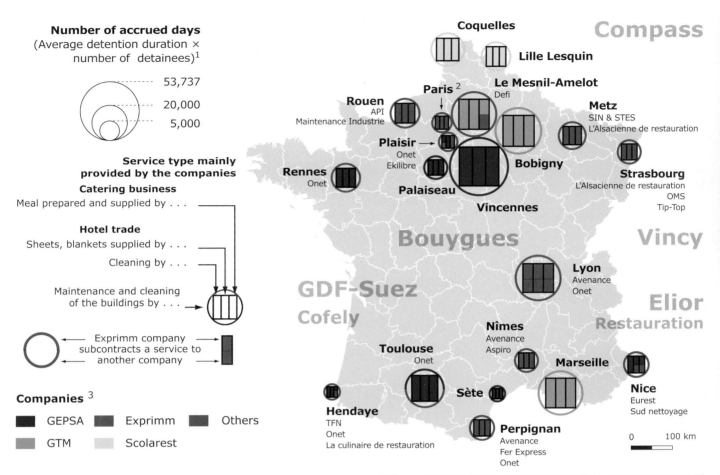

Number of accrued days
(Average detention duration ×
number of detainees)[1]

- 53,737
- 20,000
- 5,000

**Service type mainly
provided by the companies**

Catering business
Meal prepared and supplied by . . .

Hotel trade
Sheets, blankets supplied by . . .

Cleaning by . . .

Maintenance and cleaning
of the buildings by . . .

Exprimm company
subcontracts a service to
another company

Companies [3]

- GEPSA
- Exprimm
- Others
- GTM
- Scolarest

1. These two variables were taken into account because the money transferred to the companies by the state is usually calculated according to the number of accrued days of the detainees. Year reference is 2010 (*cf.* source).
2. The only administrative detention centre where the services to female detainees are taken care of by a religious congregation.
3. **GEPSA**, a subsidiary company of Cofely belonging to the **GDF-Suez** corporation, is a company which takes part in the functioning of penal institutions. It also manages the Italian detention centre of Gradisca. GTM, an important economic stakeholder in the building **trade,** belongs to **Vinci Construction corporation** (France). **Exprimm** is a real-estate service provider and subsidiary company of Bouygues Construction corporation. **Scolarest** and **Eurest** are companies operating respectively in Coquelles, Lille and Nice. They specialize in school catering. They are part of **Compass Group**, one of the world leaders in the community catering business. The names of the other companies – such as **Avenance**, part of the **Elior Restauration** corporation (catering) – are indicated above the name of the city where the administrative detention centre is established.

Transnational companies at the service of administrative detention in France

Detention centre	Detainee hygiene	
	Toiletries supplied by	Laundry
Bobigny		
Coquelles	PAF	
Hendaye		
Lesquin		
Lyon		Onet
Marseille		
Le Mesnil-Amelot		DEFI
Metz	SIN & STES	SIN & STES
Nice		
Nîmes		
Palaiseau		
Paris (Palais de justice)	Les Sœurs de la Miséricorde	Les Sœurs de la Miséricorde
Vincennes		
Perpignan	Hygy-Pro	Avenance
Plaisir		
Rennes		
Rouen-Oissel	Greffe du centre	agents de nettoyage
Sète		
Strasbourg	Gendarmerie	OMS => TIP-TOP
Toulouse		

Sources: ASSFAM, Forum Réfugiés, France Terre d'Asile, La Cimade et Ordre de Malte (2011) Centres et locaux de rétention administrative, rapport 2010; CGLPL; Melting Pot.

French fortresses in faraway seas

The Schengen Area comprises only the territories of European countries and neighbouring islands, as well as the Canary Islands, Madeira and the Azores. Why do some French overseas territories reproduce this model? How have neighbouring countries become symbols of the concept of "illegal" migration and the targets of exceptional numbers of deportations? Why does France say so little about these faraway offshoots of European policy?

Overseas borders

The ocean and cold weather render some French non-European territories unfavourable to migration. However, in the Caribbean and the Comoros archipelago, where history and geography justify close relations between neighbouring countries, overseas French territories, although poor in comparison to metropolitan France, are no less economically attractive to the populations of some surrounding countries. The French status of certain islands and enclaves transforms neighbours into foreigners and the regional movement of persons into migratory flows. Although the Schengen area is limited to the European continent, its mechanisms are reproduced and in some cases exaggerated.

Three French "ramparts" against regional movement of persons

The island of **Mayotte** is linked to the other three islands that form the archipelago of Comoros by a shared culture, close family ties and the fl uid movement of persons. In 1974, following a referendum, French decolonization led to the independence of the Union of Comoros, including all four islands. However, in 1976, overriding opinions issued by the United Nations and the Organization of African Unity, France retained Mayotte as part of the French Republic, invoking the will of the majority of inhabitants, despite the fact that the archipelago forms a single entity. Twenty years went by before France began to consider applying its national legal framework, with numerous derogations, to Mayotte. In 1995, the "Balladur visa", henceforth required by Comorans to enter Mayotte, gave concrete expression to this fracture. On 31 March 2011, Mayotte obtained the status of French department and social rights should very gradually (at best within the next 25 years) be aligned to those in metropolitan France. Mahorans paid a high price for the realization of their dream: painful social upheaval caused by the rapid change from local Muslim status to French republican civil status and from island to bunker. Comorans,

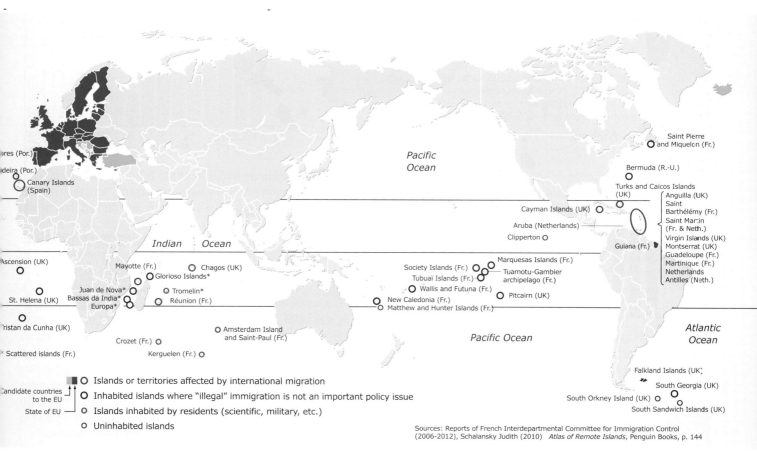

Sources: Reports of French Interdepartmental Committee for Immigration Control (2006-2012), Schalansky Judith (2010) *Atlas of Remote Islands*, Penguin Books, p. 144

The European Union in the world: the disputed territories of small islands

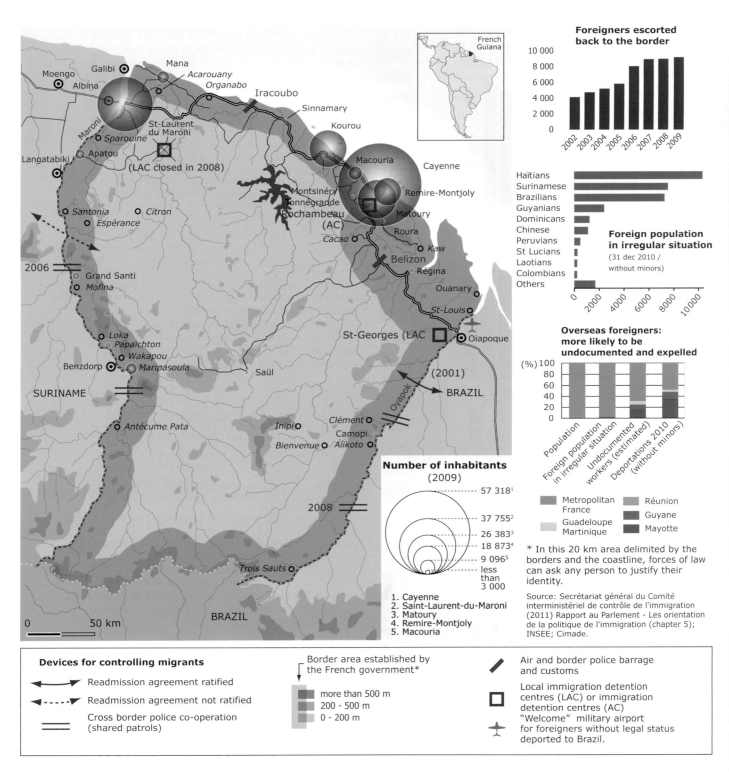

Foreigners escorted back to the border

Foreign population in irregular situation
(31 dec 2010 / without minors)

Overseas foreigners: more likely to be undocumented and expelled

Metropolitan France
Guadeloupe Martinique
Réunion
Guyane
Mayotte

* In this 20 km area delimited by the borders and the coastline, forces of law can ask any person to justify their identity.

Source: Secrétariat général du Comité interministériel de contrôle de l'immigration (2011) Rapport au Parlement - Les orientation de la politique de l'immigration (chapter 5); INSEE; Cimade.

Number of inhabitants (2009)

- 57 318[1]
- 37 755[2]
- 26 383[3]
- 18 873[4]
- 9 096[5]
- less than 3 000

1. Cayenne
2. Saint-Laurent-du-Maroni
3. Matoury
4. Remire-Montjoly
5. Macouria

Devices for controlling migrants

- Readmission agreement ratified
- Readmission agreement not ratified
- Cross border police co-operation (shared patrols)

Border area established by the French government*
- more than 500 m
- 200 - 500 m
- 0 - 200 m

- Air and border police barrage and customs
- Local immigration detention centres (LAC) or immigration detention centres (AC)
- "Welcome" military airport for foreigners without legal status deported to Brazil.

Control of migrants in French Guiana

A Schengen Area with 70,000 inhabitants

A long way from metropolitan France, the Netherlands and France share a border: that which divides the island of Saint-Martin (approximately 40,000 inhabitants on the Dutch side and 30,000 on the French side). A symbolic border! Inspired by the Schengen Agreement, an agreement signed by the two states in 1994 noted "the intensive movement of persons" on the island and established the joint control of entries, combining the criteria applied by both parties. It remained to secure the island's external borders, in keeping with the European model, but this was not possible while the territory was composed of a commune of Guadeloupe and a part of the Dutch Antilles.

In 2007, the commune became a French "overseas collectivity" and the Dutch part became an autonomous territory, opening the way for the entry into force of the 1994 agreement on 1 August. Since then, Haitians are required to have a French visa to enter the island. This had not previously been a requirement to enter the Dutch part of the island. Since May 2008, a retention centre situated in the collectivity of Saint-Martin enables administrative expulsions to be carried out without transiting through Guadeloupe, from the international airport situated in the Dutch territory.

The diplomacy of isolation

In principle, a specific visa (distinct from a Schengen visa) is required for a short stay in a French overseas territory. The countries whose citizens are exempted from this requirement are determined by bilateral agreements. A neighbourhood policy could have been applied, yet the exemption does not apply to any of the Caribbean islands or countries near French Guiana or Mayotte. Since November 2006, citizens of states in South America can travel throughout the sub-continent with only an identity card with a single exception: French Guiana. Another illustration of this incoherence: a Brazilian does not have to have a visa to enter metropolitan France but does require one to enter French Guiana.

Several readmission agreements concerning the expulsion of foreigners from French overseas territories have been concluded with neighbouring countries (Brazil in 2001, St Lucia in 2006, Dominican Republic in 2007, Mauritius in 2008). Bilateral co-operation in border controls is being strengthened, for example on either side of the bridge of Oyapock, completed in 2011, which had been supposed to facilitate travel between French Guiana and northern Brazil. On the other hand, the postponement year after year of the entry into force of readmission agreements with Guyana, Suriname, Barbados, Trinidad and Tobago, reveals the limits of this policy in relation to these states.

The conclusion of a readmission agreement between France and Haiti or the Republic of Comoros seems improbable. How could Haiti cope with the end of economic transfers from exiles in metropolitan France or the return of generally poor exiles from the Caribbean? Mass expulsions of Comorans from Mayotte to the island of Anjouan took place unhindered and without safe passage, until the eviction of the secessionist colonel in power until March 2008. Since then, the Union of Comoros has tried to stop expulsions on several occasions, underlining that Mayotte is part of its territory and that a Comoran cannot be considered to be a foreigner. Within the recently adopted arsenal of European policies, the prospect of an agreement on "concerted management of migration flows" could perhaps influence Haiti and the Comoros: offering co-development agreements in exchange for support in controlling migration and, in the case of Comoros, recognition of Mayotte as a French territory. But that would imply a strong economic commitment from France, which is not the case at present.

Denial of rights

The reproduction of European policy on a smaller scale does not alone explain the exceptional numbers of administrative expulsions from Mayotte, French Guiana and Guadeloupe, compared to those from metropolitan France, which are themselves high. These scatterings of colonialism remain the Wild West, where human rights are widely violated. Numerous reports have revealed the following:

■ An administrative machine manufacturing "illegal" migrants, based on the system applied in metropolitan France, but amplified: blocking applications for years, requiring the provision of many more documents than required by law, arbitrary decisions, avoidance of procedures granting residence permits for fear of expulsion;

■ The brutality of arrests, facilitated by the absence of a requirement to obtain prior legal authorization; accelerated expulsions outside the control of the courts; and inhuman conditions in the retention centre in Mayotte;

■ The denial of the right to an effective remedy (as guaranteed by the European Convention on Human Rights) in the case of notification of an administrative expulsion order or an obligation to leave the territory; the suspensive appeal procedure applicable in other departments does not apply in French Guiana, Guadeloupe or the "overseas collectivities".

Although the French Constitution allows for some modifications to be made to French law in their application to overseas territories, it certainly does not allow France to ignore its international human rights obligations.

French migration policies in the Caribbean and in the archipelago of Comoros are not well known. Yet their impact on human rights and the human dramas they produce are of the same nature as those caused by the policies of the European Union.

Marie DUFLO ▣

What do we know about the International Organization for Migration?

The International Organization for Migration (IOM) is an institution which is both omnipresent and little known. Those who are interested in migration have heard about it and may have sometimes come across its activities, but in contrast to the Office of the United Nations High Commissioner for Refugees (UNHCR), which has been the subject of many in-depth studies, there have been almost no independent studies on IOM.

Yet IOM has 132 (146 according to the IOM website) Member States, 460 field offices across the world, a budget of US$1.4 billion and a staff of close to 7,000 people.

In December 1951, the Intergovernmental Committee for European Migration (ICEM) was established as the successor to a "temporary" body. The ICEM's mandate was to organize the departure of displaced persons from Europe to countries seeking to increase their populations. It was created in the post-Second World War context and following the adoption of the Marshall Plan in an effort to ensure political stability in Europe. The project was initiated by the United States, a year after the establishment of the UNHCR, and was intended to counterbalance the role of the latter, which was suspected of being under communist influence.

The ICEM's mission was of a more technical and logistical nature than that of the UNHCR, which focused on the legal protection of refugees and providing material assistance. The ICEM, which had been intended to be rapidly dissolved, was renamed IOM and granted permanent status in 1989. It continues to organize the practical aspects of the displacement of migrants (legal procedures, transportation, etc.), but its approach, while diversifying, has been largely reversed: today its focus is not to organize the departure of refugees from "old Europe", for example, but to curb migration into Europe. Its activities can be divided into four categories: operational, humanitarian, political and ideological.

At the operational level, IOM provides support for the implementation of migration policies. For example, under so-called "voluntary return" programmes, IOM organizes the return of migrants from countries of destination to countries of origin and supports their reintegration. In some cases, IOM manages detention centres holding migrants in transit or awaiting deportation. Human "trafficking" constitutes another field of activity: IOM "warns" potential migrants of the dangers, "protects" victims and even transports them back to the point of departure.

The IOM's humanitarian activities have emerged more recently. During the first Gulf War in 1991, the agency was given responsibility for migrant workers fleeing Kuwait, following invasion by Iraq. Since then, it has been present in numerous conflict situations, as well as in other crises, and its activities have progressively diversified (to include reconstruction and development projects). This had the effect of increasing sources of funding and feeding its growth, but also drew criticism, both from competitors in the humanitarian "market" and certain Member States, which saw it as moving away from its initial mandate.

At the political level, IOM operates as an advisory agency to States on migration policies. Its "experts" and trainers co-operate with national bodies, providing assistance in the design and implementation of such policies, in the negotiation of co-operation agreements with other States and in strengthening border surveillance.

Finally, IOM participates in developing opinions and knowledge on migration, fostering "dialogue" both between States and with academics. It thereby generates and spreads its own descriptive and normative ideology on what migration is and should be. Under the slogan *Managing migration for the benefit of all* it proposes a framework of principles for action on migration to States, dealing with issues such as development, the workforce, health, climate change and international co-operation.

IOM thus operates like a service provider on migration. As an intergovernmental agency, in principle it acts only upon the request and according to the instructions of Member States. But its budget depends entirely on the "orders" placed by governments, so that its operation is similar to that of a private company, causing it actively to sell itself and attempt to generate demand for its services.

Under these conditions, IOM has to accept almost all demands made by States, even those related to morally questionable tasks. It therefore receives criticism for engaging in States' "dirty work". There is a contrast between its technocratic and consensual approach and its role in migration policies. The fact that it does not belong to the UN system feeds into these criticisms, because it places IOM outside of the provisions of the 1945 Charter and the 1948 Universal Declaration of Human Rights.

The expansion of the agency is characterized by standardization, since it offers more or less the same services in each situation. This raises the risk of the potential "formatting" of States, with detrimental consequences for less developed regions, where authorities are encouraged to adopt standard measures largely dictated by dominating countries (which constitute the IOM's main donors), echoing the practices of the World Bank in the name of the "Washington Consensus".

In a nutshell, the IOM plays an ambiguous role within an international context which advertises "co-operation" between

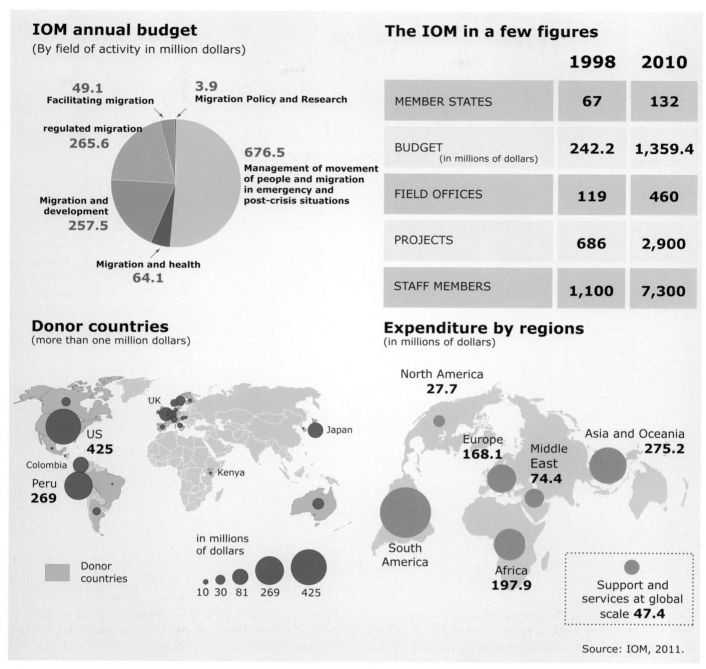

IOM annual budget
(By field of activity in million dollars)

- 49.1 **Facilitating migration**
- 3.9 **Migration Policy and Research**
- regulated migration **265.6**
- 676.5 **Management of movement of people and migration in emergency and post-crisis situations**
- **Migration and development** 257.5
- **Migration and health** 64.1

The IOM in a few figures

	1998	2010
MEMBER STATES	67	132
BUDGET (in millions of dollars)	242.2	1,359.4
FIELD OFFICES	119	460
PROJECTS	686	2,900
STAFF MEMBERS	1,100	7,300

Donor countries
(more than one million dollars)

UK, Japan, US 425, Colombia, Peru 269, Kenya

in millions of dollars

Donor countries

10 30 81 269 425

Expenditure by regions
(in millions of dollars)

- North America **27.7**
- Europe **168.1**
- Middle East **74.4**
- Asia and Oceania **275.2**
- South America
- Africa **197.9**
- Support and services at global scale **47.4**

Source: IOM, 2011.

The International Organization for Migration

States, while generalizing protectionist migration policies based on the interests of destination countries. It claims to be a supra-governmental agency sensitive to the interests of all and to the wellbeing of migrants, while thriving thanks to funding from Western countries seeking to maintain potential migrants at a distance in countries of departure or transit.

Antoine PÉCOUD

A young migrant in Patras, Greece, January 2011.
Photo: Gabriel Pécot

Part 3

Detention at the heart of asylum and immigration policies

With the proliferation of detention centres and longer detention periods, the imprisonment of migrants is becoming increasingly widespread in Europe. What was originally an improvised administrative response is today at the heart of European migration policies, to the point of becoming a structural method of managing migration. Yet this approach not only lacks political vision (other than that based on security), but also carries human and financial costs that are difficult to bear. From illegal refoulement to conditions of detention that violate human dignity, the imprisonment of children, the use of prisons and the application of multiple forms of pressure (on migrants to agree to "voluntary" returns, on third countries to sign "readmission" agreements), States are prepared to employ any means to protect themselves from what they perceive as a threat.

Developing open and closed camps in Europe and beyond

In spite of the diverse contexts and challenges (geographic, economic, demographic and political) that migratory flows present for Member States of the European Union, the number of sites for holding foreigners has considerably increased over the past few years. Identified in 2003 as a "new tool of EU migration policy", they have become the preferred instruments for the management of migrant populations. All EU Member States are pursuing the development of legal, administrative and political measures aimed at establishing camps for the reception, sifting, control and return of migrants.

The combined effects of strengthening and externalizing border controls contribute to the proliferation of such sites, which have spread not only in EU Member States but also in those at the EU's external borders (Turkey, Ukraine, Morocco, Libya) and further afield (Mauritania).

Taking the form of open camps, where migrants' freedom of movement is subjected to varying degrees of control, and closed sites, which are genuine detention centres, this trend was underlined by a study conducted in 2007 on behalf of the European Parliament (see bibliography). More recently, new camps have been established in countries situated at the external borders of the EU, including Greece.

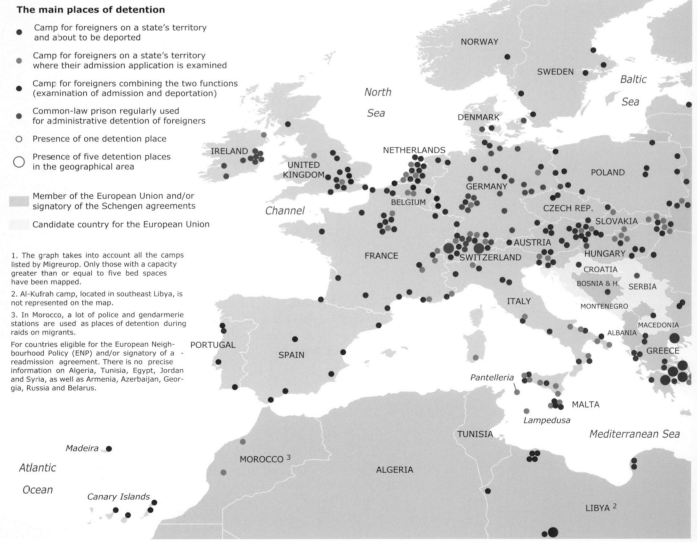

The main places of detention

- Camp for foreigners on a state's territory and about to be deported
- Camp for foreigners on a state's territory where their admission application is examined
- Camp for foreigners combining the two functions (examination of admission and deportation)
- Common-law prison regularly used for administrative detention of foreigners
- ○ Presence of one detention place
- ◯ Presence of five detention places in the geographical area

Member of the European Union and/or signatory of the Schengen agreements

Candidate country for the European Union

1. The graph takes into account all the camps listed by Migreurop. Only those with a capacity greater than or equal to five bed spaces have been mapped.

2. Al-Kufrah camp, located in southeast Libya, is not represented on the map.

3. In Morocco, a lot of police and gendarmerie stations are used as places of detention during raids on migrants.

For countries eligible for the European Neighbourhood Policy (ENP) and/or signatory of a readmission agreement. There is no precise information on Algeria, Tunisia, Egypt, Jordan and Syria, as well as Armenia, Azerbaijan, Georgia, Russia and Belarus.

Sources by country*: Austria (1-5-8), **Belarus** (Democratic Belarus), **Belgium** (Office des étrangers, Ciré), **Bulgaria** (1-4), **Croatia** (1-3-6), **Cyprus** (Kisa, TerrFerme), **Czech Republic** (1-5), of the Comité interministériel du contrôle de l'immigration, Cimade), **Germany** (Pro Asyl, 5), **Greece** (1-6-7, 8, FRA), **Hungary** (Welcome to Europe network, 1-3), **Ireland** (Irish prison service, 1-2), **Libya** (International Federation for Human Rights / FIDH, Justice Without Borders / JWB, 4), **Lithuania** (1-5), **Macedonia** (IOM), **Malta** (JRS), **Netherlands** (1-4), **Norway** (1-2), **Poland** (1-4), **Romania** (TerrFerme), **Spain** (APDHA, CIE, Derechos vulnerados, 4), **Slovakia** (1-5), **Slovenia** (1-5), **Sweden** (Swedish migration board), **Switzerland** (2), **Turkey** (HCA-RASP), **United Kingdom**
*Common sources: 1. European Committee for the Prevention of Torture (CPT); 2. Global Detention Project; 3. JRS Detention in Europe; 4. Migreurop; 5. European Parliament; 6. Human Rights Watch (HRW);

Confining migrants in Europe and the Mediterranean countries

Besides the increasing number of such centres, another trend can be observed: the objectives of these camps are increasingly vague and ambiguous. Authorities tend to distinguish between "reception centres" and detention/deportation centres. The former are either for the identification of those entering the territory in order to decide whether or not they should be admitted (in principle, following individual examinations), or for temporary accommodation (generally for asylum seekers). The latter are for the detention and deportation of people found to be in an irregular situation. The objectives used to justify the existence of these centres often conceal aims that are less palatable than those officially announced.

Identification of foreigners; examination of requests to enter the territory; reception and accommodation of asylum seekers; detention and deportation of migrants in irregular situations: any given camp may have multiple functions which are not always clearly defined. Thus, on the same site, we can find migrants in diverse situations (asylum seekers who have not been admitted or whose requests have been rejected and so-called "illegal migrants"). Furthermore, centres with different official functions can be grouped together. For

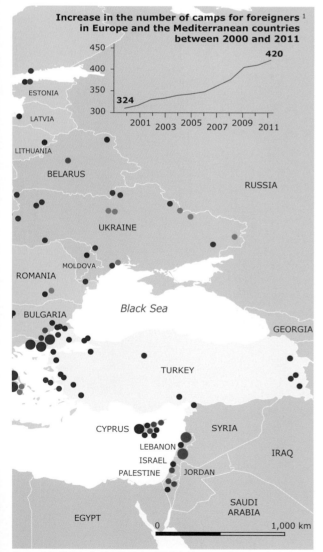

Increase in the number of camps for foreigners [1] in Europe and the Mediterranean countries between 2000 and 2011

Denmark (2-4), Estonia (1-2-5), Finland (1, Pakolaisneuvonta), France (Annual report Israel (Hotline for Migrant Workers, 2), Italy (ARCI), Latvia (1-5), Lebanon (Frontiers) Portugal (Provedor de justiça, Serviço de Estrangeiros e Fronteiras), (UK Border Agency-4), Ukraine (Border Monitoring Project Ukraine, GDISC, 1-3-6). 7. MSF; 8. Frontex.

example, Germany has put in place "multi-function" centres, aimed at bringing together sites specializing in the reception of asylum seekers and closed sites reserved for the detention of migrants.

In respect of reception measures which are not aimed at organizing the rapid return of those considered undesirable, a shift can increasingly be observed from the official purpose of receiving migrants, towards the real but less readily admitted purpose of controlling populations.

Organizing the reception of migrants can thus enable authorities to choose the place of residence to which they will be assigned: thus the former socialist countries in Central and Eastern Europe (Poland, Hungary, Slovakia, Slovenia) tend to prefer large centres, usually located far from cities (for example, in isolated former barracks situated in forests); others such as Great Britain and Ireland, or even Turkey with its satellite cities, put in place "dispersion" policies. Asylum seekers are sometimes automatically detained (Italy, Malta, Greece, Cyprus) or kept under house arrest in designated areas (Austria, Germany, Poland, Turkey). Elsewhere, in areas where groups of foreigners gather informally, camps are established, supposedly to provide reception and humanitarian assistance, but with another complementary purpose (for example, the Sangatte warehouse in France from 1999 to the end of 2002 and the Tiburtina station in Rome from 2008 to 2009). In all cases, restrictions on freedom of movement, of varying degrees of severity, enable authorities to locate and monitor migrants.

No less controversial are measures allowing for the detention of migrants for periods which in many countries significantly exceed those necessary to implement deportation orders and thus call into question the real purpose of detention. This observation led several migrants' rights associations and various other NGOs to campaign against the European "Return" Directive, referred to as the Directive of "Shame", adopted in December 2008. This text, while stipulating that the period of detention must be the shortest possible and that it can only concern a national of a third country subjected to a return procedure, provides for the possibility of extending the period of detention by up to 18 months.

The campaign against the "Return" Directive, which was insufficiently taken up by Members of the European Parliament, in particular criticized the institutionalization of excessive periods of detention for migrants, which reflects the will to distance and criminalize undesirable populations and to intimidate potential migrants and asylum seekers. It should be underlined that those detained are not accused of any offence other than those concerning entry and stay. It is therefore legitimate to question the reasons that push EU Member States to apply penal regimes (confinement in cells, limited exercise time, restricted visits or even isolation).

It is important to emphasize the worrying situation in migrant detention centres. Conditions vary considerably from one country to another. Nevertheless, certain trends were identified in the aforementioned 2007 study. The authors note, in particular, that "detention in closed centres can cause psychological disorders among detained migrants or lead to their deterioration. This can be dramatic in the case of minors". Yet the majority of European countries continue to detain accompanied and, in some cases, unaccompanied minors. In addition to the situation of minors, the lack of information for detainees on their rights and obstacles or lack of access to legal support constitute factors of significant concern. Frequent acts of violence by detainees against themselves (suicides, self-mutilation, hunger strikes) reveal their fragile psychological states and feelings of powerlessness and distress.

Acts of revolt and fires also punctuate existence in such places, in Europe (Yarl's Wood, United Kingdom, in 2002; Schiphol, Netherlands, in 2005; Vincennes, France, in 2008; and Arad, Romania, in 2012) and at its borders (three centres in Turkey during the second half of 2008). In Lampedusa, the events of January and February 2009 – protests and the escape of 700 migrants from the new Identification and Deportation Centre, followed by a fire – were met with violent repression by the authorities and led to significant mobilization of the island's inhabitants and associations condemning the poor conditions of detention of migrants and the risks of deportation. In March 2011, in Lampedusa, after the arrival of Tunisian migrants and their transfer to the mainland, protests broke out in several camps in Italy, from Gradisca to Bologna and from Turin to Bari.

Beyond the conditions in such centres, which vary considerably from one country to another, the deterioration of migrants' psychological state is a general phenomenon, as shown by a report by the Jesuit Refugee Service (JRS-Europe), entitled

Becoming Vulnerable in Detention, published in June 2010. Based on 685 individual interviews conducted in detention centres in 23 EU Member States, the report documents that the detention of asylum seekers in several countries is in violation of the EU "Procedures" Directive adopted in December 2005, which stipulates that "Member States shall not hold a person in detention for the sole reason that he/she is an applicant for asylum". Yet asylum seekers were among those detained for the longest periods. The average period of detention of those interviewed was three months, but went up to 31 months in some cases. Detainees were aged between 10 and 64 years, with minors being the most vulnerable, suffering from serious physical and mental problems as a result of detention. 83% of the minors interviewed had not received any visits. Difficulties in communicating with the outside world, the prohibition on using a mobile phone and lack of access to the internet increase the sense of isolation of detainees and limit the possibilities of obtaining legal assistance to protect their rights. The report also provides numerous testimonies on detention conditions, access to medical care and abuse by staff in centres.

The trivialization of detention and deportation systems should result in increased mobilization against the resulting

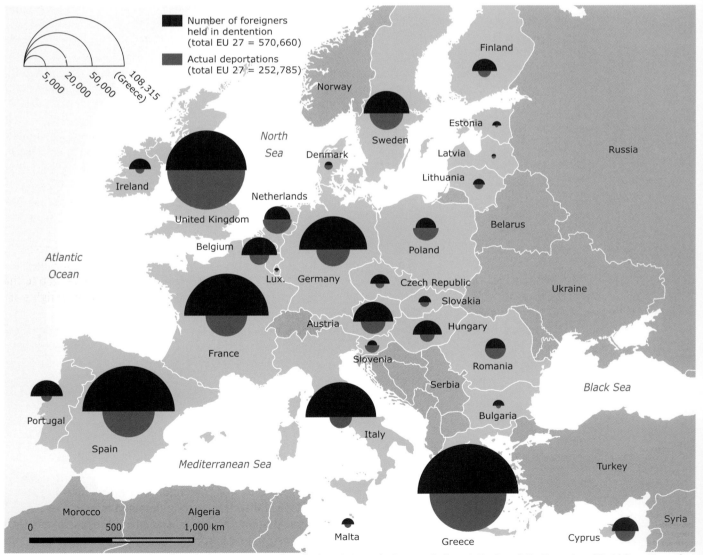

Source: European Commission, COM(2011) 248 final, *Communication from the Commission to the European Parliament, the Council, the Economic and Social Committee and the Committee of the Regions*, Communication on migration, Brussels, 4 May 2011.

Less than half the foreigners held in administrative detention were deported in 2009

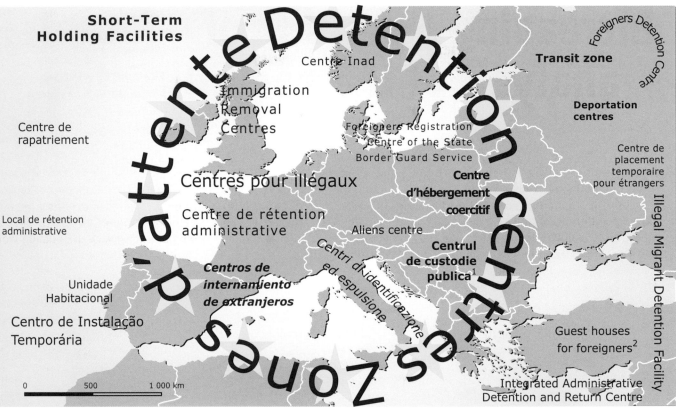

1. Centre of public care (Romania).
2. In a 2011 report of the CPT (European Committee for the Prevention of Torture and Inhuman or Degrading Treatment or Punishment), the CPT states that it prefers to use the term "detention centres" rather than the euphemism "guesthouses", "as the persons detained in these centres are undoubtedly deprived of their liberties".

Multilingual euphemisms denoting camps for foreigners

abuses. But these detention centres are particularly opaque and difficult for civil society actors to access. Associations seeking to provide support (legal, social, medical) to detainees often come up against arbitrary decisions of the authorities in charge, who limit or block visits to the centres on a discretionary basis. In most cases a right of access is not recognized by law. The absence of external monitoring contributes to conditions which foster human rights abuses.

Campaigns in Europe "for a right of access to migrant detention centres", launched between 2008 and 2012 by the networks Migreurop and European Alternatives, affirm that, confronted with the proliferation of migrant detention sites, civil society must be able to access these places in order to monitor,

alert and defend those in detention. Within these campaigns, visits to closed centres have been organized by national and European elected representatives, on "Action Days", in various countries (Italy, Portugal, Spain, France, Belgium, Germany, Bulgaria and Mauritania). Some of the campaigns' recommendations were adopted in a report issued by the European Parliament in January 2009.

These campaigns also aim to raise awareness in civil society and to encourage mobilization against the detention of migrant populations. For many participants, it is a simple step to the necessary closure of these sites where fundamental rights are violated.

Peio AIERBE and Sophie BAYLAC ▣

Increasing detention of migrants: analysis of the 2008 Directive

The diversity of migrant detention sites is reflected in the different ways they operate: length of detention, reception capacity, accommodation and hygiene conditions. Differences can be explained by the function assigned to the various sites and the administrative status of detainees, as well as by the historical relationships between States and the migration phenomenon. Such relationships have recently undergone significant upheavals in Southern and Eastern European countries.

Beyond these clear disparities, we observe two major tendencies within the European Union (EU), reinforced by the transposition of the "Return" Directive: on the one hand, an

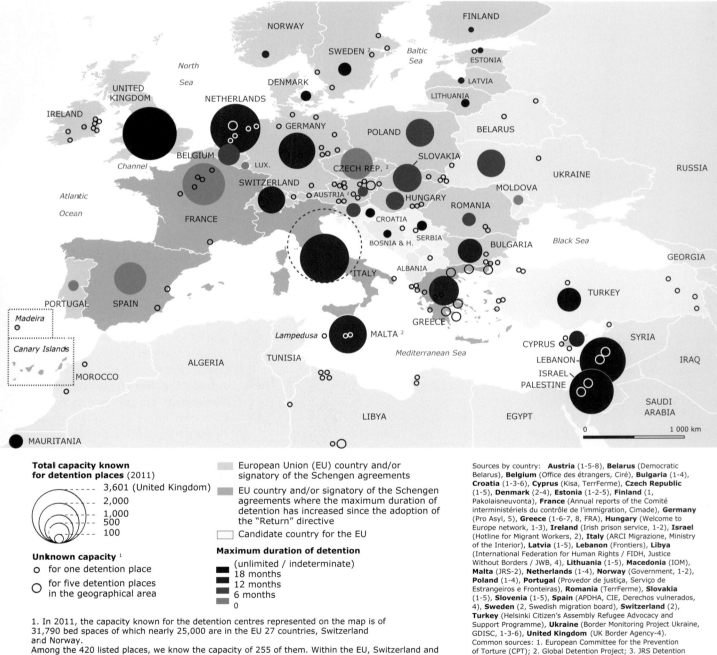

Total capacity known for detention places (2011)
- 3,601 (United Kingdom)
- 2,000
- 1,000
- 500
- 100

Unknown capacity [1]
- o for one detention place
- O for five detention places in the geographical area

  European Union (EU) country and/or signatory of the Schengen agreements

  EU country and/or signatory of the Schengen agreements where the maximum duration of detention has increased since the adoption of the "Return" directive

  Candidate country for the EU

Maximum duration of detention
- (unlimited / indeterminate)
- 18 months
- 12 months
- 6 months
- 0

Sources by country: **Austria** (1-5-8), **Belarus** (Democratic Belarus), **Belgium** (Office des étrangers, Ciré), **Bulgaria** (1-4), **Croatia** (1-3-6), **Cyprus** (Kisa, TerrFerme), **Czech Republic** (1-5), **Denmark** (2-4), **Estonia** (1-2-5), **Finland** (1, Pakolaisneuvonta), **France** (Annual reports of the Comité interministériels du contrôle de l'immigration, Cimade), **Germany** (Pro Asyl, 5), **Greece** (1-6-7, 8, FRA), **Hungary** (Welcome to Europe network, 1-3), **Ireland** (Irish prison service, 1-2), **Israel** (Hotline for Migrant Workers, 2), **Italy** (ARCI Migrazione, Ministry of the Interior), **Latvia** (1-5), **Lebanon** (Frontiers), **Libya** (International Federation for Human Rights / FIDH, Justice Without Borders / JWB, 4), **Lithuania** (1-5), **Macedonia** (IOM), **Malta** (JRS-2), **Netherlands** (1-4), **Norway** (Government, 1-2), **Poland** (1-4), **Portugal** (Provedor de justiça, Serviço de Estrangeiros e Fronteiras), **Romania** (TerrFerme), **Slovakia** (1-5), **Slovenia** (1-5), **Spain** (APDHA, CIE, Derechos vulnerados, 4), **Sweden** (2, Swedish migration board), **Switzerland** (2), **Turkey** (Helsinki Citizen's Assembly Refugee Advocacy and Support Programme), **Ukraine** (Border Monitoring Project Ukraine, GDISC, 1-3-6), **United Kingdom** (UK Border Agency-4). Common sources: 1. European Committee for the Prevention of Torture (CPT); 2. Global Detention Project; 3. JRS Detention in Europe; 4. Migreurop; 5. European Parliament; 6. Human Rights Watch (HRW); 7. MSF; 8. Frontex.

1. In 2011, the capacity known for the detention centres represented on the map is of 31,790 bed spaces of which nearly 25,000 are in the EU 27 countries, Switzerland and Norway.
Among the 420 listed places, we know the capacity of 255 of them. Within the EU, Switzerland and Norway, only the bed spaces of 223 camps are established among 351 premises listed.
2. Data related to the known capacity of one or several detention places dating from 2007 and 2009.

Ever longer detention of migrants

increase in the length of detention and, on the other, an increase in the capacities of camps. Living conditions are difficult in all such places, not only in the most precarious camps.

The length of detention reveals a paradigm shift

When discussing detention periods, we must first make the distinction between the *statutory* period, the *average* length of detention and that in *practice*. By *statutory* length, we mean the maximum limit stipulated by the law. It may be in this area that the disparity is most visible. At one end of the spectrum there is France, with the shortest statutory limit on detention in Europe: 45 days. At the other end, the United Kingdom, Denmark and Sweden have no maximum limit, so that periods of detention are potentially unlimited. In between,

it is interesting to note that southern EU countries have lower statutory limits than those in the north: 60 days in both Spain and Portugal, compared to 10 months in Austria, 12 months in Poland and 18 months in Germany. This contrast may seem surprising, given that countries in southern Europe are often most affected by the arrival of migrants. This relative leniency can be explained, in part, by the fact that, until recently, these countries were sources of emigration. In any case, the disparity is probably temporary and will tend to disappear as States begin transposition of the "Return" Directive, which is seen as an opportunity to increase maximum statutory periods of detention. Furthermore, this contrast is to a large extent counterbalanced by the systematic detention of migrants who reach their territories – or are intercepted at sea – and by often very harsh conditions of incarceration.

In *practice,* the length of detention depends on each individual case: by definition it is less visible than the statutory period. Detention periods may vary from a few hours to several years. In the majority of cases, detention periods are much shorter than the statutory limit: migrants spend a few hours or several days in a cell or a detention centre within a port or airport and are rapidly returned by boat or plane, as in Sicily or Greece. In other cases, they are intercepted at sea and immediately returned to the supposed port of departure, without even having had the opportunity to apply for asylum, as has regularly been the case around the Canary Islands and Lampedusa.

The case of 75 migrants who, in May 2009, were intercepted by Italian coastguards and turned over to a Libyan patrol, under a bilateral agreement between Italy and Libya concluded one month earlier, is a typical example. In that case, *Hirsi Jamaa and others v. Italy,* the European Court of Human Rights condemned Italy, citing multiple violations of the 1951 Geneva Convention (or "multiple violations of the European Convention"). However, in some cases, periods of detention may greatly exceed the statutory limit, on the basis of a legal pirouette: for example, in Belgium, if a deportation order cannot be executed as the result of the physical resistance of an individual, a new decision on detention is taken and the counters are reset, allowing detention for a further five months (which may be extended to eight months, in certain cases). Fortunately, migrants do not remain

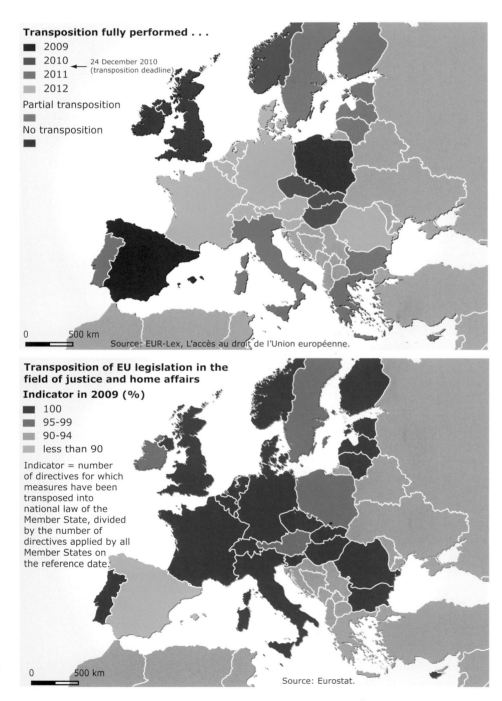

Transposition fully performed . . .
- 2009
- 2010 ← 24 December 2010 (transposition deadline)
- 2011
- 2012

Partial transposition

No transposition

0 ——— 500 km

Source: EUR-Lex, L'accès au droit de l'Union européenne.

Transposition of EU legislation in the field of justice and home affairs
Indicator in 2009 (%)
- 100
- 95-99
- 90-94
- less than 90

Indicator = number of directives for which measures have been transposed into national law of the Member State, divided by the number of directives applied by all Member States on the reference date.

0 ——— 500 km

Source: Eurostat.

The "Return" Directive does not apply in all EU countries (State of play as of April 2012)

"When it appears that a reasonable prospect of removal no longer exists for legal or other considerations...

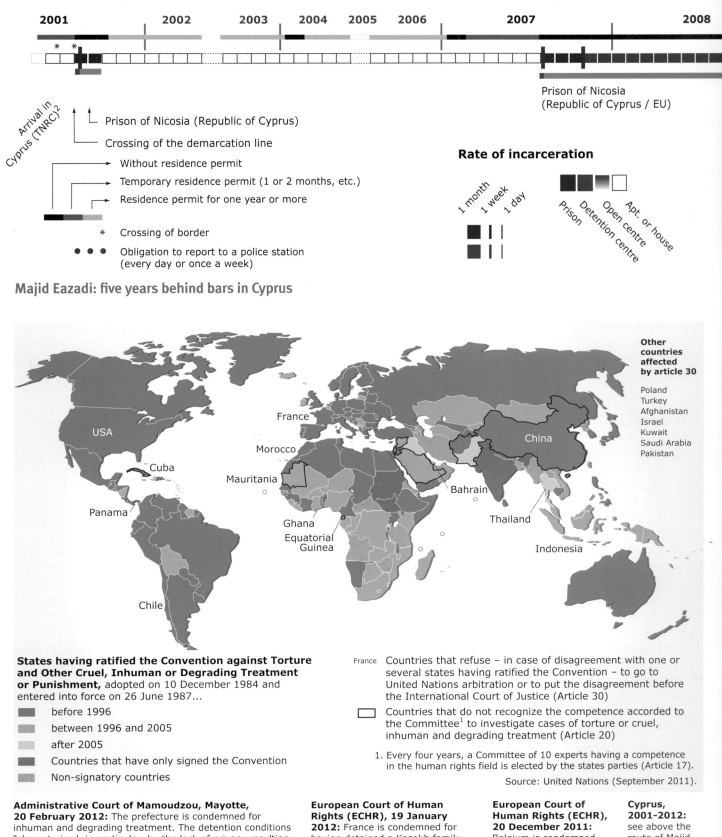

2001 **2002** **2003** **2004** **2005** **2006** **2007** **2008**

Prison of Nicosia
(Republic of Cyprus / EU)

Arrival in Cyprus (TNRC)[2]

Prison of Nicosia (Republic of Cyprus)

Crossing of the demarcation line

Without residence permit

Temporary residence permit (1 or 2 months, etc.)

Residence permit for one year or more

* Crossing of border

• • • Obligation to report to a police station
(every day or once a week)

Rate of incarceration

1 month   1 week   1 day

Prison   Detention centre   Open centre   Apt. or house

Majid Eazadi: five years behind bars in Cyprus

Other countries affected by article 30

Poland
Turkey
Afghanistan
Israel
Kuwait
Saudi Arabia
Pakistan

USA
Cuba
Panama
Chile
France
Morocco
Mauritania
Ghana
Equatorial Guinea
China
Bahrain
Thailand
Indonesia

States having ratified the Convention against Torture and Other Cruel, Inhuman or Degrading Treatment or Punishment, adopted on 10 December 1984 and entered into force on 26 June 1987...

before 1996

between 1996 and 2005

after 2005

Countries that have only signed the Convention

Non-signatory countries

France Countries that refuse – in case of disagreement with one or several states having ratified the Convention – to go to United Nations arbitration or to put the disagreement before the International Court of Justice (Article 30)

Countries that do not recognize the competence accorded to the Committee[1] to investigate cases of torture or cruel, inhuman and degrading treatment (Article 20)

1. Every four years, a Committee of 10 experts having a competence in the human rights field is elected by the states parties (Article 17).

Source: United Nations (September 2011).

Administrative Court of Mamoudzou, Mayotte, 20 February 2012: The prefecture is condemned for inhuman and degrading treatment. The detention conditions "characterized, in particular, by the lack of privacy resulting from an overpopulated centre, its dilapidation, the impossibility of accessing an outside space, the climate of tension ensuing from the permanent anxiety of expulsion and the absence of any reception arrangements for the children are likely to infringe the right to respect the dignity, not only of the minors concerned, de facto, by the decision of placement in administrative detention aimed at their parents, but of the whole family as well."

European Court of Human Rights (ECHR), 19 January 2012: France is condemned for having detained a Kazakh family with a three-year-old girl and a baby in a detention centre unsuitable for their two very young children. "The living conditions of the applicants' children (...) could only lead to a situation of anxiety and of serious psycological repercussions," declared the ECHR.

European Court of Human Rights (ECHR), 20 December 2011: Belgium is condemned for having inflicted an inhuman and degrading treatment on a Cameroonian woman, detained for nearly five months in a closed detention centre, without the necessary care while she was HIV-positive.

Cyprus, 2001-2012: see above the route of Majid Eazadi, an Iranian national.

"Numerous States have ratified the Convention but inhuman and degrading treatments continue"

…ention ceases to be justified and the person concerned shall be released immediately."[1]

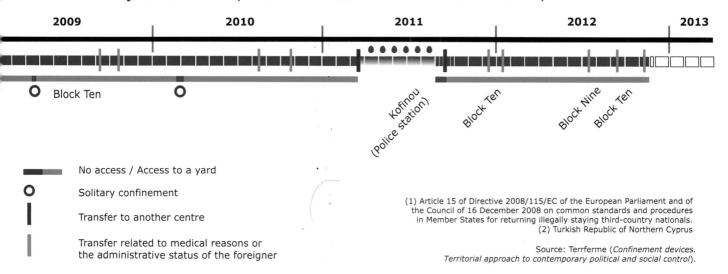

2009   2010   2011   2012   2013

Block Ten

Kofinou (Police station)

Block Ten

Block Nine

Block Ten

No access / Access to a yard

Solitary confinement

Transfer to another centre

Transfer related to medical reasons or the administrative status of the foreigner

(1) Article 15 of Directive 2008/115/EC of the European Parliament and of the Council of 16 December 2008 on common standards and procedures in Member States for returning illegally staying third-country nationals.
(2) Turkish Republic of Northern Cyprus

Source: Terrferme (*Confinement devices. Territorial approach to contemporary political and social control*).

in detention indefinitely, even in those countries where there is no statutory limit on detention. But detention periods can still turn out to be very long: Cyprus holds the record, with migrants having been detained up to three years. Detention is all the more psychologically difficult to endure when its duration is uncertain. Thus, statistics on the *average* length of detention provide an unreliable picture, given that differences are significant depending on the individual case.

These periods of imprisonment are extremely lengthy for people who have not committed any offence other than residing on a territory in an irregular situation. They infringe the rights of migrants and reveal a genuine paradigm shift in terms of the function assigned to detention. At the outset, it is necessary to know the origin of the person to be deported and to secure the co-operation of the supposed country of origin. When it is taken into consideration that public authorities require no more than two or three weeks to determine whether or not a migrant may be deported, it is clear that detention is not only used in order to organize the logistical aspects of deportation, but also as an instrument of repression against "undesirables". Thus, it is no exaggeration to suggest that administrative detention has been established as a method of managing "illegal" immigration. Combined with the possibility of imposing a ban on re-entering the territory for several years following deportation, this system treats migrants in the same way that, until recently, European States treated the most dangerous criminals. Thomas Hammarberg, the former Commissioner for Human Rights of the Council of Europe, repeatedly underlined, without being heard, that imprisonment should be reserved for criminals, which migrants are not.

Increasing capacities

The diversity of detention centres is also reflected in their "reception capacity": they can be informal open-air camps, prisons or any type of building converted into a detention centre, and they may accommodate anything from a few dozen to more than 3,300 people.

In March 2011, in Italy, new temporary detention centres were opened to deal with migrants from Libya and Tunisia,

who had arrived in Lampedusa. At the end of September 2011, the Italian Interior Minister went as far as converting boats into detention centres where more than 600 migrants were deprived of their freedom.

If we consider only the closed centres listed in 2011, the total known capacity – representing two-thirds of camps within the EU – is approximately 25,000 places (see map, page 86). But theoretical capacity is only an indicator: many places significantly exceed it, while others have an indeterminate capacity in practice, which fluctuates according to arrivals, as in Lampedusa and certain Greek islands.

Although the tendency to increase capacity is partly induced by the increase in the length of detention, this is not the only factor. Policies setting yearly targets for deportations, like that adopted by the French government, lead to an increase in the number and capacity of detention centres.

Difficult material conditions

The issue of capacity cannot be completely detached from that of material conditions. Here again, there are disparities. Detention conditions in newly built centres specifically designed for the purpose are relatively decent. Nevertheless, living conditions are very difficult: denial of rights; cohabitation difficulties between people having trouble coming to terms with their imprisonment. Even those centres said to be "models" are not spared frequent incidents such as riots, hunger strikes, various acts of violence, arson – which are met with "tough" police interventions – as well as regular deaths and suicides.

Such incidents remind us of the material and hygiene conditions prevailing in more informal, under-equipped camps, with chronic overcrowding and without genuine democratic control: conditions are often appalling and border on inhuman and degrading treatment. This is particularly the case in Malta, Lithuania, Greece and Turkey, where migrants are subjected to aggravated police violence, while other EU Member States close their eyes for the sake of border control. Conditions are similarly difficult and opaque in police facilities used as temporary detention centres in the United Kingdom, France, Greece and Cyprus: in most cases, such premises are not equipped for detention exceeding a few hours, though in practice it may stretch over lengthy periods, in violation of official regulations which in any case provide little protection for the rights of migrants.

A first assessment of the Return Directive

Differences in periods of detention were highlighted during the debates preceding the adoption of the "Return" Directive in June 2008. The purpose of this directive was to harmonize conditions of detention and deportation of migrants in EU Member States. As of 15 September 2011, that is nine months after the deadline for transposition as set by the text (24 December 2010), 19 of the 27 Member States had incorporated it into their national law. Since then, Belgium, Cyprus and the Netherlands have started to transpose the directive. As feared by critics of the directive, several countries took advantage of the opportunity to extend the statutory limit on detention: from 40 to 60 days in Spain; from 2 to 18 months in Italy; from 3 to 6 months, renewable up to a maximum of 12 months, in Greece. In France, the statutory limit was increased from 32 to 45 days in July 2011. Foreigners convicted of terrorist acts may be held for up to six months. Countries including Bulgaria, the Netherlands and Cyprus, which previously had no statutory limit on the administrative detention of foreigners, opted for the maximum authorised limit of 18 months when transposing the text.

Since the directive only sets minimum standards, it leaves a significant margin of appreciation for implementation. States are more prone to transpose provisions restricting the rights of migrants than those which would protect them. Choices made by national legislators clearly apply a repressive approach. Thus, in Spain, the ban on re-entering the territory was increased from three to five years and the deportation of unaccompanied foreign minors was made easier. In Italy, one of the provisions of the law on internal security created the offence of "illegal immigration and residency", punishable by a fine of 5-10,000 euros, and solidarity with migrants was made an offence. Any person who provides shelter or rents accommodation to "illegal" immigrants may be punished with up to three years' imprisonment.

The first assessment of the implementation of the directive is therefore disappointing, given its minimalist positions on protection of migrants' rights. However, the failure of Member States to transpose all or part of the directive provides new tools for the defence of migrants' rights before the courts. By invoking provisions of the directive considered to be sufficiently precise and unconditional to make them directly applicable – such as the obligation to specify a deadline for voluntary return when notifying migrants of an expulsion order – French lawyers have secured the release of numerous clients.

Marie CHARLES and Pierre-Arnaud PERROUTY ◖

Permanent protest in the camps

The industrialized countries of the European Union (EU) – the first trading bloc in the world, with a total of 20% of imports and exports – continue to set up costly barriers to keep away those displaced by globalization, neoliberal policies, economic crises and wars. The militarization of land borders and of the Mediterranean Sea has significantly increased over the past few years, as has the externalizing of immigration controls, under bilateral agreements concluded with States in Africa and the Middle East.

To complete this strategy of protection against new arrivals, European countries have also established a vast detention complex, designed to hold those who manage to enter the territory and whom they seek to deport. This system of imprisonment of asylum seekers and migrants comprises a range of sites, from centres specifically designed to hold migrants, to former military barracks near coastal areas – as in Italy, where thousands of people are imprisoned, sometimes in squalid and disastrous conditions – waiting zones in international airports and even prisons. In the 2000s, with the development of "return" programmes by the EU and its Member States, social tensions in detention centres intensified year on year.

In 2010, numerous crises took place in camps as a result of overcrowding, poor sanitary conditions, institutional neglect and lack of medical care. Thus, unrest, demonstrations and hunger strikes punctuate life in these centres, including Yarl's Wood, Oakington, Campsfield (United Kingdom), Ponte Galeria (Rome, Italy), Zona Franca (Barcelona, Spain), Stange, Haslemoen, Lier and Fagerli (Norway) and Gävle (Sweden)... (see map, page 93).

In Norway, in the Fagerli "transit centre" (*ventemottak*), located in the municipality of Akershus, and in the centre in Lier, 2010 was marked by a number of serious incidents. In both centres, buildings were set on fire. According to the Norwegian Immigration Agency, the damage resulting from these incidents cost almost 12 million kroner, representing double the amount spent in 2009.

Protests have also been initiated by asylum seekers and migrants who are not in detention. Living in informal camps, hostels, squalid hotels or "simply" on the street, migrants despairing at their miserable living conditions have organized hunger strikes. This was the case for 300 migrants, mainly from northern Africa, in Athens and Thessaloniki. Smaller protest actions were carried out in 2010 and during the first months of 2011 in Mosney, County Heath (Ireland) and in camps in Böbrach, Denkendorf and Nostorf-Horst in Germany.[1] This unrest and these acts of protest can also be explained by continuous pressure from governments to increase the number of deportations and by the actions of the European Agency for the Management of Operational Co-operation at the External Borders (Frontex), which has been organizing increasing numbers of joint "returns" flights.

Unrest and hunger strikes

Since its establishment in October 2005, Frontex has seen its annual budget and workforce increase yearly and it now has an annual budget of 87 million euros and a staff of around 280. In March 2010, the European Commission published plans to enlarge Frontex's role so as to give it extra powers to charter aircraft for joint returns operations. The increase in the number of such flights is one of the factors to be taken into account in explaining the incidents that have taken place in detention centres. In addition, laws have been adopted aimed at limiting migrants' rights: making it impossible to appeal against administrative decisions, and making access to centres more difficult for organizations defending those detained. With external support, detainees sometimes start protest actions and/or hunger strikes to make their voices heard.

The authorities have responded to the surge in such incidents in detention centres with disciplinary measures; cases of self-mutilation and suicide attempts have also been dealt with from a security perspective and detainees suffering from serious illness have not always been spared. In the United Kingdom, protest actions and hunger strikes have been suppressed by force. For example, in 2010, in the Yarl's Wood Centre (Bedfordshire), over 40 women who went on hunger strike were corralled into a corridor and subjected to the public order crowd-control technique known as "kettling". The women were also subjected to physical and verbal abuse by some of the employees at the centre. The organization Public Interest Lawyers has issued a lawsuit for inhuman and degrading treatment. In April 2010, riot police were called in to restore order at Oakington immigration removal centre following the death of Eliud Nguli Nyenze, a 40-year-old Kenyan man. According to a migrant solidarity group, unrest broke out after detainees, fearing a cover-up, tried to prevent the dead man's body being removed from the centre. In May 2010, the death of Mohamed Abagui in the Foreigners' Internment Centre of Zona Franca, in Spain, also gave rise to demonstrations by detainees, denouncing what they described as structural violence at the centre. All these cases illustrate the lack of attention given to the situation of migrants in detention, as detainees have been claiming for a long time.

Hunger strikes do not only take place in the large detention centres. In Sweden, Cyprus and Austria, this kind of incident has occurred when asylum seekers have been detained for long periods of time in solitary confinement or transferred to other police holding facilities. Commenting on a 31% increase in hunger strikes in Austria, the Ludwig Boltzmann Institute of Human Rights, in Vienna, pointed out that, under Austrian law, asylum seekers and migrants can be held in preventive detention for as long as 10 months. But these premises, some dating back to the 19th century, are not suitable for long-term detention. According to a spokesperson for the Institute, poor conditions, inadequate medical care and restricted access to legal services are the reasons so many of those

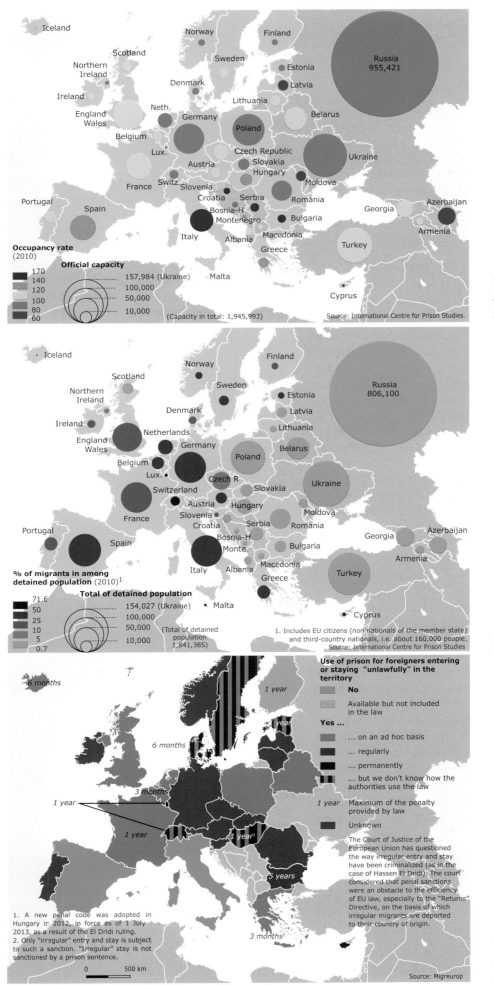

Occupancy rate
(2010)

Official capacity

170	
140	
120	157,984 (Ukraine)
100	100,000
80	50,000
60	10,000

(Capacity in total: 1,945,993)

Source: International Centre for Prison Studies.

Prisons in Europe: a capacity of nearly 2 million

% of migrants in among detained population (2010)[1]

Total of detained population

71.6	
50	154,027 (Ukraine) • Malta
25	100,000
10	50,000
5	10,000
0.7	

(Total of detained population 1,841,385)

1. Includes EU citizens (non nationals of the member state) and third-country nationals, i.e. about 160,000 people.
Source: International Centre for Prison Studies

Migrants in jail

Use of prison for foreigners entering or staying "unlawfully" in the territory

- No
- Available but not included in the law

Yes ...

- ... on an ad hoc basis
- ... regularly
- ... permanently
- ... but we don't know how the authorities use the law

1 year Maximum of the penalty provided by law

- Unknown

The Court of Justice of the European Union has questioned the way irregular entry and stay have been criminalized (as in the case of Hassen El Dridi). The court considered that penal sanctions were an obstacle to the efficiency of EU law, especially to the "Returns" Directive, on the basis of which irregular migrants are deported to their country of origin.

1. A new penal code was adopted in Hungary in 2012, in force as of 1 July 2013, as a result of the El Dridi ruling.
2. Only "irregular" entry and stay is subject to such a sanction. "Irregular" stay is not sanctioned by a prison sentence.

0   500 km

Source: Migreurop

The criminalization of entry and stay of migrants

**Reported events
in detention centres**
(January 2010-May 2012)

- ● Arsons
- ● Riots and/or demonstrations
- ● Escape / attempted escape
- ● Hunger strikes

Note: This document does not pretend to be exhaustive, but rather seeks to connect events that are often presented as isolated phenomena.

Source: Fortress Europe, Migreurop, Terra.

Resistance from within: not an exceptional phenomenon

detained go on hunger strike. In Cyprus, such incidents have occurred regularly in Block Ten (Nicosia) and Larnaca. Such incidents are known at the highest levels of the EU, but the situation has remained the same for almost 10 years. In Sweden, the UNHCR and the United Nations Committee against Torture (CAT) underlined that there was no time limit on the detention of asylum seekers, leading to the opening of a federal investigation into the detention of foreigners. According to the Parliamentary Ombudsman, asylum seekers should not be detained for more than one night in police holding facilities or preventive detention centres. Yet this limit is regularly exceeded. In 2010, 232 detainees were detained in such locations on security grounds, for periods ranging from a few days to several months.

European governments try to avoid noise being made about

the treatment of asylum seekers and migrants in detention centres. They seek to deal with such persons as if they have no rights: as a Greek human rights activist, Costas Douzinas, wrote, these exiles are the new *homines sacri*, people without any legal recognition.[2] For how much longer?

Liz FEKETE[3] ●

1 The Nostorf-Horst Centre is located in former army barracks in eastern Germany. Situated in the heart of a forest, it has been named *Guantánamo* by detainees.
2 Costas Douzinas, "These hunger strikers are the martyrs of Greece", *The Guardian*, 28 February 2011.
3 This article is based on a briefing paper, published by the Institute of Race Relations in London, entitled "Accelerated removals: a study of the human cost of EU deportation policies", 2009-2010. The full report can be consulted at: www.irr.org.uk/europebulletin/index.html

Mediterranean Sea

Kyrenia

Nicosia prison
(TRNC) [2]

Ercan

Nicosia central
prison[1]

Nicosia

Famagusta

Paralimni

New detention centre
established in 2012

Larnaka

Dhekelia
British base

Paphos

Limassol

0   10   20 km

Akrotiri
British base

Detention capacity (Nicosia prison, detention centres, police stations)

- - - 150

- - - 50

- - - 10

● Official immigrant detention centre

● Prison or police station used for immigration detention

● Other police stations where migrants can be detained

Other sites where "irregular" migrants may be detained

𝗫 Crossing points for cars or pedestrians

𝗜 Pedestrian crossing point

✖ International airports

☐ Ports for commercial maritime lines (travelers)

Republic of Cyprus (European Union)

Turkish Republic of Northern Cyprus
(only recognized by Turkey)

British military bases

- - - - Turkish demarcation line

- ∙ - ∙ Greek demarcation line

☐ Demilitarized buffer zone
(monitored by UNFICYP)

Sources: Co-operation Directorate Cyprus Police Headquaters (Human Rights Office), UNFICYP.

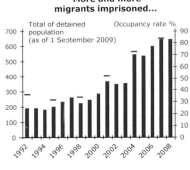

More and more migrants imprisoned...

Total of detained population (as of 1 September 2009)   Occupancy rate %

In Cyprus, the number of migrants among detainees is the highest in Europe (after Luxembourg and Switzerland), i.e. 61.9% of the whole detained population as of 1 September 2009. Many intercepted migrants (including asylum seekers) are imprisoned for irregular entry and then brought to immigration detention once their sentence has been served. This troubling situation has been highlighted as an issue many times by the Commissioner on Human Rights of the Council of Europe. This recurrent practice by the authorities partly explains the rise in the detention of migrants since 2004 (when Cyprus entered the EU).

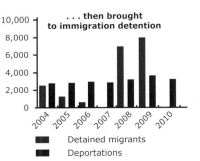

... then brought to immigration detention

■ Detained migrants
■ Deportations

1. Nicosia central prison, the only prison in the southern part of the island, comprises the immigration detention centre (Block 9 for women, and Block 10 for men) and a former cinema room turned into a place of detention (capacity of about 60) where "irregular" migrants are imprisoned.
2. Prison used as an immigration detention centre (unknown capacity).

Prisons and police stations as immigration detention centres

EU readmission policy: co-operation to increase removals

As the centrepiece of migrant deportation policy, readmission is an inherent issue in the external relations of Member States of the European Union (EU). It aims at facilitating the deportation of irregular migrants by compelling States to accept their nationals and, in some cases, persons who have merely passed through their territory in transit.

Although the bilateral approach remains predominant, since 1999 the European Commission has had the competence to negotiate readmission agreements at the EU level. During the Seville Summit in 2002, the EU declared that "any future co-operation (...) agreement (...) should include a clause on joint management of migration flows and on compulsory readmission in the event of illegal immigration". The European Pact on Immigration and Asylum, adopted by the European Council in October 2008, called for the continued negotiation of readmission agreements "at EU or bilateral level". Following the entry into force of the Lisbon Treaty in December 2009, such international commitments are submitted to the European Parliament for approval. However, owing to the lack of transparency in the negotiation and implementation of such agreements, the Parliament has seen its role significantly reduced to that of a democratic guarantor.

Seeking to overcome all administrative and legal obstacles

standing in the way of deportations, Member States have established the so-called "simplified readmission" procedure, which allows police services to send back, without delay or formalities, an undocumented migrant who has been questioned. Obsessed with forced returns, Member States have ridden roughshod over obligations to respect fundamental rights.

Nobody knows what happens to those deported in "receiving" countries: what about the right of asylum and the prohibition on "*any inhuman and degrading treatment*"?

Such violations have been documented in Ukraine and denounced by international organizations, including Human Rights Watch. Like a spider spinning its web, the EU calls on third countries and candidate countries for EU membership (see the box on page 97 on the readmission agreement with Turkey) to conclude similar agreements with their neighbours. Through this "cascade" readmissions system, the EU clears itself of any responsibility for the fate of those it has banished.

Of 20 mandates for negotiation entrusted to the European Commission, 13 agreements have entered into force (with Hong Kong, Macao, Sri Lanka, Albania, Russia, Ukraine, Macedonia, Bosnia-Herzegovina, Montenegro, Serbia,

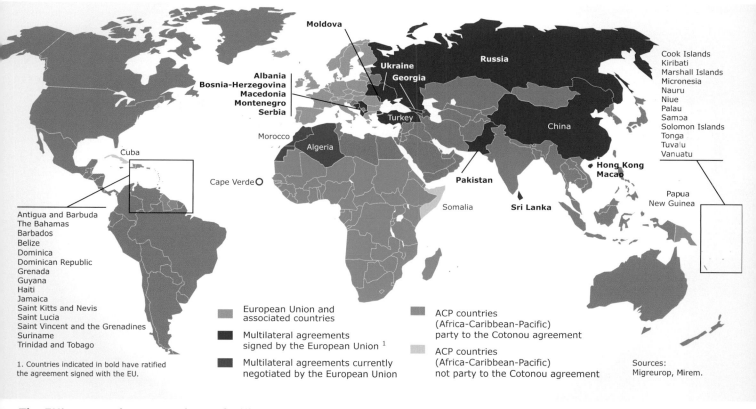

The EU's external co-operation to facilitate expulsions

Moldova

Albania
Bosnia-Herzegovina
Macedonia
Montenegro
Serbia

Ukraine
Georgia

Russia

Morocco

Turkey

China

Cook Islands
Kiribati
Marshall Islands
Micronesia
Nauru
Niue
Palau
Samoa
Solomon Islands
Tonga
Tuvalu
Vanuatu

Cuba

Cape Verde ○

Algeria

Pakistan

Hong Kong
Macao

Papua
New Guinea

Somalia

Sri Lanka

Antigua and Barbuda
The Bahamas
Barbados
Belize
Dominica
Dominican Republic
Grenada
Guyana
Haiti
Jamaica
Saint Kitts and Nevis
Saint Lucia
Saint Vincent and the Grenadines
Suriname
Trinidad and Tobago

1. Countries indicated in bold have ratified the agreement signed with the EU.

- European Union and associated countries
- Multilateral agreements signed by the European Union [1]
- Multilateral agreements currently negotiated by the European Union
- ACP countries (Africa-Caribbean-Pacific) party to the Cotonou agreement
- ACP countries (Africa-Caribbean-Pacific) not party to the Cotonou agreement

Sources:
Migreurop, Mirem.

France

Sources: Migreurop, French Ministry of Foreign and European Affairs, MiReM.

Italy

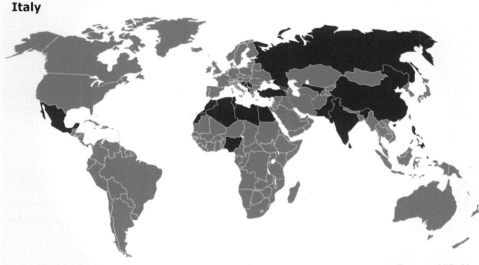

Source: MiReM.

Spain

■ Readmission
agreements
in force

Source: MiReM.

France, Italy, Spain: bilateral readmission agreements... but diverging interests

Moldova, Pakistan, Georgia). An agreement concluded with Turkey was signed on 21 June 2012, while negotiations with Morocco, Cape Verde, Armenia and Azerbaijan have been continuing. China and Algeria have refused to hold talks as long as the EU does not agree to their demands for less stringent visa regimes in return. For these countries, drawing out negotiations is a means of putting pressure on the EU and thereby raising the stakes, since readmission is above all in the interests of the EU.

In order to incite mostly reluctant States to conclude such agreements, the EU pursues this policy within the framework of a broader system of exchanges. Blackmail practices are used: there will be no economic or trade co-operation or development aid, without a readmission agreement. The establishment of an enhanced partnership between the EU and Pakistan in 2005 was dependent on the signature of such an agreement. Targeted by the EU because of their supposed "high migration risk", these countries are offered quotas for "legal migration" – that is, the cheap labour needed in some sectors of the European economy – as compensation. Whether in the form of so-called "co-ordinated management of migratory flows", as initiated by France, or the "mobility partnerships" concluded by some EU States with Georgia, Cape Verde and Moldova, no one is fooled by the label attached to readmission or its consequences.

In February 2011, the European Commission presented a "*mixed picture*"[1] emerging from the evaluation of this policy and noted the rigidity of Member States, insufficiently concerned with human rights obligations, miserly with "*incentives*" and obsessed by "*an increase in illegal immigration*". The EU must urgently account for the consequences of this policy, especially given the prevailing situations in Afghanistan, Iraq and Bangladesh,

READMISSION AGREEMENT WITH TURKEY

Turkey provides a good example of the intricate connection between the EU and bilateral agreements. In 2001, Greece and Turkey signed a readmission agreement as part of a more general agreement aimed at "fighting crime and, in particular, terrorism, organized crime, illegal drug trafficking and illegal migration". Turkey, a transit country, has officially become the country to which migrants who reach Greece are returned. However, since its entry into force, this agreement has not worked well, in any case not as well as Greece intended. According to figures from the Greek Ministry of the Interior, between 2003 and 2007, of the 21,000 readmission applications submitted by Greece to Turkey, only 1,200 were accepted. In response to Turkey's lack of co-operation, Greece has carried out illegal deportations, both at the land border, along the Evros River, and in the Aegean Sea, with Greek border guards pushing back illegal migrants. In May 2010, nearly 10 years after the signature of the bilateral readmission agreement between Greece and Turkey, the two countries signed a new agreement aimed at enforcing the former accord. Turkey undertook to implement the agreement including by:

- Accepting at least 1,000 readmission applications per year
- Designating a port in Izmir or near Izmir for the opening, within three months, of a border post for the readmission of migrants from Greece.

Turkey expressed its willingness to collaborate closely in this area. However, co-operation has not improved under the new agreement: Turkey has remained reluctant to take back migrants who pass through its territory in transit. At the beginning of January 2011, Greece decided to adopt a new strategy to prevent migrants from reaching its territory and to deal with what it considers to be an "invasion" of migrants. The political response resembled that designed by the United States and Mexico: the construction of a 12-kilometre long wall along the Evros River on the land border, in order to block migrants' journeys, in violation of human rights principles.

Developments have also taken place with regard to the negotiation of a readmission agreement with the European Union. In 2002, the European Commission was mandated to enter into negotiations with Turkey. On 24 February 2011, during a meeting of the EU Council, Interior and Immigration Ministers approved the terms of a readmission agreement between the EU and Turkey. In return, Turkey asked for the relaxation of visa requirements, as had been the case for the Balkan States in 2007. The EU raised the possibility of facilitating visas for certain categories of persons, including businesspeople and students, all the while calling on Turkey to conclude readmission agreements with countries of origin or transit of migrants. The EU agreed to provide funding for the construction of new detention centres, as well as a training programme for law-enforcement bodies on the processing of migrants and border surveillance.

Owing to its geographical position, Turkey has become an important player in the fight led by the EU against migrants. The EU has been prepared to pay a high price to ensure that the country plays the role of buffer state for those heading towards its territory.

FACILITATING THE READMISSION OF IRREGULAR MIGRANTS

Since 2007, following the examples of agreements signed by Spain with several African countries within the framework of its "Africa Plan" and agreements for the "co-ordinated management of migratory flows" concluded by France with, to date, nine third countries, the European Union has been developing a new political tool to serve the so-called "global approach to migration". They are referred to as "mobility partnerships" or agreements on migration management. While the content of each partnership is defined according to the specificities of each third country concerned, they generally include four main components:

1 Opportunities for "legal migration", mostly temporary depending on the labour needs of EU Member States and subject to the principle of Community preference;

2 Support from the EU to build "capacity to manage migration flows", whether migration towards European territory or intra-regional migration;

3 Development aid, in particular for the prevention and reduction of the brain drain phenomenon and support for so-called "voluntary" returns, by facilitating the reintegration of migrants in their countries of origin;

4 Combating irregular immigration, which encompasses a whole series of measures including border management, cross-border co-operation, strengthening security in relation to travel documents and, above all, the implementation of readmission agreements.

According to the European Commission, in order to be able to establish and develop such mobility programmes with third countries, certain conditions must be met, in particular in relation to co-operation on irregular immigration and the conclusion of readmission agreements. This is a clear means of conditioning so-called "development" policies on co-operation in the area of border control and the negotiation, signature and implementation of such agreements. To date, four mobility partnerships have been signed: with Moldova and Cape Verde in 2008, Georgia in 2009 and Armenia in 2011. The Commission has been granted a negotiating mandate to conclude similar agreements with Senegal and Azerbaijan.

where the European Commission plans to pursue negotiations. Moldova and Georgia have already signed readmission agreements with the EU while negotiations are under way with Cape Verde and Armenia.

The use of this new tool of EU external policy has made it possible to shift the balance of power in the implementation of deportation policies, to further benefit European national interests, establishing even greater inequality for EU "partners". Indeed, while a readmission agreement between the EU and a third country involves all EU Member States, the mobility partnerships existing to date only concern interested EU Member States. As a consequence, a third country's

obligation to readmit its nationals as well as third country nationals in an irregular situation, who passed through its territory in transit, applies in respect of all EU Member States, yet related meagre financial benefits are only provided by the few EU Member States that agree to participate in the "mobility partnership".

Pascaline CHAPPART, Claudia CHARLES and Lola SCHULMANN ◘

---

1 European Commission, Evaluation of EU Readmission Agreements, COM(2011) 76 final, 23.2.2011, p. 14.

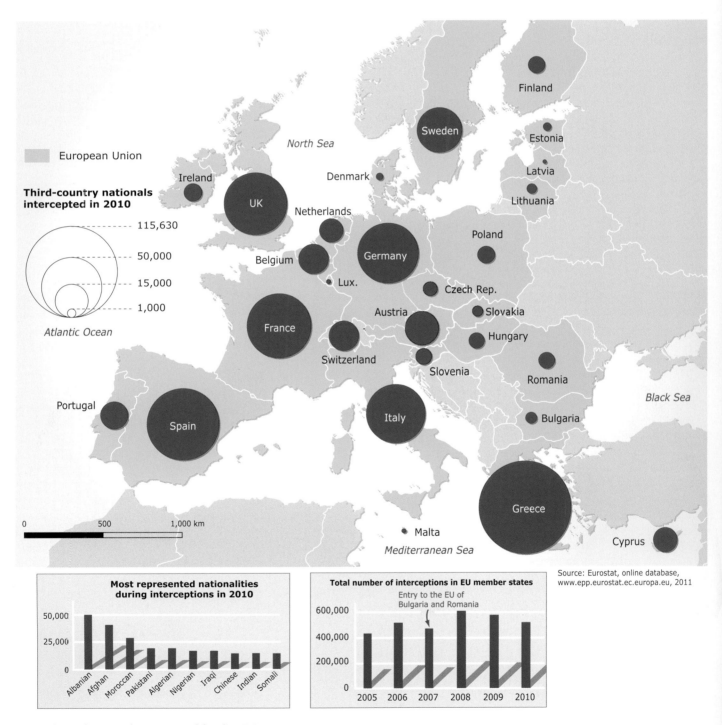

Source: Eurostat, online database, www.epp.eurostat.ec.europa.eu, 2011

Irregular migrants intercepted in the EU

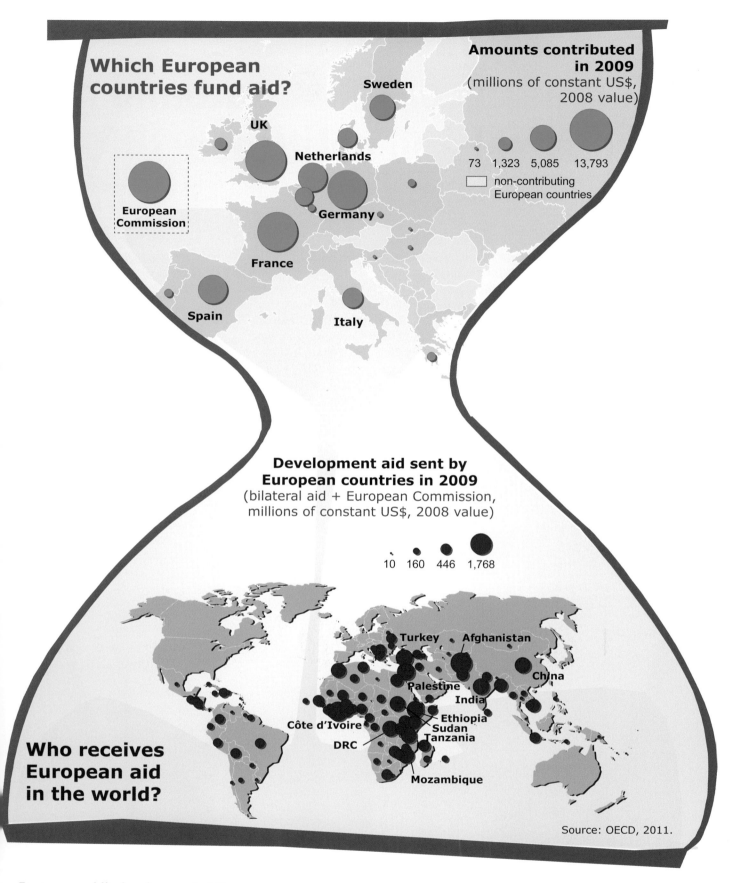

Which European countries fund aid?

Amounts contributed in 2009
(millions of constant US$, 2008 value)

73   1,323   5,085   13,793

□ non-contributing European countries

Sweden

UK

Netherlands

European Commission

Germany

France

Spain

Italy

Development aid sent by European countries in 2009
(bilateral aid + European Commission, millions of constant US$, 2008 value)

10   160   446   1,768

Turkey   Afghanistan

China

Palestine

India

Côte d'Ivoire   Ethiopia   Sudan   Tanzania

DRC

Mozambique

Who receives European aid in the world?

Source: OECD, 2011.

European public development aid in 2009

"Voluntary returns": European consensus around a numerical and political artifice

Considered to be "an effective, humane and cost-effective mechanism for returning irregular migrants"[1], voluntary return programmes are today widely promoted in Europe. In November 2002, the Council of the European Union (EU) adopted the "Plan for Return to Afghanistan" aimed at "facilitat[ing] early return", preferably "voluntary", otherwise "forced". On the strength of its experience in assisting departures[2], the International Organization for Migration (IOM) was assigned responsibility for repatriating and reintegrating Afghan migrants, to whom it also provided "advice to raise their awareness on the risks posed by unexploded mines and munitions". Under the humanitarian label of "safe, dignified and sustainable" return, States aim to ensure low-cost return in financial, political and social terms. Adopted in 2008, the EU

"Return" Directive encourages States to resort to this method in their expulsion policies. As in the case of forced returns, "voluntary" returns can be accompanied with a measure prohibiting re-entry into EU territory, formally for five years in the case of the United Kingdom and three years in the case of Spain.

At the national level, most EU Member States have developed an arsenal of incentives which can be presented as alternatives to detention and deportation, according to the priority given to the return of certain targeted groups. In Belgium, since October 2008, families who can be returned are lodged in "return houses" under the supervision of a "coach" who encourages them to go back. "Open voluntary return centres", specifically designed for rejected asylum seekers, are

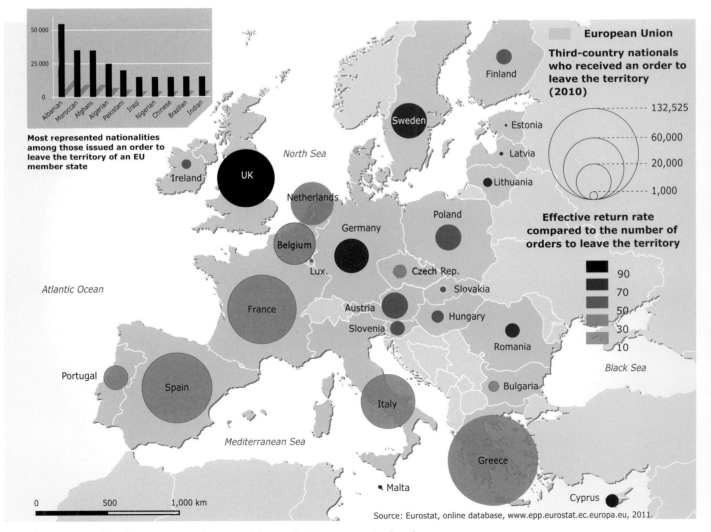

Source: Eurostat, online database, www.epp.eurostat.ec.europa.eu, 2011.

Nearly 225,000 foreigners were deported from the European Union in 2010

currently under consideration. In France, guidance given for the implementation of the system of assisting returns and resettlement by the French Office of Immigration and Integration (Ofii, formerly Anaem) illustrates the artifice and practical effects of a deportation policy which aims to "maximize recourse to choice". The French Member of Parliament, Philippe Cochait, considered in his opinion on the Finance Law of 2011 that "for 'immigration, asylum and integration' missions, the solution of voluntary return... presents only advantages: migrants who choose it spare themselves the ordeal of police escort and return to their countries of origin with dignity, sometimes with a not insubstantial sum of money[3]; this formula is less costly for the State and the result is guaranteed, since either the person provides his or her travel documents, or his or her country of origin grants a consular pass more easily". Since 2008, "voluntary departures" represent more than a third of the annual target figure for expulsions fixed by the French government. The budget allocated to the 28,000 deportations planned for 2011 integrated this factor: "It is estimated that funding will be necessary for 18,760 forced returns, responsibility for voluntary returns being assumed by Ofii." In the end, the organization of 15,840 returns by Ofii enabled France to announce a record-breaking 32,912 returns in 2011.

Relaunched in 2006, despite its failure since the beginning of the 1970s, assisted return is a flexible system, appreciated by officials for its versatility since it can be "adapted as necessary". Ofii and the relevant prefecture thus conduct joint visits to reception centres holding asylum seekers. And although the law prohibits voluntary returns to be carried out when migrants are in detention centres, an officer from Ofii confirmed that "there are centres where detainees' passports are taken and we ensure that they ask to be returned". Those who "are the subjects of major mobilization by organizations supporting migrants" and nationals from countries that have signed agreements on "concerted management of migration flows" are encouraged to resort to this system. In 2009, this public agency recorded 15,236 departures, of which 72% concerned Romanian and Bulgarian nationals who were legally free to circulate within the EU, while they are subjected to a transitory regime concerning their right to reside in the EU. Made illegal, as "unreasonable burdens on the State", these European citizens were deported under escort by Ofii under the "humanitarian return" procedure. This has enabled France, since the adoption of a circular in December 2006, to organize illegal forced returns of European citizens, justifying them by the poverty of deported populations.

"It's Ofii or the police", migrants are told. While a xenophobic campaign was launched in the political sphere during the

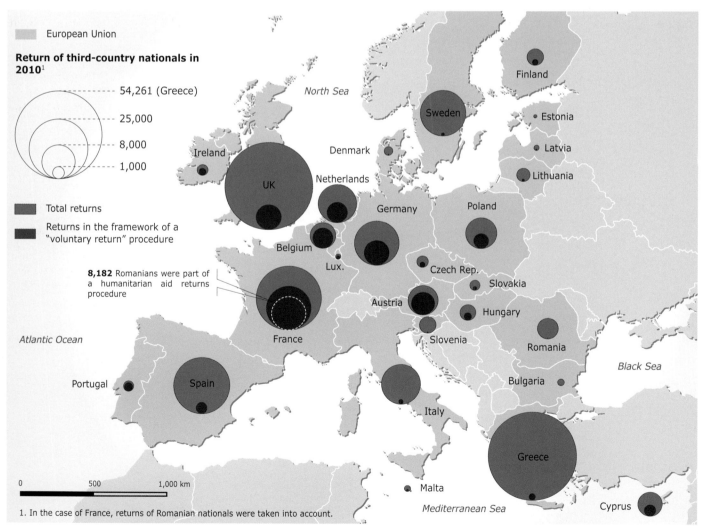

Sources: Data compilation - European Commission, Communication from the Commission to the European Parliament and the Council, Annual Report on Immigration and Asylum, 2011; Office Français de l'immigration et de l'Intégration, Rapport d'activité 2010; International Organization for Migration, Assisted Voluntary Return and Reintegration, EU Year Report 2010; International Organization for Migration, Assisted voluntary return and reintegration, Annual report of activities 2010.

"Voluntary" returns: another way to deport?

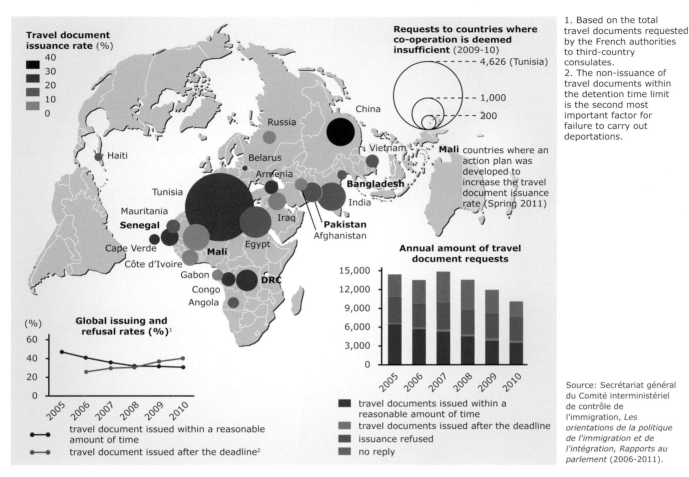

Travel document issuance rate (%)
- 40
- 30
- 20
- 10
- 0

Requests to countries where co-operation is deemed insufficient (2009-10)
- 4,626 (Tunisia)
- 1,000
- 200

Mali countries where an action plan was developed to increase the travel document issuance rate (Spring 2011)

1. Based on the total travel documents requested by the French authorities to third-country consulates.
2. The non-issuance of travel documents within the detention time limit is the second most important factor for failure to carry out deportations.

Haiti, Russia, China, Vietnam, Belarus, Armenia, Bangladesh, India, Tunisia, Iraq, Pakistan, Afghanistan, Senegal, Mauritania, Egypt, Cape Verde, Mali, Côte d'Ivoire, Gabon, DRC, Congo, Angola

Annual amount of travel document requests

(chart: 2005–2010, values 0 to 15,000)

Global issuing and refusal rates (%)[1]

(chart: 2005–2010, values 0 to 60%)

- travel document issued within a reasonable amount of time
- travel document issued after the deadline[2]

- travel documents issued within a reasonable amount of time
- travel documents issued after the deadline
- issuance refused
- no reply

Source: Secrétariat général du Comité interministériel de contrôle de l'immigration, *Les orientations de la politique de l'immigration et de l'intégration, Rapports au parlement* (2006-2011).

Not enough co-operation from consulates, according to the French Interior Ministry

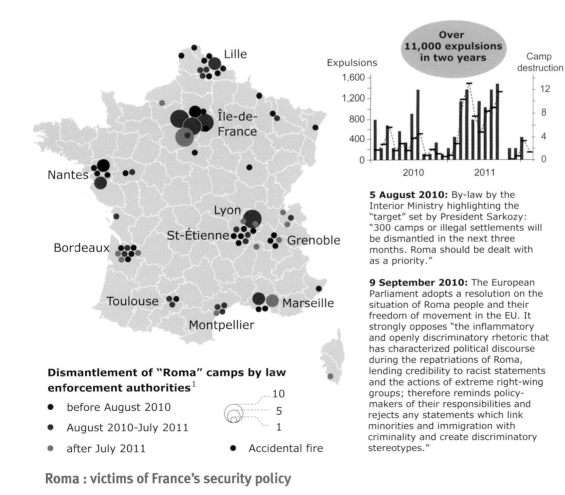

Lille, Île-de-France, Nantes, Lyon, St-Étienne, Grenoble, Bordeaux, Toulouse, Marseille, Montpellier

Dismantlement of "Roma" camps by law enforcement authorities[1]
- before August 2010 — 10
- August 2010-July 2011 — 5
- after July 2011 — 1
- Accidental fire

Over 11,000 expulsions in two years

Expulsions (0–1,600)
Camp destruction (0–12)
2010 — 2011

5 August 2010: By-law by the Interior Ministry highlighting the "target" set by President Sarkozy: "300 camps or illegal settlements will be dismantled in the next three months. Roma should be dealt with as a priority."

9 September 2010: The European Parliament adopts a resolution on the situation of Roma people and their freedom of movement in the EU. It strongly opposes "the inflammatory and openly discriminatory rhetoric that has characterized political discourse during the repatriations of Roma, lending credibility to racist statements and the actions of extreme right-wing groups; therefore reminds policy-makers of their responsibilities and rejects any statements which link minorities and immigration with criminality and create discriminatory stereotypes."

13 September 2010: Interior Minister Brice Hortefeux wants to "avoid any misunderstanding about what may be viewed as a potential stigmatization" and "personally signs" a new by-law whereby prefects are required to carry on the dismantlement of illegal settlements "whoever their occupiers".

7 April 2011: The Council of State annuls the by-law of 5 August 2010. It argues that the government should not have acted "with disregard for the equality principle enshrined in law" when conducting a dismantlement policy of illegal settlements that identified some of their occupiers based on their ethnicity".

1. Non-comprehensive census. Moreover, the authorities have generally labelled these settlements as "Roma" camps even if not all residents were Roma.

Sources: Romeurope (2012), "Les Roms, boucs émissaires d'une politique sécuritaire qui cible les migrants et les pauvres", 2010-2011 report; Goossens Philippe et Cousin Grégoire (2011), "Recensement des évacuations forcées de lieux de vie occupés par des Roms migrants en France (Répression des bidonvilles Roms)", unpublished report; press review on Romeurope's website.

Roma : victims of France's security policy

"INTEGRATION VILLAGES": BETWEEN SECURITY PARADIGM AND IMPROVISED HOSPITALITY REGIME

Since 2006, "integration villages" have been established in France. These shelters designed for Roma families consist of plots of land adapted for caravans and mobile homes and are presented by public authorities as a solution to the eradication of slums.

Behind the stated social and humanitarian motives, these measures are aimed at dissimulating "foreign poverty" or freeing up land for urban development.

Yet these projects take little account of individual circumstances. They are all the more destined to fail since they are based on cultural and political assumptions.

The French authorities consider it necessary to develop intermediary forms of shelter, before allowing access to more permanent forms of accommodation, and to limit the number of beneficiaries through the draconian selection of families, in order to avoid an inevitable invasion.

While such initiatives can seem to favour the integration of migrants, in practice they lead to the creation of ethnic ghettos and the adoption of freedom-crushing regulations. Such sites are strictly supervised: a guard filters entries into the village during the day (from 8am to 10pm) and only families with accommodation or friends, in limited numbers, are allowed in, on condition that they have requested prior authorization. At night, floodlights facilitate surveillance. The paradoxical nature of the State's approach should be underlined: on the one hand the State provides such projects with significant funding and on the other it refuses to grant these people the right to work,

depriving them of the opportunity to gain financial and residential independence.

A cross between ethnic villages and humanitarian programmes, which are spreading as examples of "best practice" in Europe, are these operations a new experiment in regulating foreign poverty?

Alexandre LE CLÈVE

Source: Libération (Sept.2011)

summer of 2010, a circular issued by the Ministry of the Interior called on prefects to initiate the "systematic dismantling of illegal camps, prioritizing those inhabited by Roma". The mobilization of police services and Ofii revealed the repressive practices and systematic harassment with which Romanian and Bulgarian populations have been targeted since 2007, in order to encourage them to leave the territory.

The prefects co-ordinated activities aimed at ensuring that Ofii officers, with support from the Regional Health and Social Services Agency (*Direction départementale des affaires sanitaires et sociales*), the police and border guards, intervened day and night, conducting joint operations to evacuate all such persons and arrange the departure of many. In 2009, Ofii organized 44 joint returns flights to Romania and Bulgaria. In August 2010, the Minister of Immigration announced that "8,328 Romanian and Bulgarian nationals have already been deported to their countries of origin and 29 flights especially chartered". These massive and discriminatory returns provoked strong reactions, over and above those of the Romanian and Bulgarian governments, from international bodies. Although at first the European Commission threatened France with legal action for non-application of European law and stigmatization of the Roma population, it withdrew rapidly in the face of the rigid position of the French authorities. Since 2009, France has required Romania to control the entries and exits of its nationals, by threatening to delay Romania's entry into the Schengen Area. In addition to the strengthening of police and judicial cooperation between the two States, in September 2011 a biometric index called Oscar (*Outil statistique et de contrôle de l'aide au retour –*

statistical tool for controlling assisted returns) was installed in Ofii. Officially it is aimed at preventing multiple requests for assisted return, but campaign groups have denounced it as an "anti-Roma tracking system". Ofii officers are not unaware of the absurdity of these eviction practices which condemn these populations to eternal wandering. "The Minister asked us to keep on with this procedure so we don't have any alternative... At Ofii we think it's a lot of money for not much result," one of the officers stated. Within Ofii, as among partner associations, expectations in terms of "development solidarity" have been largely disappointed: not all "voluntary" deportees are eligible for reintegration assistance in their country of origin. In 2011, only 2% of returnees received "assistance for economic reintegration". Such assistance, which was non-existent in Bulgaria, only concerned 72 of the 8,307 Romanians deported by Ofii in 2010. In July 2010, all reintegration assistance, other than in Senegal and Mali, was frozen because of insufficient funding or, in the case of Romania, as a retaliatory measure. How long will manufacturing the irregularity of Roma EU citizens continue to serve as an adjustment measure in the race to reach deportation targets in France?

Pascaline CHAPPART

1   Council of Europe, doc. 12277, 4 June 2010.
2   According to the Council of Europe, the IOM has repatriated more than 1.6 million persons in more than 160 countries over the past 30 years, under its "assisted voluntary return" programmes.
3   Within the framework of a "humanitarian return", stipends can reach up to 300 euros for an adult and 100 euros per child, while for a "voluntary return", a couple can receive 3,500 euros, an adult 2,000 euros and 1,000 euros each for up to three children, then 500 euros per additional child.

Detention of migrants in France: words hide the reality

In France, administrative detention of migrants has existed since the beginning of the 1960s, but it was only legalized in 1980. It is a unusual regime since, for historical reasons, two systems, governed by two different legal organizations, co-exist. On the one hand, there are administrative holding centres and facilities (*centres et locaux de rétention adminis-* *trative*) for migrants who are in the process of being deported. On the other hand, there are "waiting zones" for those who have been denied entry by border police, pending assessment of their situation. In both cases, laws were adopted to validate – at a very late stage – practices of arbitrary detention which had long been denounced by lawyers and campaign groups.

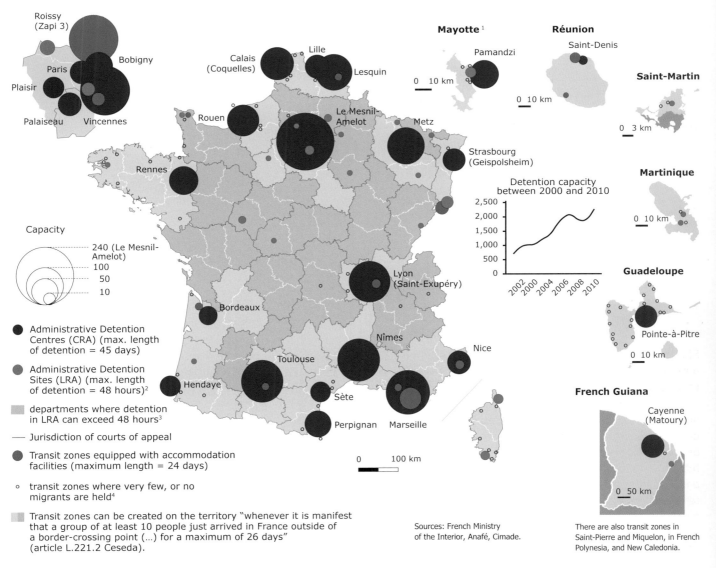

Sources: French Ministry
of the Interior, Anafé, Cimade.

There are also transit zones in
Saint-Pierre and Miquelon, in French
Polynesia, and New Caledonia.

1. Pamandzi administrative detention centre has an official capacity of 60 but 150 to 200 persons are regularly detained in the centre, although Article R.551.2 of the Ceseda states that "administrative detention centres (...) shall not exceed their capacity".

2. Pursuant to Article R.553.5 of the Ceseda, a copy of the prefect order announcing the creation of administrative detention sites (LRA), whether permanent or temporary, shall be transmitted to the General Inspectorate of Detention Sites (Contrôleur général des lieux de privation de liberté – CGLPL). This never happens, and it is therefore difficult to know exactly how many temporary and permanent LRAs are in use.

3. Pursuant to Article R.551.3 of the Ceseda: "if the decision by the judge of freedoms and detention is appealed, and if there is no administrative detention centre within the jurisdiction of the court of appeal where the LRA is located, the migrant can be maintained in the LRA pending the decision of the president of the court of appeal. Similarly, in the case where a removal order is challenged, and if there is no administrative detention centre within the jurisdiction of the administrative tribunal where the LRA is located, the migrant can be detained pending the examination of the appeal".

4. These transit zones are, like any other, established pursuant to a prefecture order. However, they do not comprise any accommodation facility. A migrant arrested and held in one of these sites is usually put in a hotel room – requisitioned by the prefecture – or even held on board a merchant navy vessel in a port.

The detention archipelago (2012)

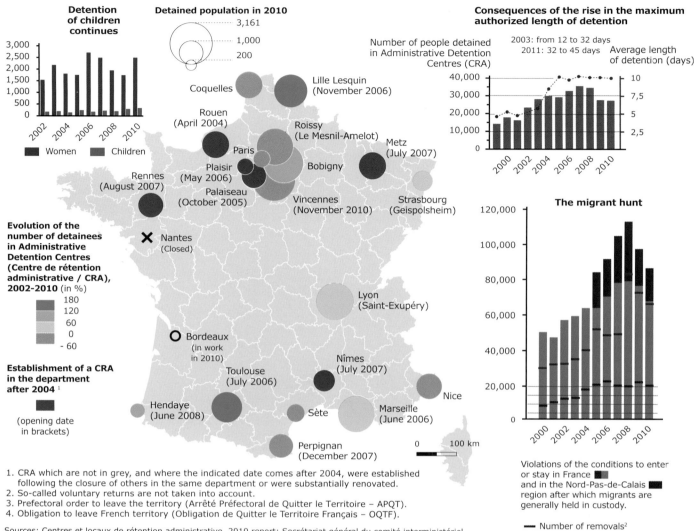

Detention of children continues

3,000
2,500
2,000
1,500
1,000
500
0

2002 2004 2006 2008 2010

■ Women   ■ Children

Detained population in 2010

3,161
1,000
200

Consequences of the rise in the maximum authorized length of detention

Number of people detained in Administrative Detention Centres (CRA)

2003: from 12 to 32 days
2011: 32 to 45 days   Average length of detention (days)

40,000 — 10
30,000 — 7,5
20,000 — 5
10,000 — 2,5
0

2000 2002 2004 2006 2008 2010

Coquelles
Lille Lesquin (November 2006)
Rouen (April 2004)
Roissy (Le Mesnil-Amelot)
Paris
Metz (July 2007)
Plaisir (May 2006)
Bobigny
Rennes (August 2007)
Palaiseau (October 2005)
Vincennes (November 2010)
Strasbourg (Geispolsheim)

Evolution of the number of detainees in Administrative Detention Centres (Centre de rétention administrative / CRA), 2002-2010 (in %)

180
120
60
0
- 60

Establishment of a CRA in the department after 2004 [1]

(opening date in brackets)

✗ Nantes (Closed)

○ Bordeaux (in work in 2010)

Lyon (Saint-Exupéry)

Nîmes (July 2007)

Toulouse (July 2006)

Nice

Hendaye (June 2008)
Sète
Marseille (June 2006)

Perpignan (December 2007)

0   100 km

The migrant hunt

120,000
100,000
80,000
60,000
40,000
20,000
0

2000 2002 2004 2006 2008 2010

1. CRA which are not in grey, and where the indicated date comes after 2004, were established following the closure of others in the same department or were substantially renovated.
2. So-called voluntary returns are not taken into account.
3. Prefectoral order to leave the territory (Arrêté Préfectoral de Quitter le Territoire – APQT).
4. Obligation to leave French territory (Obligation de Quitter le Territoire Français – OQTF).

Violations of the conditions to enter or stay in France ■ and in the Nord-Pas-de-Calais ■ region after which migrants are generally held in custody.

— Number of removals [2]
— Non implemented APRFs [3] (and OQTFs [4] since 2008)

Sources: Centres et locaux de rétention administrative, 2010 report; Secrétariat général du comité interministériel de contrôle de l'immigration, *Les orientations de la politique de l'immigration et de l'intégration, Rapports au Parlement (2006-2011)*; Bulletin statistique de l'Observatoire national de la délinquance et des réponses pénales, No.26, Oct. 2011.

10 years of French immigration policy: the results

Since 1964, public authorities had been holding migrants, outside any legal framework, in premises located in the port of Marseille before deporting them by boat. As time passed, this practice became standard and the length of detention increased to the extent that lawyers representing several detainees initiated a complaint for illegal detention. It was only then that the government passed a law which provided that "*a foreign national who cannot immediately comply with a decision denying him or her the right to enter the French territory may, if necessary, be kept in detention, subject to a written decision providing reasons, in premises which are not under the authority of the prison administration, for a period strictly required to organize his or her departure*". The law also stated that "*the person to be deported [...] may, if necessary, be kept in detention until his or her effective deportation [in a prison facility]*".

Despite strong criticism from activists and lawyers, who compared it to administrative detention practised during the Algeria War, the system was approved in 1980 by the Constitutional Court (*Conseil constitutionnel,* which reviews the conformity of laws with the French Constitution). Since then, it has never been challenged and the period for which migrants may be deprived of their freedom while awaiting deportation

has increased: through successive reforms, it went from less than 7 days to 12 days, and then to 32 days, reaching 45 days in 2011.

Euphemisms conceal the reality

Having been a clandestine practice for many years, French public authorities have never fully recognized the imprisonment of migrants and they continue to use euphemisms to describe it: the terms "holding" *("rétention")* or "administrative holding" ("*rétention administrative*") are used, in place of "detention" ("*détention*"). Yet these terms only appeared in the law in 1994. Until then, the law provided that migrants could be "*held in premises which are not under the authority of the prison administration*". This phrase evokes a temporary arrangement, less restrictive than "detention", especially as it takes place in premises described in a purely negative manner, without explicitly stating that they are under police surveillance. The verb "hold" is used to hide a form of imprisonment that dare not – or cannot – speak its name. Indeed, those defending migrants' rights reject the terms "internment" ("*internement*") and "detention".

Another euphemism is used to designate the modalities of

imprisonment that apply to migrants who have been denied entry into France because they do not have the necessary documents. The "waiting zone" was also invented in 1992 to provide a legal basis for the practice of holding migrants who have been denied access to the territory or who have requested access to seek asylum in the international transit areas of ports and airports. Until then, "holding" could last several days, sometimes several weeks, without being provided for in any law, in order to give the police sufficient time to organize departure. In defence of the practice, the public authorities claimed that, contrary to "administrative holding", there was no deprivation of liberty, since foreigners were "free" to leave the international area at any time to go to a country other than France. Consulted once again, the Constitutional Court approved this legal fiction in part, considering that it was a

form of detention but that it only "slightly" hindered freedom of movement. However, it limited its duration to 20 days. The creation of waiting zones illustrates a recurring process in the fight against irregular immigration: the eagerness to fill all gaps in the statutory framework which might allow "flows" of undesirable immigrants to enter or remain in France.

In 2012, there were 26 administrative holding centres, 25 other administrative holding facilities and nearly 80 waiting zones in France. The gradual extension of the length of detention, combined with the "target-setting policy" (for the numbers of deportations) launched by the former French Interior Minister, Nicolas Sarkozy, in 2003, caused the number of migrants detained in France to double between the beginning and the end of the first decade of the century.

Claire RODIER ◗

"Detention centres" in Belgium: state-sponsored violence against human rights

There are five detention centres in Belgium, which are managed by the Immigration Office. The total detention capacity in these centres is 628 persons.

These sites are the subject of regular criticism by NGOs and international bodies pointing to repeated violations of human rights. Over the last 10 years, the European Court of Human Rights has condemned Belgium on eight separate occasions[1] for facts related to the detention or deportation of migrants.

Material conditions vary greatly from one centre to another and are not among the worst in Europe. However, Belgian detention centres are clearly employed to put pressure on migrants: prison regulations are applied and detention periods are very long.

Since 2005, more than 50,000 migrants have been detained in these centres, which are not officially prisons but places *"where a migrant is detained, [to be] made available to the government"*.

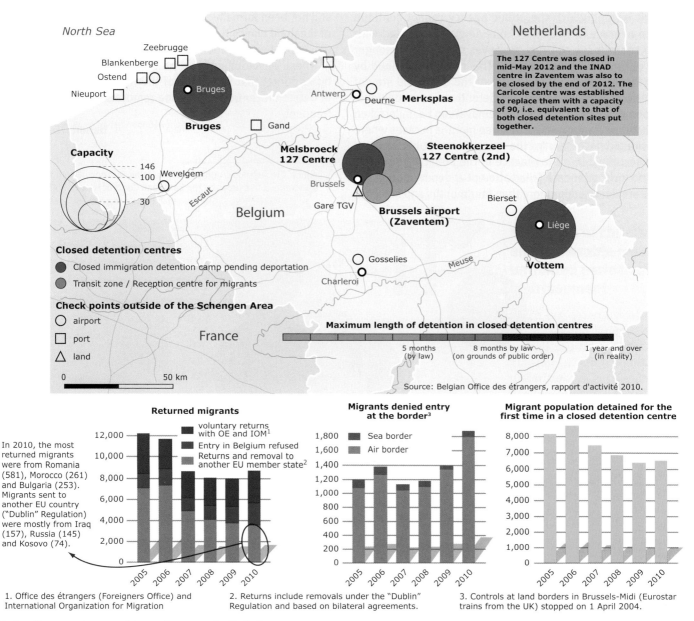

In 2010, the most returned migrants were from Romania (581), Morocco (261) and Bulgaria (253). Migrants sent to another EU country ("Dublin" Regulation) were mostly from Iraq (157), Russia (145) and Kosovo (74).

Returned migrants
- voluntary returns with OE and IOM[1]
- Entry in Belgium refused
- Returns and removal to another EU member state[2]

Migrants denied entry at the border[3]
- Sea border
- Air border

Migrant population detained for the first time in a closed detention centre

Source: Belgian Office des étrangers, rapport d'activité 2010.

1. Office des étrangers (Foreigners Office) and International Organization for Migration
2. Returns include removals under the "Dublin" Regulation and based on bilateral agreements.
3. Controls at land borders in Brussels-Midi (Eurostar trains from the UK) stopped on 1 April 2004.

Detention centres and transit zones in Belgium

Detention of migrants in Eastern Europe: human and financial costs

The accession of new Member States in 2004 and 2007, followed by the integration of some of them into the Schengen Area in December 2007, moved the external borders of the European Union towards the east. During the enlargement process, the EU encouraged and supported policies aimed at the identification, detention and expulsion of migrants in order to control arrivals at its new borders.

To the east, from the end of the 2000s, considerable amounts of money were devoted to the control and "management" of migrants transiting through Ukraine. From 2000 to 2006, Ukraine was part of the TACIS programme, under which it received a total of 35 million euros. Eight million euros were allocated to building the capacity of the government to manage migration flows, with the support of the IOM, and four million were dedicated to the development of holding centres in northern Ukraine (in Lutsk and Chernikov). At the same time, within the framework of the Aeneas programme (2004-2006), the International Centre for the Development of Migration Policy in Ukraine received 2.3 million Euros for the construction of five new camps, including in Zhuravichi (near the Polish border) and Rozsudiv (near the Russian and Belarusian borders) and improving facilities in the eight existing camps.

Despite appeals from international organizations denouncing arbitrary detention and the difficulties faced by migrants in accessing legal support, the first grants were allocated well before the law on migrants was revised. In a report issued in September 2008 evaluating the effectiveness of financial support to the construction of new facilities in Ukraine, the European Court of Auditors underlined that, at the time that audits were conducted in 2005 and 2006, migrants in detention centres suffered *"severely from overcrowded living conditions, insufficient sanitation and poor diet"*. Living conditions of detainees were described as "inhuman and degrading", especially in the centres in Pavchino and Chop. Presumably believing that violations of human rights would disappear in less dilapidated buildings, the Court was concerned about delays in completing the work. In reality, funding migration control systems in Ukraine takes priority over supporting improvements to respect the human rights of migrants and asylum seekers.

After the entry into force of the readmission agreement

In 2008, Ukraine received 35 million euros of EU funding under the European Neighbourhood and Partnership Instrument (ENPI) programme, to cover 24-month projects called GDISC and ERIT. The development of new holding sites accelerated following the entry into force of the EU-Ukraine readmission agreement in January 2008, aimed at Ukrainian nationals found to be in an irregular situation in the EU. Since 2010, the agreement provides for the Ukrainian authorities to "take back" all those who have passed through Ukraine in transit. As of 2010, infrastructures were of three types: there were 73 special facilities comprising "screening centres" and "special rooms"; ten "temporary holding facilities" under the responsibility of border guards; and two "migrant accommodation centres" under the authority of the Interior Ministry.

After arrest, migrants are directed to screening centres within the premises of border guards, mainly situated in a 50-kilometre-long border area between Ukraine and Russia. These centres are supposed to identify the migrants and separate "irregular" migrants from asylum seekers. Then migrants are transferred to a temporary holding facility where they remain until they obtain a place in an accommodation centre. In order to reduce costs and increase the effectiveness of controls, new mobile units were constructed, intended to be easy to dismantle and move, depending on the transit routes adopted by migrants. Three temporary holding centres and two special facilities were established in Shatsk, Malniv, Mosticku, Chernivtsi and Ismail. Furthermore, under the GUMIRA project, from February to April 2010, the EU financed the construction of mobile camps in Pysarivka, Lugansk, Seredina Buda, Kharkiv and Odessa. At the end of 2008, just after the holding centre in Pavchino was closed down on sanitary grounds, the two new centres in Zhuravichi and Rozsudiv quickly became overcrowded and the Ministry of Defence donated three buildings to the Ministry of the Interior in order to build more holding centres.

The construction of "modern gulags" continues

The new camps, built on the sites of former Soviet military bases, meet high standards, according to an observer. The centre in Lutsk, for example, has clean and well-lit cells, the buildings are *"freshly renovated"*, from the outside everything appears *"clean and sterile"*, and the centre is *"surrounded by a high, white wall topped with sparkling barbed wire"*. Despite the good intentions proclaimed by the EU, which continues to underline its commitment to human rights, the fate of migrants detained in the new centres raises concerns. In 2010, the NGO Human Rights Watch reported that detainees in Ukraine were at risk of being subjected to torture and that some had been severely beaten, deprived of food or subjected to other inhuman and degrading treatment. Violations included arbitrary detention, lack of access to asylum procedures, detention of children and holding unrelated men and women together and children with adults.

In November 2010, after the Minister of the Interior proposed increasing the number of migrant accommodation centres from two to eight and doubling the number of temporary holding centres, the European Commission granted Ukraine funding of 66 million euros in order to "*develop and implement an integrated border management strategy*", adding that the "*funding is [also] intended to significantly improve conditions in the temporary holding facilities for irregular migrants*". The Commissioner for Enlargement and European Neighbourhood Policy stated that, with this decision, the Commission was supporting "*the efforts of the Ukrainian*

Government to achieve an effective balance between secure borders and the facilitation of legal movements of persons and goods". By providing further financial assistance to Ukraine, the EU continues to externalize its detention system and to institutionalize the expulsion of migrants under the readmission agreement. Detention of migrants thus becomes the price to be paid for agreements on visa facilitation for Ukrainian nationals, despite the risks it carries for the rights of those deported.

Paulina NIKIEL ▣

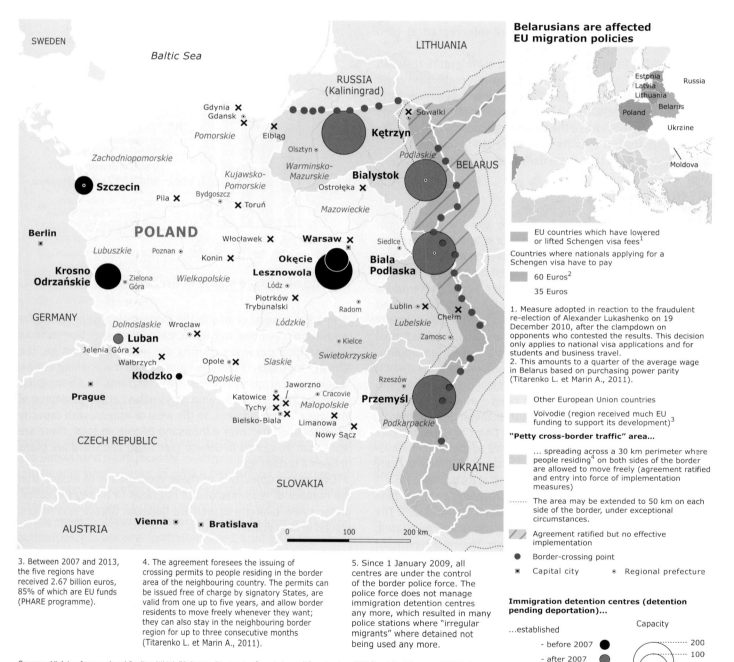

Belarusians are affected EU migration policies

EU countries which have lowered or lifted Schengen visa fees[1]

Countries where nationals applying for a Schengen visa have to pay

60 Euros[2]

35 Euros

1. Measure adopted in reaction to the fraudulent re-election of Alexander Lukashenko on 19 December 2010, after the clampdown on opponents who contested the results. This decision only applies to national visa applications and for students and business travel.
2. This amounts to a quarter of the average wage in Belarus based on purchasing power parity (Titarenko L. et Marin A., 2011).

Other European Union countries

Voïvodie (region received much EU funding to support its development)[3]

"Petty cross-border traffic" area...

... spreading across a 30 km perimeter where people residing[4] on both sides of the border are allowed to move freely (agreement ratified and entry into force of implementation measures)

The area may be extended to 50 km on each side of the border, under exceptional circumstances.

Agreement ratified but no effective implementation

● Border-crossing point

▣ Capital city   ◉ Regional prefecture

Immigration detention centres (detention pending deportation)...

...established   Capacity

- before 2007   ●   200
- after 2007   ●   100
... closed after 2007[5] ✗   20

3. Between 2007 and 2013, the five regions have received 2.67 billion euros, 85% of which are EU funds (PHARE programme).

4. The agreement foresees the issuing of crossing permits to people residing in the border area of the neighbouring country. The permits can be issued free of charge by signatory States, are valid from one up to five years, and allow border residents to move freely whenever they want; they can also stay in the neighbouring border region for up to three consecutive months (Titarenko L. et Marin A., 2011).

5. Since 1 January 2009, all centres are under the control of the border police force. The police force does not manage immigration detention centres any more, which resulted in many police stations where "irregular migrants" where detained not being used any more.

Sources: Violaine Jaussaud and Paulina Nikiel, "Pologne, Roumanie: être de bons éléments dans l'UE élargie"*in* Migreurop (2010) *Aux frontières de l'Europe : contrôles, enfermements, expulsions*, pp. 47-72; Larisa Titarenko and Anaïs Marin, "Les Bélarusses victimes du rideau Schengen", *Regard sur l'Est*, 15 November 2011, www.regard-est.com; Laurent Geslin and Sébastien Gobert "La Pologne orientale passe à l'Ouest", *Le Monde diplomatique*, June 2012.

Eastern Poland: the double frontier

Migrant holding centres in Spain: a story of human rights abuses

Migrant "holding centres" appeared in Spain following the adoption of the first "law on immigration". The basic function of these centres is to deprive "irregular" migrants' who are the subject of administrative sanctions of their liberty. Since such sanctions can end in removal from the country, centres are supposed to ensure the enforcement of expulsion orders. A new law adopted in 2009, transposing European Directive 2008/115/CE (the "Return" Directive), extended the maximum period of detention in a holding centre from 40 to 60 days. The legislation in force provides that the holding centres must not resemble prisons and that only the freedom of movement of those detained should be limited; other rights must be scrupulously respected. However, nearly 30 years after the establishment of migrant holding centres, the adoption of an internal regulation, as required by the 2009 law, is still pending.

The holding centres have been strongly criticized since their opening. Spain's Ombudsperson and Attorney General have denounced living conditions and regular violations of human rights in the centres. NGOs and activists have repeatedly exposed the appalling sanitary and social conditions and outdated infrastructures. Cases of ill-treatment, sexual abuse and violations of the right to asylum have also been documented. Reports by the Spanish Commission for Refugee Aid (Comisión Española de Ayuda al Refugiado – CEAR), Pueblos Unidos and the Spanish coalition of Migreurop have regularly drawn attention to the ill-treatment suffered by detainees in the centres.

Several international bodies have also voiced their concerns about the failings of detention procedures applied by the Spanish authorities to migrants in an irregular situation. The UN Human Rights Committee, for example, expressed concern

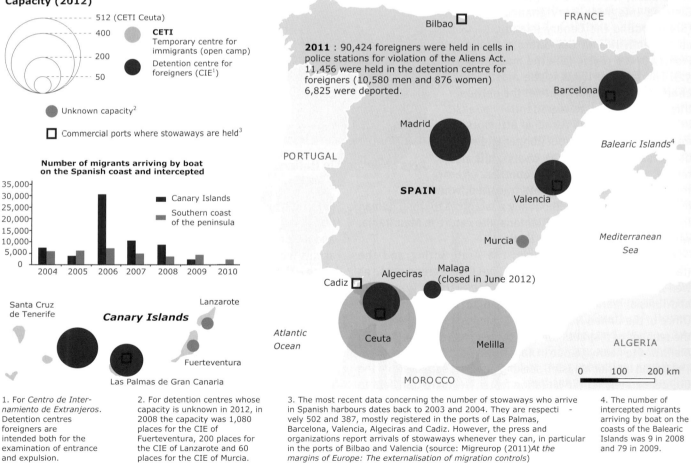

Capacity (2012)

512 (CETI Ceuta)
400
200
50

CETI
Temporary centre for immigrants (open camp)

Detention centre for foreigners (CIE[1])

Unknown capacity[2]

☐ Commercial ports where stowaways are held[3]

Number of migrants arriving by boat on the Spanish coast and intercepted

- Canary Islands
- Southern coast of the peninsula

35,000
30,000
25,000
20,000
15,000
10,000
5,000
0

2004 2005 2006 2007 2008 2009 2010

Canary Islands

Santa Cruz de Tenerife

Lanzarote

Fuerteventura

Las Palmas de Gran Canaria

Bilbao ☐

FRANCE

2011 : 90,424 foreigners were held in cells in police stations for violation of the Aliens Act. 11,456 were held in the detention centre for foreigners (10,580 men and 876 women) 6,825 were deported.

Barcelona ☐

Madrid

PORTUGAL

Balearic Islands[4]

SPAIN

Valencia ☐

Murcia

Mediterranean Sea

Malaga (closed in June 2012)

Algeciras

Cadiz ☐

Atlantic Ocean

Ceuta ☐

Melilla

ALGERIA

0   100   200 km

MOROCCO

1. For *Centro de Inter- namiento de Extranjeros*. Detention centres foreigners are intended both for the examination of entrance and expulsion.

2. For detention centres whose capacity is unknown in 2012, in 2008 the capacity was 1,080 places for the CIE of Fuerteventura, 200 places for the CIE of Lanzarote and 60 places for the CIE of Murcia.

3. The most recent data concerning the number of stowaways who arrive in Spanish harbours dates back to 2003 and 2004. They are respecti - vely 502 and 387, mostly registered in the ports of Las Palmas, Barcelona, Valencia, Algeciras and Cadiz. However, the press and organizations report arrivals of stowaways whenever they can, in particular in the ports of Bilbao and Valencia (source: Migreurop (2011)*At the margins of Europe: The externalisation of migration controls*)

4. The number of intercepted migrants arriving by boat on the coasts of the Balearic Islands was 9 in 2008 and 79 in 2009.

Sources: Asociación Pro Derechos Humanos de Andalucía (APDHA); Comisión Española deAyuda al Refugiado (CEAR); El Pais; Publico; Spanish Ministry of Labour and Immigration; *El defensor del pueblo*; presentation in the regional experts workshop responding to boat arrivals and mixed migration flows in the Mediterranean, organized by ICMC in the framework of the DRIVE project, 10-13 May 2011, Catania, Sicily in International Catholic Migration Commission (ICMC), *Mayday! Strengthening responses of assistance and protection to boat people and other migrants arriving in Southern Europe*, 2011, p. 132.

Confinement of migrants in Spain

over "arbitrary" decisions on detention and expulsion. The UN Committee on the Elimination of Racial Discrimination, meanwhile, criticized the way in which migrants who are released when expulsion orders cannot be implemented are abandoned; it also underlined the absence of norms regulating the enjoyment of rights inside the centres. The European Commission against Racism and Intolerance of the Council of Europe has also highlighted the poor detention conditions and failings in asylum procedures and access to legal assistance.

There has recently been a significant increase in public interest in the conditions in Spain's holding centres. This can be linked to the denunciations and awareness-raising actions of civil-society organizations. In particular, the winter of 2011-2012 was marked by the deaths of two detainees: Samba Martine on 20 December 2011 in Madrid and Idrissa Diallo on 6 January 2012 in Barcelona. These deaths were caused by a lack of access to medical assistance and were widely reported in the media. Despite strong political and public pressure on the government, as of summer 2012 no investigations had been undertaken and no-one had been held accountable.

The lack of transparency within this system increased under the new People's Party government. In 2010, within the framework of the campaign "For a right of access to migrant detention centres", Migreurop gained access to three centres (in Madrid, Malaga and Barcelona). In 2012, similar requests made by the campaign "Open Access" were all rejected. Today, authorization for access is granted on an individual and discretionary basis by the management of each centre. It is only through legal action that associations can obtain recognition of a temporary right of access.

Under the People's Party government, migrants who have completed prison sentences and are subject to judicial expulsion orders are increasingly placed in holding centres. This contributes to media portrayals conflating different categories of migrants and encourages the criminalization of those detained merely on the basis of their irregular administrative situation. Such transfers have been made possible by the fall in the numbers of migrants arriving on the Canary Islands, caused by the activities of Frontex and the militarized surveillance of migratory routes, which proves deadly for hundreds of passengers in *cayucos* and other boats.

In June 2012, the holding centre in Malaga closed its doors. As a result of these developments and the mobilization of activists, calls for the closure of all the holding centres are increasing. In the meantime, the platform "For the application of the law beyond the threshold of holding centres" is demanding that regulations currently under discussion guarantee respect for the human rights of detainees.

Carlos ARCE and Peio M. AIERBE ▣

Egyptian migrants awaiting expulsion in a Libyan
detention camp, June 2012.
Photo: Sara Prestianni

Part 4

Impact on departure and transit areas

In the context of the globalization of migration, the movement of people around the planet is organized into desirable and undesirable flows. In order to maintain migrants deemed undesirable under house arrest, Europe engages in the development of a control system involving countries further and further away from its territory. As a result, interference in the policies applied by countries of departure and transit of migrants is increasing, with the effect of impeding the movement of people even beyond Europe's borders. In countries in the South, informal camps emerge in deserts and forests, along the coastlines and on the fringes of cities. Migratory journeys often culminate in a rootless existence, brief or lengthy periods spent in lawless zones, violence and even death. The countries where such abuses are committed bear direct responsibility. But European States know that they suffer from numerous shortcomings and a democratic deficit. And their friendly relations with corrupt and dictatorial regimes correspond to the dismissal of part of humanity as subhuman.

Buffer zones around Morocco: Oujda, the enclaves of Ceuta and Melilla, and Western Sahara

As borders close, migratory routes are displaced, increasing the dangers faced by those travelling and creating *buffer zones*. These are areas in territories bordering the European Union, which "protect" Europe from the arrival of migrants, with the authorities of the countries concerned agreeing to take on the role of border guards.

Until 2004, an important migratory route from Africa to Europe passed between the north of Morocco and the south of Spain via the Strait of Gibraltar where, at the closest point, 14 kilometres separate the two countries. With the establishment of increasingly developed surveillance systems, points of departure have gradually moved to the south of Morocco, to the occupied territory of Western Sahara. From there, migrants attempt to reach the Canary Islands, necessitating a crossing seven times longer than the route through the Strait of Gibraltar, in much more perilous waters. These two factors considerably increase the risks of accidents at sea. Yet more stringent controls continue to push points of departure further and further south, to Mauritania and Senegal and east, to Libya.

Europe and Morocco: friendly relations around a policy on the "management of migratory flows"

Since the end of the 1990s, the European Union (EU) has provided considerable financial aid to transit countries to strengthen border controls on those exiting those territories. In Morocco, the MEDA I (1996-2001) and II (2001-2006) programmes largely funded the "Moroccan strategy on combating illegal immigration".

Morocco also benefits from the European Neighbourhood and Partnership Instrument (ENPI), under which it receives assistance to co-operate in the EU policy on externalization of asylum and border control. The EU-Morocco Association Agreement, concluded in 1996, opened up the prospect of Morocco acquiring "advanced status", enabling co-operation to be developed in other domains. Immigration, border security and fighting terrorism constitute the main priority areas.

At the seventh EU-Morocco Association Council in October 2008, the EU welcomed "the efforts by Morocco to deal with

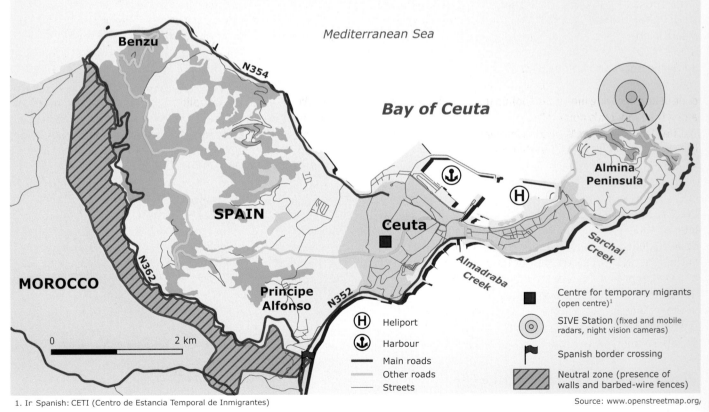

1. In Spanish: CETI (Centro de Estancia Temporal de Inmigrantes)

Source: www.openstreetmap.org/

Ceuta is increasingly isolated from Morocco

illegal immigration, which have led to a substantial reduction in immigration flows from Morocco".

Since 1999, Morocco is also engaged in a co-operation agreement with France entitled "State action at sea". The agreement focuses on the co-ordination of maritime surveillance, prioritizing the fight against drug trafficking and combating illegal immigration. In the framework of this co-operation, Morocco has a maritime control centre in the Strait of Gibraltar, near Tangier, and a navigation surveillance system along the coast.

Together, these resources form what the Moroccan authorities refer to as the "system". The costs of the equipment necessary for its operation and the majority of the labour costs are financed by the EU.

In 2003, under the "national strategy on the management of migratory flows", Morocco adopted a law on "the entry and stay of foreigners, irregular emigration and immigration" (Law No. 02-03). This legislation was proposed and adopted in the context of negotiations between the EU and Morocco on migration issues and was presented to Parliament at the same time as Law No. 03-03 on terrorism.

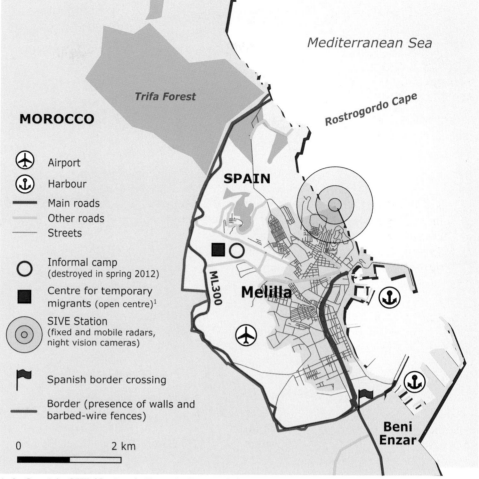

1. In Spanish: CETI (Centro de Estancia Temporal de Inmigrantes)   Source: www.openstreetmap.org/

Melilla: the other Spanish enclave on Moroccan territory

In 2005, the institutional component of the Moroccan strategy "on combating illegal immigration" was implemented, with the creation of a Department for Migration and Border Surveillance and a Migration Monitoring Centre. Their role is to apply the policy on management of flows and in particular to "optimize the deployment of operational units for surveillance, control and securing infiltration points used by illegal migrants along the Kingdom's borders".

The effectiveness of Morocco's implementation of the neighbourhood policy is carefully observed by the most directly affected European countries. Thus, when, in the first months of 2011, Morocco lessened its efforts as a result of the movements of the "Arab Spring"[1] and the drafting of a new Constitution, the Director General of International Relations of the Spanish Interior Ministry, Arturo Avello, and the Director General of the Spanish Police and Guardia civil came to remind the Moroccan authorities what was expected of them.[2] In the months that followed, repression against migrants resumed.[3] From August 2011, the Moroccan authorities organized "sweep" operations in the regions of Fnideq, Nador and Oujda, as well as in large towns in the interior of the country (Fes, Casablanca and Rabat), creating de facto prohibited zones for migrants.

Buffer zones in and around Morocco

* Border regions
Of the 12 administrative regions into which Morocco has been

divided since 2011, three are on the borders: the occupied territory of Western Sahara in the south, which Morocco calls the Laâyoune-Saqia Al Hamra region (capital Laâyoune), the Eastern-Rif region (around Nador and Oujda) and the Tangier-Tetouan region in the north (capital Tangier). Frequent roadblocks in these three regions, whether for military reasons as in Western Sahara or political reasons as in the north and east, mean that these areas are highly controlled. In practice, it is impossible to travel more than 30 kilometres without being stopped at a checkpoint by the royal police or national security at the entrance to and exit from towns.

Migrant camps are regularly destroyed and inhabitants find themselves pushed towards towns inland, where their presence is tolerated because they fill a gap in the Moroccan labour market, accepting work at half wages and in very difficult conditions. This is the case in Agadir, with agricultural work, and in the Western Saharan town of Dakhla, with fishing. The security machine starts up as soon as they approach the buffer zones.

* Oujda
Most migrants arrested under the system of managing migratory flows are returned to the eastern region, which it is then difficult to leave. Indeed, the region itself has become a large open-air detention centre. Blocked by the border zone with Algeria, at best migrants manage to reach the Oujda university campus, which has become an informal

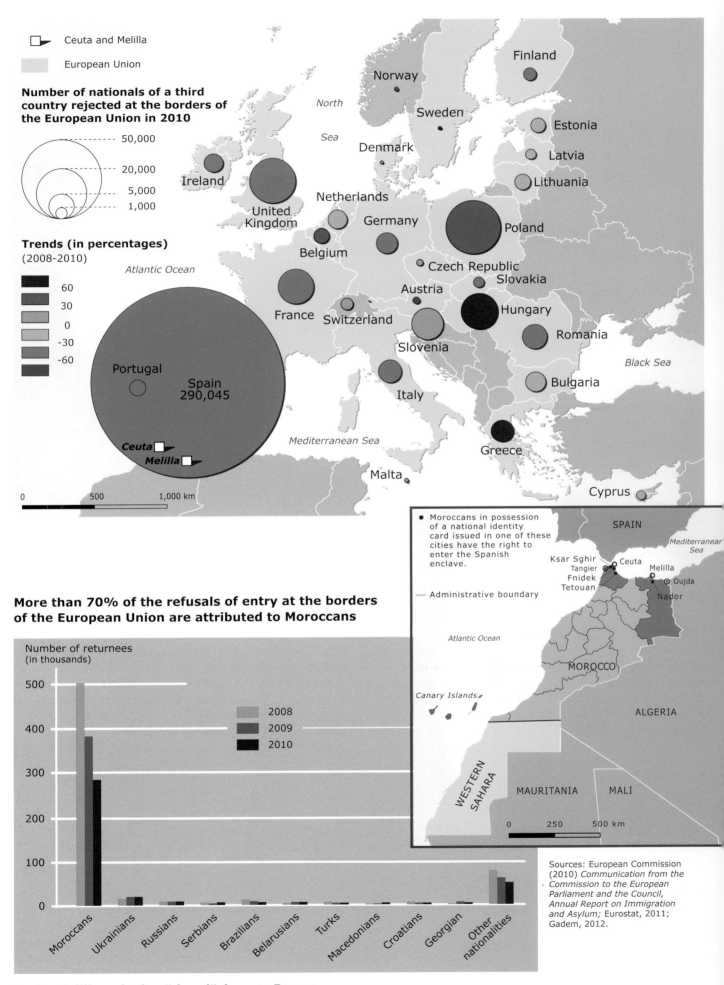

Number of nationals of a third country rejected at the borders of the European Union in 2010

50,000
20,000
5,000
1,000

Trends (in percentages)
(2008-2010)

60
30
0
-30
-60

Ceuta and Melilla

European Union

Atlantic Ocean

North Sea

Portugal

Spain
290,045

Ceuta
Melilla

Mediterranean Sea

Malta

Ireland

United Kingdom

Netherlands

Germany

Belgium

France

Switzerland

Slovenia

Italy

Greece

Norway

Sweden

Denmark

Finland

Estonia

Latvia

Lithuania

Poland

Czech Republic

Slovakia

Austria

Hungary

Romania

Bulgaria

Black Sea

Cyprus

0   500   1,000 km

More than 70% of the refusals of entry at the borders of the European Union are attributed to Moroccans

Number of returnees
(in thousands)

500
400
300
200
100
0

2008
2009
2010

Moroccans
Ukrainians
Russians
Serbians
Brazilians
Belarusians
Turks
Macedonians
Croatians
Georgian
Other nationalities

- Moroccans in possession of a national identity card issued in one of these cities have the right to enter the Spanish enclave.

— Administrative boundary

SPAIN

Mediterranean Sea

Ksar Sghir
Tangier
Fnidek
Tetouan

Ceuta

Melilla

Oujda

Nador

Atlantic Ocean

MOROCCO

Canary Islands

ALGERIA

WESTERN SAHARA

MAURITANIA

MALI

0   250   500 km

Sources: European Commission (2010) Communication from the Commission to the European Parliament and the Council, Annual Report on Immigration and Asylum; Eurostat, 2011; Gadem, 2012.

Ceuta, Melilla and other "closed" doors to Europe

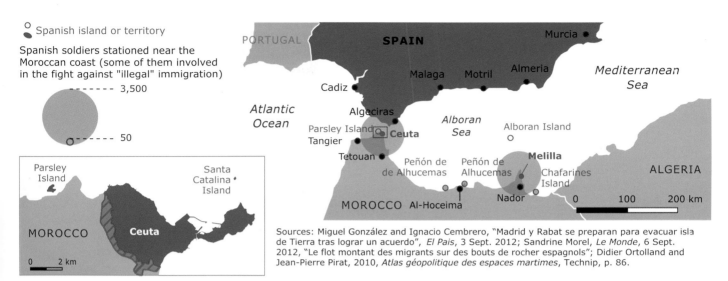

Sources: Miguel González and Ignacio Cembrero, "Madrid y Rabat se preparan para evacuar isla de Tierra tras lograr un acuerdo", *El País*, 3 Sept. 2012; Sandrine Morel, *Le Monde*, 6 Sept. 2012, "Le flot montant des migrants sur des bouts de rocher espagnols"; Didier Ortolland and Jean-Pierre Pirat, 2010, *Atlas géopolitique des espaces maritimes*, Technip, p. 86.

Off Morocco, troops aim to stop migrants reaching Spanish soil (May-September 2012)

accommodation centre where migrants from sub-Saharan Africa reside for longer and longer periods. Moving around is very difficult. For example, it is almost impossible to take a bus into the centre of Morocco, since drivers have received strict instructions to refuse to "pick up blacks", as has been observed in bus stations.

On the railway line linking Oujda and Rabat, two filters have been put in place: at Oujda station, with police posted in front of the access to the platforms, and in the small town of Taourirt, 30 kilometres from Oujda. When trains stop there, police climb aboard and make "blacks" get off. The scenario is the same on the line between Tangier, Tetouan and Fnideq in the north.

* Western Sahara

The occupied territory of Western Sahara, which Morocco invaded in 1975, is bordered to the west by the Atlantic Ocean, facing the Canary Islands. Since 2003, a system to fight "illegal emigration"[4] has been erected along the coast. A 2,720-kilometre security wall has also been built to protect against incursions from the Frente Polisario – Western Sahara's liberation movement, recognized as the legitimate government by the African Union. Morocco's armed forces have over 100,000 soldiers permanently mobilized to defend this security belt, which also has a surveillance system comprising simple alarms and Rasura and AN/PPS-15 radars, as well as a range of security instruments capable of detecting any movement up to 60 kilometres away.

* Ceuta and Melilla

Ceuta (with a surface area of 8 square kilometres) is dominated by the imposing Belyounech mountains to the west. Melilla (14 square kilometres) is situated on the eastern side of the peninsula of the Cape of the Three Forks and near Mount Gurugú in the south.

Since 1995, the two towns have had the special status of "autonomous cities". The borders of Ceuta and Melilla are secured by dual six-metre-high fences and watchtowers,

in order to dissuade potential emigrants, who have made Belyounech and Gurugú into departure platforms for the European continent.

Incidents regularly break out at the borders to these two enclaves. The first major events were in September 2005, when migrants tried to break through the border fences and were trapped between Spanish rubber bullets and Moroccan guns. At least 13 were killed and 50 injured in Ceuta, drawing major international attention and condemnation. In Ceuta, which is soon to become a military base, "sweep" operations are frequently organized. Migrants, in groups, attempt to force their way through the fences around the two enclaves. On several occasions, the Moroccan and Spanish security forces have fired real bullets at those trying to access these gateway territories to Europe. Migrants are generally arrested and returned to Oujda.[5] Of course, this system does not stop migrants continuing to attempt to cross the barriers.

Shortly after the 2005 events in Ceuta and Melilla, the numbers responsible for patrolling the region almost doubled and since then the Moroccan Royal Marines have deployed significant resources at sea and on the coast to conduct maritime surveillance.

The Moroccan and Spanish security forces regularly attempt to intercept migrants at sea. On several occasions this has resulted in migrants drowning. Survivors are generally violently removed.[6]

Hicham RACHIDI ◘

---

1   See en.wikipedia.org/wiki/2011-2012_Moroccan_protests
2   See elpais.com/diario/2011/07/15/espana/1310680814_850215.html
3   See www.gadem-asso.org/Les-forces-de-l-ordre-marocaines
4   It should be underlined that the fight against "illegal emigration" violates international instruments and in particular Article 13 of the Universal Declaration of Human Rights of 1948, which recognizes everyone's right to "leave any country".
5   www.gadem-asso.org/
6   See www.gadem-asso.org/Les-forces-de-l-ordre-marocaines,125

Wanderings and encampments

The most striking aspect of many migrants' journeys is the "zigzagging" routes they involve, even after arrival in Europe. "Illegal passage", the only alternative to restrictions on "regular" entry into the European Union, is made up of toing and froing, bypassing obstacles and thwarted attempts.

The European Union (EU) has set the objective of containing migrants outside its territory and it is the "border countries" – both external, like Libya, and internal, such as Greece – that are responsible for working to achieve this. Under the pretext of "shared responsibility", European countries on the periphery of the Union must prevent migrants entering the EU, while third countries must prohibit departures.

Among the many consequences of these policies, the most serious are the multiplying deaths at the borders. Other tragic situations are generated. Forced wandering, through deserts and oceans, over fences and walls, in camps, prisons, "ghettos" and "jungles", crammed into lorries, 4x4s, canoes or cargo ships. For many years, trap-like places, buffer zones from where one can neither move forward nor turn back, have been developing at borders. Among the best known are Calais (France), Patras (Greece) and Oujda (Morocco). More recently, other such sites have appeared, such as the jungle in Subotica (Serbia) and formal camps in Chucha (Tunisia) and Salloum (Egypt), run by the UNHCR.

The jungles in Calais and the ghettos in Patras have endured for more than 10 years, despite destruction by bulldozers and collective arrests under the media spotlight. Such camps, stopping points on the route from one country to another, are rebuilt or moved elsewhere. Migrants come up with strategies to circumvent obstacles. After the informal camps near the Spanish enclaves of Ceuta and Melilla in Morocco (at the beginning of the 2000s), Nouadhibou in Mauritania (2006), and the Tunisian and Libyan coasts (2008), since 2009, the route to Europe has become even longer, passing through the Greek borders (see map opposite), and via the east of Europe, through the Balkans.

Beyond the European Union...

In 2011, the Tunisian Revolution and the conflict in Libya reconfigured migratory routes. The conflict in Libya, but also the disappearance of controls in Tunisia and Libya, contributed to the departure of several thousand people towards Italy. Despite the extensive media coverage orchestrated by the Italian government of their arrival on Lampedusa, the numbers are unexceptional in comparison with previous years, at other points of entry into Europe.

The numbers are also derisory. Of the hundreds of thousands of people who fled Libya in 2011, only approximately 4% tried to reach European States (Italy and Malta). The majority flocked to the camps in Salloum and Chucha.

These so-called "transit" camps, run by the UNHCR, were supposed to accommodate refugees from Libya for the time necessary to organize their repatriation or protection. But as of 18 months later, several thousand persons were still stuck there.

Ibrahim[1] is one of them. He fled Somalia in 2008 for Libya. Suffering from racism and arbitrary detention, Ibrahim planned to head for Europe, where he hoped to receive protection. "That was in August 2009. We left in a small overloaded boat. There were 85 of us. After one day, we had nothing left to eat. We had an accident as we were getting close to Malta. Four people died. Shortly afterwards, an Italian boat approached us and we thought that we were going to be rescued. But they took us back to Libya." Ibrahim and his companions were victims of one of the numerous illegal push-backs carried out by Italy, which were condemned by the European Court of Human Rights on 23 February 2012. "When we arrived in Libya, we were detained in a camp near Tripoli for nine months." On his release, Ibrahim went to Benghazi and he was there when the conflict started. With the advance of Qadafi's troops and the threat of NATO bombing, he fled to Egypt. He spent over a year in the camp at Salloum, waiting to obtain refugee status and to be resettled in another country.

In the Chucha camp, at the Tunisian-Libyan border, there are similar stories. The 3,000 people still in the camp cannot or will not return to their countries of origin, affected by wars and political instability. The majority of them have been granted refugee status but have little hope of resettlement. A Somalian refugee repeats tirelessly, "Resettlement is not a right. That's what the UNHCR tells us."

Chucha also receives people who *a priori* do not have a reason to be there and risks becoming a containment site for "undesirables". Ounia arrived in March 2012[2], brought to the camp by the Tunisian security forces with 72 others. They had left Libya by boat, bound for Europe, but rapidly found themselves in difficulty: "Water was coming in," she explained. The Italian coast guards were contacted using a satellite phone, then a Tunisian fishing boat came to their assistance and took the passengers aboard. "After one day and one night," the fishing boat was intercepted by a Tunisian military ship. "Six men with guns came on to the boat." The soldiers assured the migrants that they would take them to Sicily, but they were taken to Sfax in Tunisia and then by bus to the Chucha camp.

Ounia and her group already know that they have no hope, even though a request for asylum has been registered. The resettlement plan launched by the UNHCR in 2011 had few takers in northern European States, which were reluctant to "share the burden", and it was closed on 1 December 2011.

The only alternatives proposed by the UNHCR were to wait until Tunisia, which is in the process of adopting a new Constitution, adopted a law on asylum (at the earliest in mid-2013), or to return "voluntarily" to their countries of origin – an incongruous solution for people who had just been recognized as refugees. Other "solutions" include staying in Tunisia in an irregular situation, or returning to Libya...

Thus, in Saloum, as in Chucha, trying to reach Europe becomes a genuine option, despite the risks involved in the crossing: in 2011, more than 1,500 people died or disappeared[3] in the Mediterranean Sea, while it was under the intense surveillance of Frontex patrols and military ships under NATO command.

... and in Europe

Migrants' travels do not end on arrival in Europe. Abdul reached Calais after a five-year "voyage" through more than 10 countries[4]. His unfinished journey illustrates the consequences of tightening border controls, refoulement practices and the strategies invented by migrants to avoid these obstacles.

Abdul, who was an interpreter for an Italian NGO, was forced to flee Afghanistan after receiving threats from the Taliban. He walked for 48 hours through Iran to reach the Turkish border and paid 1,000 euros to cross the mountains separating the two countries. In Istanbul, he prepared for departure to Greece. "We crossed the sea on an inflatable dinghy. A young guy who had been deported from England to Afghanistan organized it. He already knew the route! Our boat was intercepted by the Greek coastguards, who took us to the Mitilini camp on the island of Lesbos. Life was very difficult there, there were 80 of us sleeping in one cell and everything was very dirty."

After 16 days, the police gave him an order to leave the country within one month. He decided to go to Patras to make his way to Italy. "I ran behind lorries to hide under them, between the wheels, to get onto a boat. One night, the *commando* [harbour police] found me and beat me violently. They took me to the Venna camp, near Komotiní. There were 30 of us to a cell, without air or light, and we were only allowed out for one hour every two or three days. The police told me that I would be detained for three months but I ended up staying for six months. Then they transferred us to another camp near Alex-andropolis and took us in a military truck to the Evros river. They made us get into

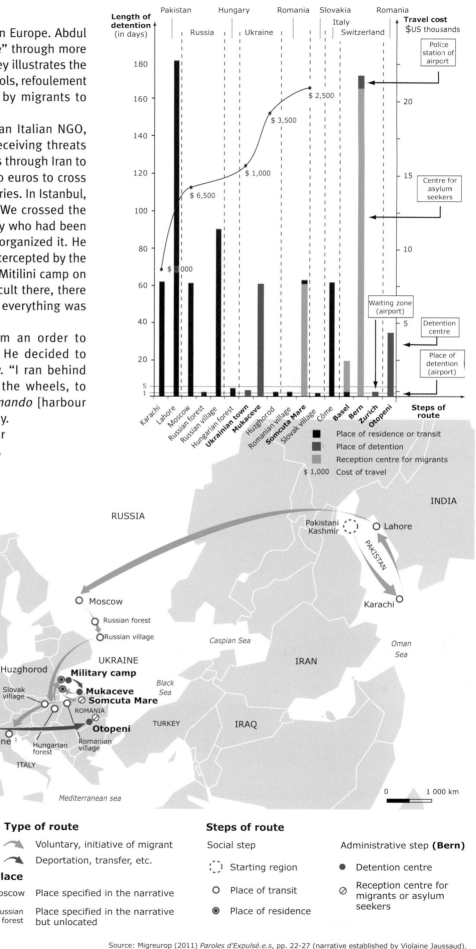

1. Length of presence unspecified in the narrative: the city is not mentioned in the chart.

Source: Migreurop (2011) *Paroles d'Expulsé.e.s*, pp. 22-27 (narrative established by Violaine Jaussaud).

The burden of detention on a Pakistani's route to Europe

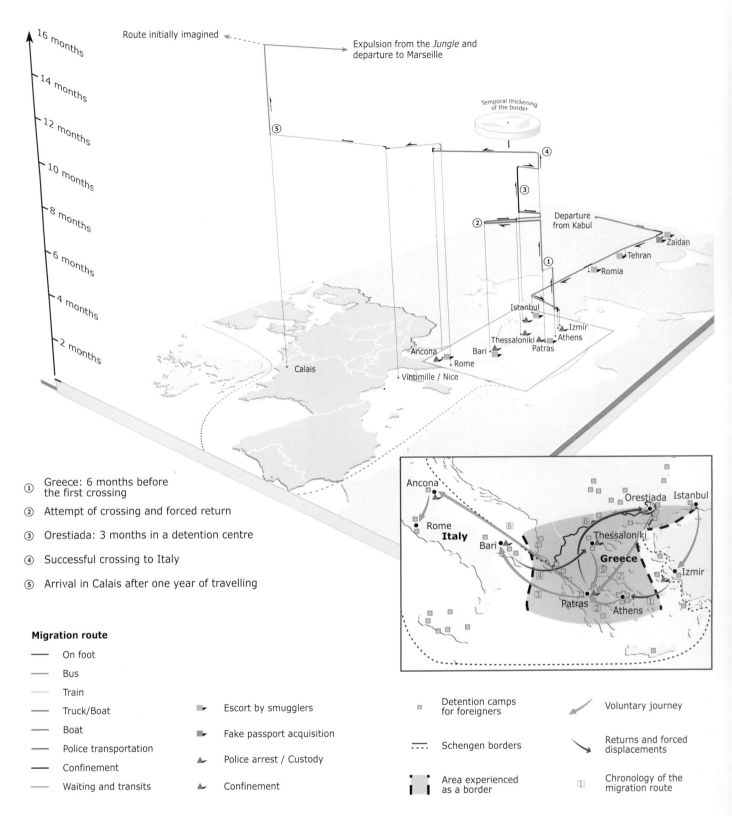

① Greece: 6 months before the first crossing

② Attempt of crossing and forced return

③ Orestiada: 3 months in a detention centre

④ Successful crossing to Italy

⑤ Arrival in Calais after one year of travelling

Migration route

—— On foot

—— Bus

—— Train

—— Truck/Boat

—— Boat

—— Police transportation

—— Confinement

—— Waiting and transits

▪► Escort by smugglers

▪► Fake passport acquisition

▲► Police arrest / Custody

▲► Confinement

▫ Detection camps for foreigners

···· Schengen borders

▨▌ Area experienced as a border

✎ Voluntary journey

↘ Returns and forced displacements

[1] Chronology of the migration route

"I tried to come by plane with a fake passport, but I failed because my face is not very suitable!" (Khan)

Three years ago, in Kabul, Khan started his journey to England. It lasted 16 months and cost more than 15,000 euros.

Mapping the migration route of Khan, including its temporal dimension, is an attempt to show that the borders of the European Union cannot be understood without focusing on experiences of those who face them.

For example, to cross the EU Greek border, Khan needs to travel a distance more temporal than spatial (steps 1,2,3,4). The crossing time causes a grey area to appear on the map. This is what we call the "temporal thickness" of the border.

Blocked for more than 10 months between Greece and Italy, he will be arrested numerous times, returned, displaced and confined.

During this period of transit, he lives outdoors or in improvised camps, near places that appear appropriate to cross. But these places get closed over and over again. Once in Ancona, Italy, his journey becomes relatively fluid until the next stumbling block of the trip, the Calais-UK border.

After three months of unsuccessful attempts to enter England, Khan is beaten by a group of police as he is about to return to the *Jungle* migrant camp. Hosted by an old woman until his recovery, he finally decides to make his application for asylum in France. The announcement of the evacuation of the *Jungle* in Calais at the end of September forces him back on the road: he goes to Marseille, where a new journey begins, a legal one, to obtain a right of residence.

Interview conducted by Emmanuelle Hellio, Marseille, February 2012.

From Kabul to Calais, the thickness of the European border as revealed by the route of an Afghan migrant

little boats, 20 people at a time, and pushed us towards the Turkish coast."

"In Turkey, we walked through a forest without knowing where we were going. We were cold and scared. We saw a house where we asked for something to eat. The owner said he could help us but that he would have to call the police, otherwise there would be problems. The Turkish army arrived... and took us to the Edirne camp. After 10 days, they said that they were going to deport us to Afghanistan but that we had to pay for our plane ticket. If we refused, they said they would deport us over the Iranian border. The Turkish police know very well that migrants are kidnapped and threatened there, demanding money from the migrants' families. Sometimes they cut off migrants' fingers or noses if the money doesn't arrive. So my family sent 500 dollars so that I would be deported."

As soon as he arrived back in Afghanistan, Abdul organized another departure to Europe, despite the traumas of detention, violence and deportation that had marked his previous journey. He decided to avoid the Turkish-Greek border zone and to pass through Bulgaria. "It was night-time. I was very scared; the Bulgarian border guards had dogs... I went back to Patras. The situation had changed. It was more difficult to travel under a

truck and the barbed-wire fences around the port were higher. We didn't have enough money to go that way so with two other people we decided to go through Macedonia and Serbia... We were arrested in Belgrade in a park. After 40 days in detention, I left for Hungary... I was arrested in a train on the way to Austria and I was held in a camp for 26 days. I was let out on the advice of a psychologist. I continued my journey to Italy and then to Calais. I'm trying to get to England but I know that I risk being sent back to Greece again, where they have my fingerprints."

Violaine CARRÈRE, Sara PRESTIANNI and Anne-Sophie WENDER ◐

1 Real names have not ben used. Interview conducted by Migreurop in March 2011.
2 Interviewed in Chucha in April 2012 (La Cimade / Forum tunisien pour les droits économiques et sociaux)
3 UNHCR, News Stories, 30/01/2012
4 Interviewed in Calais, in July 2009

Arrival phase, first eight months: house-hunting, trying to get papers, refusal of the application for asylum, appeal to the CDNA, learning French, help from associations and individuals.

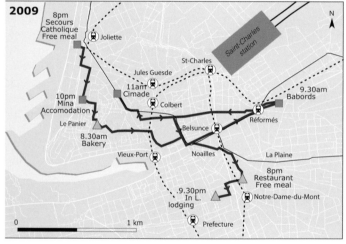

Stabilization phase, for the next 16 months: improving language, obtaining subsidiary protection, right to have a job, certificate of entitlement to social rights.

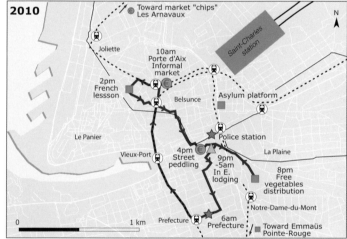

Settling phase: renting a flat, getting a contract of employment, family entry and settlement.

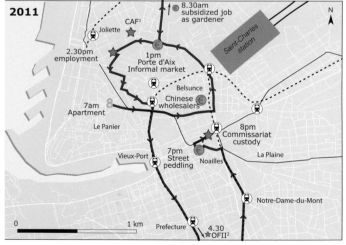

"Marseille belongs to Exile. This city will never be anything else, the world's last port of call. Its future belongs to those who arrive. Never to those who leave!"
(Jean-Claude Izzo (1996), Chourmo, Paris, Gallimard: p 102.)

🚇 Metro station   ----- Metro line   ——— Tramway line

Main places where Khan went

△ Help from individuals: meals, accommodation, administrative assistance

■ Community association places

★ Administrative / legal places

€ Day job and moonlighting places

8 Rented flat

➜ One-day urban route

Sources: Based upon an interview by E. Hellio, Marseille, February 2012.
Map data by *les contributeurs d'OpenStreetMap, CC BY-SA*.

1. French governmental agencies for family-supporting subsidies
2. French Office for Immigration and Integration

Khan's three periods in Marseille

In Africa, the EU disrupts migration that does not concern it

The externalization of European migration policies represented a fundamental change: in addition to preventing migrants from entering European Union (EU) territory and deporting migrants in an "irregular" situation, the EU signalled its will to contain populations within the borders of their own countries. A direct consequence of this policy is the disruption of intra-African migration. Applied in particular in north and northwest Africa – from Senegal to Libya, via Niger – the policy is both unfair and incoherent, in so far as the majority of migrants from sub-Saharan Africa head first to neighbouring countries: in 2007, 69% of migration in sub-Saharan Africa was South-South migration; in 2008, 86% of migration from West African countries was exclusively intra-regional. Furthermore, this policy is being developed in the context of increasingly complex migratory flows in the region, marked by the emergence of new transit countries (Mauritania) and receiving countries (Morocco, Algeria, Tunisia, Libya) and the conflict in the north of Mali. Regional migration is deeply affected by temporary – or circular – labour migration and by intensive trade.

The externalization of migration controls on the African continent was approved by the European Pact on Asylum and Immigration (2008), which promoted the concept of "global partnership with countries of origin and transit". While its rhetoric is based on the synergy between migration and development, the primary aim of this partnership is to make departure and transit countries in sub-Saharan Africa and North Africa operate as the EU's delocalized, mobile customs offices. To this end, such States, especially those on the coast, act as buffer states at the limits of Europe, multiplying obstacles to migration. This set-up is the fruit of the EU's mobilization of economic, political and commercial incentives, at the bilateral and multilateral level.

One of the characteristic features of permanent negotiations on migration between European and African States is the connection made over the last decade between public development aid and the "management of migration flows". Today, it is standard to integrate migration-related undertakings from States in the Global South into development aid agreements, thereby instrumentalizing such aid. Various benefits are added, in particular within the framework of the European Neighbourhood Policy (ENP): visa relaxation measures (limited in practice to élites who are already more mobile than ordinary citizens) and funding for development programmes aimed at ensuring that populations remain in their countries of origin, such as the Return to Agriculture Plan (REVA) in Senegal, funded by Spain. There are many different incentives, as some European leaders admit. In 2006, Franco Frattini, then European Commissioner responsible for Justice and Home Affairs (JHA), described as "carrots" the means employed by Europe in negotiations with third countries, aimed at persuading third countries to sign readmission agreements.

Any analysis would, however, be partial and incomplete if it were to clear African States of any responsibility in the repressive turn their policies have taken. Between complacency and political instrumentalization, these governments operate as frontline actors in the restrictions imposed on intra-African migration. In concrete terms, the widespread tightening of controls on migration has taken several forms: in addition to awareness-raising campaigns, we have seen increases in police and military co-operation on border surveillance, the construction of border stations and migrant detention centres (in Mauritania, Morocco, Algeria and Libya in particular), the adoption of repressive laws against irregular emigration, culminating in the creation, in Morocco, Tunisia and Algeria, of an unprecedented "offence of illegal emigration", and, above all, the incorporation of the restrictive, security-based laws in force in the EU into their national legislation.

Without strong safeguards, and in a climate of stigmatization or even xenophobia, migrants not only face legal insecurity (failure to respect their rights or the absence of any status) but also physical insecurity. Recurring episodes of arrest, detention and deportation – sometimes repeated from one country to another, often ending in no-man's land in the heart of the Sahara desert – are marked by degrading, humiliating and inhuman treatment, appalling conditions of detention and physical violence which may go as far as torture or rape, as for example in Libya.

Beyond the human rights violations indirectly caused by its actions, the EU in attempting to protect its borders contributes

São Tome and Príncipe

Comoros

The Community of Sahelo-Saharan States (CEN-SAD)

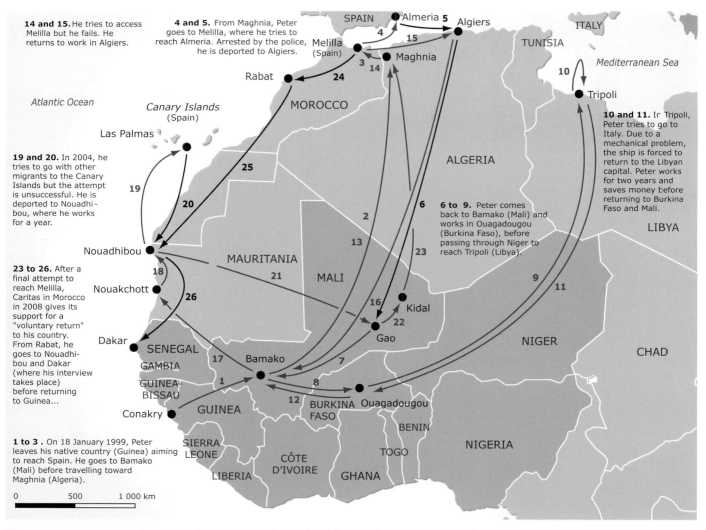

14 and 15. He tries to access Melilla but he fails. He returns to work in Algiers.

4 and 5. From Maghnia, Peter goes to Melilla, where he tries to reach Almeria. Arrested by the police, he is deported to Algiers.

19 and 20. In 2004, he tries to go with other migrants to the Canary Islands but the attempt is unsuccessful. He is deported to Nouadhibou, where he works for a year.

23 to 26. After a final attempt to reach Melilla, Caritas in Morocco in 2008 gives its support for a "voluntary return" to his country. From Rabat, he goes to Nouadhibou and Dakar (where his interview takes place) before returning to Guinea…

1 to 3. On 18 January 1999, Peter leaves his native country (Guinea) aiming to reach Spain. He goes to Bamako (Mali) before travelling toward Maghnia (Algeria).

6 to 9. Peter comes back to Bamako (Mali) and works in Ouagadougou (Burkina Faso), before passing through Niger to reach Tripoli (Libya).

10 and 11. In Tripoli, Peter tries to go to Italy. Due to a mechanical problem, the ship is forced to return to the Libyan capital. Peter works for two years and saves money before returning to Burkina Faso and Mali.

Migratory movements between ECOWAS and North Africa are increasingly difficult

to the destabilization of the migratory system of a whole region, and thus its political, cultural and socio-economic balance. This is particularly the case in the Economic Community of West African States (ECOWAS), composed of 15 sub-Saharan States. Created in 1975 to reinforce regional co-operation and integration, ECOWAS is based on a fundamental principle, the freedom of movement, which is today badly affected by pressure from Europe. The same applies to the Community of Sahelo-Saharan States (CEN-SAD). Similarly, securing borders

raises questions within the West African context, where the issue of refugees scattered throughout the region has not been solved. For example, for refugees from Côte d'Ivoire, return is a slow and complex process, further hindered by the closure of borders. In a context of continuing internal conflicts in several countries of the region, it is equally important to question the potential humanitarian impact of such policies.

Nicolas PERNET

131

Three to four million Afghan exiles held hostage by international power relations

How many Afghan exiles will remain in Pakistan and Iran in several months' time? With the upcoming withdrawal of NATO forces from Afghanistan, scheduled for 2014, the question of the repatriation of these refugees is being raised urgently by the Pakistani and Iranian governments. There are between four and five million Afghans currently residing there: 2.7 million refugees in a regular situation (1.7 million in Pakistan and 1 million in Iran) and hundreds of thousands of others without residence permits (approximately 1 million in Pakistan and between 700,000 and 1 million in Iran). For Afghanistan, with a population of 33 million, the stakes are high, in economic and security terms.

It is not the first time that the authorities of Islamabad and Tehran have threatened to deport the citizens of their common neighbour, whom they have hosted or tolerated for over 30 years. Over five million Afghans have already returned to their country of origin: the first wave of returns took place following the retreat of the Soviet Union in 1989, the second after the fall of the Taliban regime in 2011. Until now, such threats have not had significant consequences, although for the past three years Iran has been deporting 50,000 Afghans each month, following police sweep operations.

Over a 30-year period, Afghans who have remained in exile in Pakistan and Iran have made a place for themselves, often

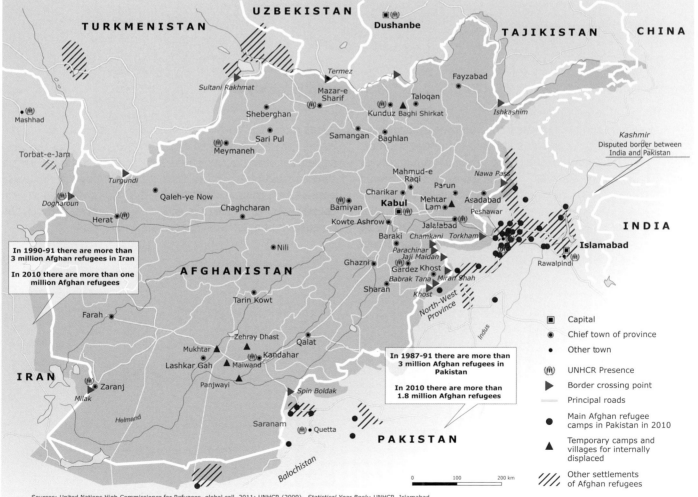

Sources: United Nations High Commissioner for Refugees, global call, 2011; UNHCR (2009), *Statistical Year Book*; UNHCR, Islamabad, Census of Afghans in Pakistan, Top 35 Camps by Province of Residence, February-March 2005.

The majority of Afghans took refuge close to home

living in precarious conditions. Nearly half of them were born there. The prospect of going (back) to Afghanistan raises as many political calculations as economic imperatives. Almost 40% of those repatriated since the fall of the Taliban have been unable to carve out a place for themselves and Islamist fighters take advantage of their misery, recruiting them for paid employment, much to the concern of the West.

In Pakistan: bargaining chips in negotiations with the United States

In Pakistan, the unpopularity of US policy continues to grow. According to surveys, three-quarters of the population can no longer bear the brutal military operations carried out by the United States in Pakistani territory (including targeted drone and missile attacks launched from Afghanistan and the assassination of Osama bin Laden in Abbottabad, in May 2011). In this context, the announcement of the imminent deportation of Afghans and the non-renewal of residence permits presents at least two advantages for the government: it sends a sign to those Pakistanis who consider the Afghans responsible for the rise in terrorism,

while encouraging Washington to provide economic aid in exchange for a continued Afghan presence.

In fact, the 400,000 Afghans from the Khyber Agency, at the border with Afghanistan, who were supposed to be the first to be sent back at the end of June 2012, are still there. Are we to believe this to be a coincidence? On 3 July 2012, Hillary Clinton, then US Secretary of State, announced $1.1 billion of funding for the Pakistani army, in addition to a monthly payment of $100 million for the resumption of transit of NATO military equipment from the port of Lahore to Afghanistan.

It was the same story in 2009, when Afghan exiles in Pakistan had become undesirable. Barack Obama provided $150 million for them to remain, to which the United Nations Office of the High Commissioner for Refugees (UNHCR) added a further $8 million. The extension of permission for Afghan exiles to remain in Pakistan was set to expire at the end of 2012. It should thus soon become clear whether the return of some of these people is part of the newly concluded deal between the two States. This seems probable, despite the parliamentary elections in Pakistan at the beginning of 2013, which saw the ousting of the party in power – the Pakistan People's Party (PPP).

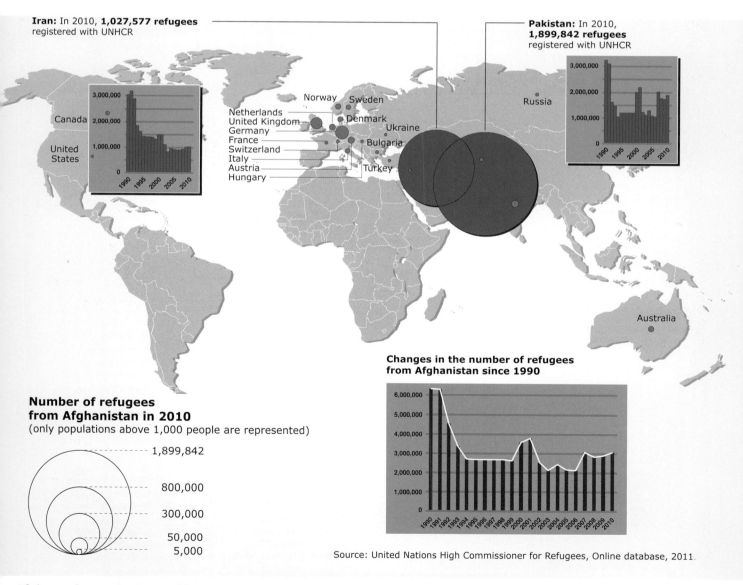

Iran: In 2010, **1,027,577 refugees** registered with UNHCR

Pakistan: In 2010, **1,899,842 refugees** registered with UNHCR

Number of refugees from Afghanistan in 2010
(only populations above 1,000 people are represented)

- 1,899,842
- 800,000
- 300,000
- 50,000
- 5,000

Changes in the number of refugees from Afghanistan since 1990

Source: United Nations High Commissioner for Refugees, Online database, 2011.

Afghan refugees in the world

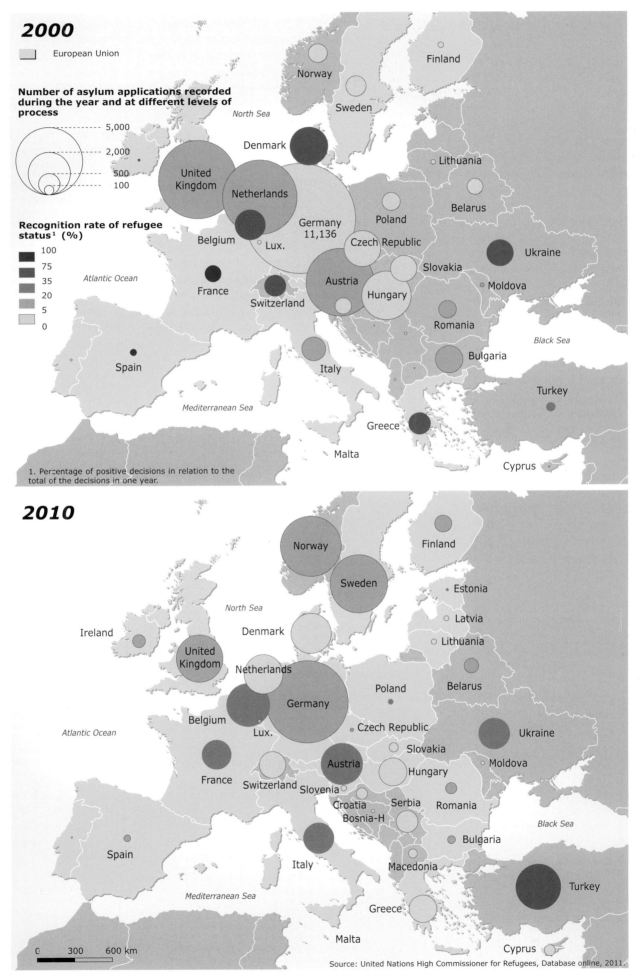

2000

European Union

Number of asylum applications recorded during the year and at different levels of process

- 5,000
- 2,000
- 500
- 100

Recognition rate of refugee status[1] (%)

- 100
- 75
- 35
- 20
- 5
- 0

North Sea

Norway
Finland
Sweden

Denmark
Lithuania
Belarus

United Kingdom
Netherlands
Poland

Belgium
Germany 11,136
Czech Republic
Ukraine

Lux.
Slovakia
Moldova

Atlantic Ocean

France
Austria
Hungary

Switzerland
Romania

Spain
Italy
Bulgaria

Black Sea

Turkey

Mediterranean Sea

Greece

Malta
Cyprus

1. Percentage of positive decisions in relation to the total of the decisions in one year.

2010

Norway
Finland

Sweden
Estonia

North Sea

Denmark
Latvia

Ireland
Lithuania

United Kingdom
Belarus

Netherlands
Poland

Belgium
Germany
Czech Republic
Ukraine

Lux.
Slovakia
Moldova

Atlantic Ocean

France
Austria
Hungary

Switzerland
Slovenia
Serbia
Romania

Croatia
Bosnia-H

Spain
Italy
Bulgaria

Black Sea

Macedonia
Turkey

Mediterranean Sea

Greece

Malta
Cyprus

0   300   600 km

Source: United Nations High Commissioner for Refugees, Database online, 2011.

Since 2001, the European Union has been less open to receiving Afghans

In Iran: a tool of influence, half carrot, half stick

"If President Karzai signs the strategic partnership agreement with Washington, Iran will deport all Afghan refugees," the new Iranian Ambassador in Kabul announced on 8 May 2012. The threat did not stop the Afghan parliament approving the agreement, raising the country to the rank of United States "Ally Special Security Status", with a view to the upcoming withdrawal of NATO troops.

Iran quickly reacted with retaliatory measures, at the same time as a discussion on the regularization of some undocumented Afghans was launched. The Iranian police continues to deport tens of thousands each month, while new arrivals and returns fill the gaps left by these forced departures. In several regions, local authorities have ordered shopkeepers and artisans to establish the residence status of "foreign nationals" (a synonym for Afghan immigrants) before concluding a sale. There were serious racist attacks in June 2012 in the province of Yadz, where such incidents are not uncommon. However, in Kabul, people firmly believe in the imminent adoption of an Iranian regularization programme, presented as potentially benefiting one million Afghans. The Iranian authorities say nothing about such a programme.

In Iran, xenophobic mood swings are regular and ambiguous. On the one hand, the economic crisis linked to Western sanctions – imposed because of the Iranian nuclear programme – provokes intolerance towards migrants. On the other hand, Afghans undertake many tough and badly paid jobs that Iranians do not want. In addition, most Afghan exiles in Iran belong to the Shia minority, Hazaras, and their disappearance would deprive Iran of one of its only tools of influence in Afghanistan.

In these conditions, public hostility towards Afghans is aimed more at curbing arrivals than drastically reducing their presence, which would be impossible in practice and politically damaging.

At the UNHCR, ideological stubbornness over the "biggest mistake" in its existence

Despite public statements by the United Nations, the West and Afghanistan's neighbours that Afghan exiles should return to their country, each actor on the Afghan stage has its own reasons not to want such repatriation to take place:
- Afghanistan, where poverty and insecurity is among the highest in the world, already has at least 500,000 internally displaced persons and the integration of 5 million returnees

since the fall of the Taliban regime has been very problematic;
- Pakistan experiences friendly pressure from the West for a delay on deportations, combined with significant financial compensation;
- Iran, currently the least sensitive to external economic and strategic pressure in the area of migration policy, could one day give in to the desire to influence Europe, in the knowledge that any mass deportation of Afghan exiles would convince many of them – especially the young – to choose the route to the West;
- The West, in general, fears that mass returns would strengthen the Taliban and other Islamist fighters.

Everywhere, Afghan exiles are treated as bargaining chips, hostages to international diplomacy. Their fate will not be determined by concerns for their human rights.

The UNHCR is well aware of this and continues to meet the needs of these exiles, while going through the motions of encouraging them and supporting them to return to their country. For the last few years, its voluntary return programme has systematically failed and the *cri du cœur* of its representative in Kabul, Peter Nicolaus, who at the end of 2011 publicly called this policy "the biggest mistake the UNHCR ever made", has changed nothing.

What does it matter that the Afghans have voted "with their feet" against the UNHCR's claims? There were only 60,000 "voluntary" returns in 2011 from Iran and Pakistan and, as of 2011, Afghans still had first place among asylum seekers in industrialized countries, with 38,000 new applications.

In 2012, the UNHCR persisted in maintaining the myth of return at a spectacular conference held at the beginning of May in Geneva. In the presence of representatives from Pakistan and Iran, presented as the "pillars" of an innovative strategy, the UNHCR requested $1.9 billion to repatriate 2.7 million Afghans over three years, promising to improve their reception and integration conditions. No-one believes in the possibility that such a programme, which only repeats past errors, will succeed. Several days after the conference in Geneva, the UN Office for the Co-ordination of Humanitarian Affairs (OCHA) – the UNHCR's sibling organization – was unable to contain its astonishment in an article published by its press agency, the Integrated Regional Information Networks (IRIN)[1], which went as far as to ask this vital question: "Is the strategy [of the UNHCR] politicized?"

Of course, only political objectives can explain such a manifestly absurd plan. The UNHCR is funded to maintain an ideological vision of humanity: its *raison d' être* requires that, whatever the reasons for and the duration of their exile, displaced populations from the Global South go (back) to the parcel of land corresponding to their nationality, whatever it costs, even when – as is the case for more than two million Afghans – they were not born there.

Jean-Pierre ALAUX

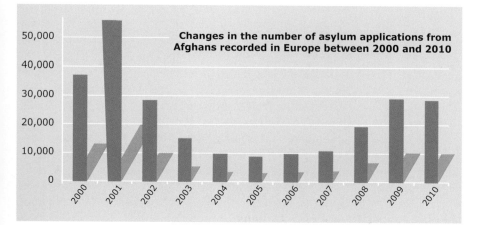

Changes in the number of asylum applications from Afghans recorded in Europe between 2000 and 2010

---

1   In the article, "Briefing: The right way forward for Afghan refugees?", 7 May 2012, IrinNews asks, for example, "Is it the right time to encourage returns to Afghanistan?" and *"Will return really be voluntary?"*

International conventions called into question?

Non-exhaustive statistics on migrant deaths at borders highlight the fact that many women and men pay with their lives for travelling in search of a better or safer future. Yet a number of international conventions on refugee and maritime law impose on States an obligation to grant such people protection.

Which are the relevant international conventions and what principles do they contain?

First, there are rules governing the movement of ships at sea. Their application depends on whether the ship is in the territorial waters of a coastal State, its contiguous zone, its exclusive economic zone (EEZ) or the high seas.

According to the United Nations Convention on the Law of the Sea adopted in 1982 in Montego Bay (Jamaica), which entered into force in 1994, all ships enjoy a right of "innocent passage" through the territorial sea of a coastal State "so long as it is not prejudicial to the peace, good order or security of the coastal State" (Article 19 of the Convention, based on customary law). However, it also provides that the "loading" or "unloading" of any person in such zone, in violation of the law applicable in the coastal State, shall be deemed to constitute such an infringement. In such circumstances the coastal State can exercise its enforcement powers, but only if the infringement affects its territory, for example if migrants attempt to disembark there.

In the high seas, the principles of freedom of navigation and the jurisdiction of the flag State apply. In such areas, a ship flying the flag of another State may not exercise any power of restraint, without the authorization of the flag State, except if a suspected ship flies the flags of several States or is deemed without nationality (Article 110). These rules could therefore allow Member States of the European Union (EU) to control boats suspected of illegally transporting migrants. However, such control may only be exercised under limited circumstances and the applicable rules must be read and interpreted in the light of other international standards, in particular the duty to render assistance to any person found at sea in distress and the principle of non-refoulement of refugees and asylum seekers.

There are two international conventions that concern rescue at sea: the 1974 Convention for the Safety of Life at Sea and the 1979 Convention on Maritime Search and Rescue. The latter emphasizes, in particular, that any person found in danger at sea must be rescued, whatever his or her nationality and beyond any consideration relating to the management of migratory flows. International co-operation must be established for search and rescue operations, which may involve the conclusion of agreements between adjacent States. The same conventions provide that States rendering assistance must bring those rescued to a safe place.

In addition, there are rules on the protection of refugees and respecting human rights.

Article 33 of the 1951 Geneva Convention Relating to the Status of Refugees provides that no State Party shall expel or return a refugee in any manner whatsoever to a country where his life or freedom would be threatened. The prohibition on refoulement is also contained in Article 3 of the Convention against Torture and Other Cruel, Inhuman or Degrading Treatment or Punishment of 1984 and Article 7 of the International Covenant on Civil and Political Rights of 1966. Similarly, under Article 3 of the European Convention on Human Rights of 1950, the European Court of Human Rights considers not only that a State Party to the Convention must not subject anyone to cruel, inhuman or degrading treatment but also that it must not return anyone to a country where he or she might be exposed to the risk of such treatment (ECHR, *Soering v United Kingdom*, 7 July 1989).

Despite the clarity of these principles, a question remains: do these obligations bind EU Member States when they operate outside their territories, in the high seas or in the territorial waters of third countries, in particular through joint maritime patrols set up by Frontex? According to the Office of the UN High Commissioner for Refugees (UNHCR), the geographical application of the 1951 Geneva Convention is not limited and therefore applies in any area. The European Court of Human Rights has also underlined that the extra-territorial scope of this Convention must be taken into account when a State exercises its jurisdiction over a person outside of its borders (ECHR, *Issa v Turkey*, 16 November 2004; *Illascu v Moldavia and Russia*, 8 July 2004). The Court considers this to be a "dynamic interpretation" of human rights, to ensure that States are compelled to respect the standards laid down in international treaties, which they have undertaken to respect, beyond their borders. This principle of extra-territorial application of the Geneva Convention could be extended to the international conventions on rescue at sea. On 25 March 2010, the European Parliament adopted "guidelines" in plenary which provide that Member States must render assistance to any person found in danger at sea, whatever their nationality, status or the circumstances leading to their discovery. They also specify that during joint operations led by the Frontex Agency, the latter must take into consideration a potential request for assistance, the situation of the boat, and the possibility that children, pregnant women or persons requiring medical assistance are on board. These rules were recently invoked by Amnesty International in relation to the arrival of Tunisian migrants on the island of Lampedusa, following the fall of Ben Ali in February 2011. Amnesty called for the safety of persons intercepted at sea to be guaranteed and any requests for asylum to be considered.

Yet there are numerous examples of EU Member States failing to respect principles on sea rescue, the obligation to process an asylum application or the non-refoulement of people seeking protection. For example, on 21 June 2004, the *Cap Anamur*, a boat belonging to a German NGO of the same name, rendered assistance to 37 migrants who were on board a Zodiac boat between Malta and Italy. Access to Porto-Empedocle (Sicily) was refused to them at first on the grounds that the migrants had been rescued closer to the Maltese coast than to the Italian island of Lampedusa. Malta put forward a similar argument and Germany, the flag State, did not intervene. The boat remained in international waters until 11 July, when authorization to dock in Sicily was given. The migrants' crossing lasted a total of 22 days. The captain, the second-in-command and the president of the NGO were arrested for having "*promoted illegal immigration*" (Article 12 of the 2002 Bossi-Fini Law on immigration) and the boat was seized. The three were released five days later and banned from entering Italy. The migrants were transferred to detention centres in Agrigente and Ponte Galeria (Rome) where they applied for asylum; 22 of them had their applica

tions reviewed under an accelerated procedure and they were deemed "manifestly unfounded". Less than 15 days later, 25 of them were deported to Ghana – which Italy assumed to be their country of origin – despite the fact that the Court in Rome had yet to examine appeals against the decisions refusing asylum and that the European Court in Strasbourg, to which the cases had been referred under emergency provisions, had requested Italy to suspend all deportation measures pending the review of cases.

In July 2006, the same States re-offended, refusing to allow a Spanish trawler, the *Francisco Catalina*, to dock. The boat had rescued 51 Eritrean refugees, 100 nautical miles from the Libyan coast. Following a six-day odyssey, an agreement was reached between Spain, Andorra, Italy, Malta and... Libya. It provided that once the boat arrived in Malta, Spain and Andorra would accept 23 migrants, Malta 8, Italy 10 and Libya 10. Thus, European States agreed for 10 Eritrean nationals to be sent back to a regime which had consistently violated

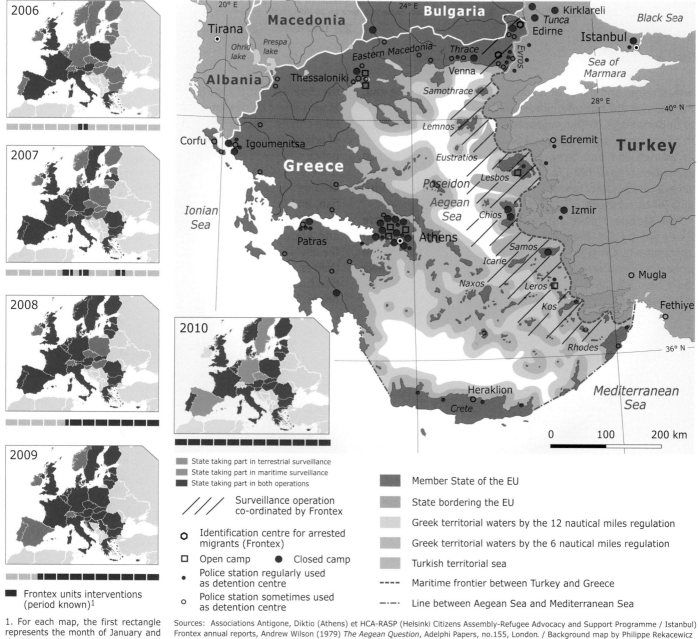

1. For each map, the first rectangle represents the month of January and the last one the month of December.

Sources: Associations Antigone, Diktio (Athens) et HCA-RASP (Helsinki Citizens Assembly-Refugee Advocacy and Support Programme / Istanbul) Frontex annual reports, Andrew Wilson (1979) *The Aegean Question*, Adelphi Papers, no.155, London. / Background map by Philippe Rekacewicz (1997) *Greek and Turkish claims in the Aegean Sea*, www.monde-diplomatique.fr/cartes/meregeemdv1997.

General mobilization against migration in the Aegean Sea

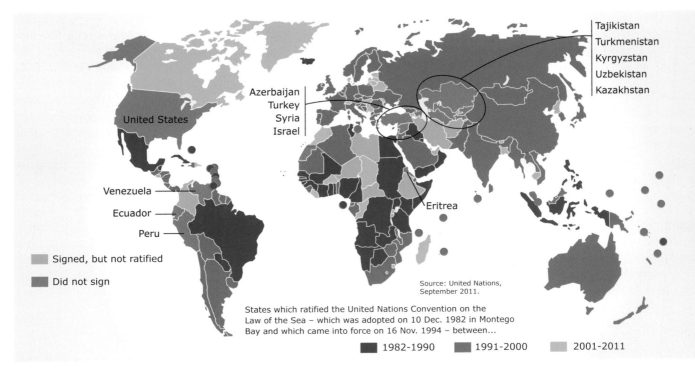

Tajikistan
Turkmenistan
Kyrgyzstan
Uzbekistan
Kazakhstan

Azerbaijan
Turkey
Syria
Israel

United States

Venezuela
Ecuador
Peru

Eritrea

Signed, but not ratified

Did not sign

Source: United Nations,
September 2011.

States which ratified the United Nations Convention on the
Law of the Sea – which was adopted on 10 Dec. 1982 in Montego
Bay and which came into force on 16 Nov. 1994 – between...

1982-1990   1991-2000   2001-2011

The Law of the Sea

human rights and those of migrants in particular. In the end, the transfer did not take place, as Libya refused to respect its undertakings. Other migrants have met a different fate: on 7 June 2010, 25 Eritrean and Somalian migrants, including six women and one baby, alerted the Maltese and Italian authorities of their need for assistance in the high seas. Their call was deliberately ignored, leaving Libya with the responsibility for their rescue.

The *Marine I* case further illustrates this deliberate disregard by EU Member States of their international commitments. On 31 January 2007, a boat carrying 369 people broke down in international waters off the coast of Mauritania and a Spanish maritime rescue ship, the *Luz del mar*, came to its assistance. However, it was not until 12 February that

the Spanish ship entered the port of Nouadhibou, after Mauritania had obtained an undertaking that Spain would take charge of repatriating all the migrants to their countries of origin. Between 12 and 14 February, more than 100 Spanish police officers came to identify the migrants and, in particular, to determine their nationality. Meanwhile the migrants were detained in former fishing huts, used for the preparation of fish, and no information was provided to them. Those 35 of them who had declared that they were from Burma, Sri Lanka and Afghanistan were transferred to the Canary Islands to file asylum applications. Nine Sri Lankan asylum seekers had their applications denied – despite a favourable recommendation from the UNHCR – and were sent back to their country of origin. Meanwhile, 35 nationals from several African countries

Source: United Nations, 2012.

States party to the Protocol against the Smuggling of Migrants by Land, Sea and Air, supplementing the United Nations Convention
against Transnational Organized Crime – adopted by the United Nations on 15 November 2000 and which came into force on
28 January 2004 – between...

2001-2003   2004-2006   2007-2009   2010-2012   Did not sign   Signed, but not ratified

Many states are inclined to fight transnational crime...

(such as Liberia and Sierra Leone) were sent back to Guinea-Conakry after transiting through Cape Verde. During their "stay" in the archipelago, they were detained without notification of any administrative or judicial decision. All but 23

of the other passengers on *Marine I*, who were of Indian and Pakistani origin, finally agreed to "voluntary repatriation", which took place on 27 and 28 March.

Claudia CHARLES ▣

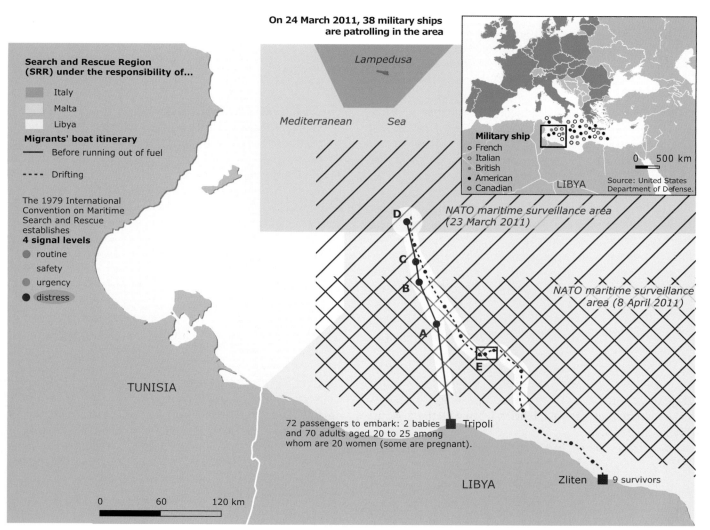

On 24 March 2011, 38 military ships are patrolling in the area

Search and Rescue Region (SRR) under the responsibility of...
- Italy
- Malta
- Libya

Migrants' boat itinerary
—— Before running out of fuel
- - - - Drifting

The 1979 International Convention on Maritime Search and Rescue establishes **4 signal levels**
- routine
- safety
- urgency
- distress

Lampedusa

Mediterranean   Sea

Military ship
- French
- Italian
- British
- American
- Canadian

0   500 km

Source: United States Department of Defense.

LIBYA

NATO maritime surveillance area (23 March 2011)

D
C
B
A
E

NATO maritime surveillance area (8 April 2011)

72 passengers to embark: 2 babies and 70 adults aged 20 to 25 among whom are 20 women (some are pregnant). ■ Tripoli

TUNISIA

LIBYA

Zliten ■ 9 survivors

0   60   120 km

The migrants' boat leaves Tripoli's harbor between midnight and 2am (GMT) with 72 people aboard (47 Ethiopians, 7 Eritreans, 7 Nigerians, 6 Ghanaians and 5 Sudanese).

(A) At 2.55pm, a French aircraft flies over the boat and gives the Maritime Rescue Co-ordination Centre in Rome their geographic position with the following co-ordinates: LAT 33°N – LONG 13°05'E (LAT = latitude; LONG= longitude).

(B) After heading for Lampedusa for 15 to 18 hours, the migrants send a distress signal via a satellite phone. The boat is located by GPS on 27 March 2011 at 4.52pm at LAT 33°58.2'N – LONG 12°55.8'E by satellite phone operator Thuraya. Shortly after this signal, the Italian coastguards transmit an Enhanced Group Call (EGC) locating the boat in distress and broadcast its geographic position. This message is broadcasted every four hours until 6 April 2011. The Maltese coastguards are directly informed by their Italian counterparts, as well as the NATO headquarters, which spreads the information to the ships under its command.

(C) The ship sails for about two hours before a military helicopter flies over it. After this meeting, the satellite phone is thrown overboard. The last signal detected

by the satellite operator is LAT 34°07.11'N – LONG 12°53.24'E on 27 March 2011 at 7.08pm. The boat stays approximately in the same area for 6 hours before a military helicopter appears above the boat and throws down water and biscuits, then leaves. The boat doesn't move much from the position corresponding to the last signal sent, and the migrants pass several fishing boats which don't assist them. So they take the decision to carry on their route between midnight and 1am probably in a northerly direction for Lampedusa for 5 to 8 hours, at an estimated average speed of 4.43 knots (average speed on water from Tripoli to point A).

(D) On 28 March around 7am, the boat runs out of fuel and starts drifting within an 8 nautical miles radius (indicated by a white shading) from position LAT 34°24.79'N – LONG 12°48.58'E.

(E) The boat is drifting (the estimated drifting of the boat was strongly due to southeast prevailing winds) and the migrants cross a military ship which doesn't assist them.

On 10 April 2011, the boat washes up in Zilten once again. At that time, 11 migrants are still alive. Two of them were to die shortly after. ▭

A group of associations (ARCI, Boats 4 People, Ciré, FIDH, GISTI, LDH, Migreurop, Progress Lawyers Network, REMDH) have since registered a complaint against the French army.

The United States and France launch their operations, respectively "Odyssey Dawn" and "Harmattan".

Canada sets up the "Mobile" operation.

NATO takes full command of the military operations.

NATO brings help to shipwrecked migrants. EU refuses them.

End of NATO military operation.

February	March	April	May	June	July	August	September	October
26	17 19 31				11			20

The United Nations put a weapons embargo on Libya (UN Security Council Resolution 1970).

The civil war shaking Libya provokes the first massive exodus towards Tunisia and Egypt.

The United Nations decides to establish a ban on all flights in the airspace of Libya and allows the Member States to intervene with the aim of protecting the civilian population (UN Security Council Resolution 1973).

Nearly 346,000 foreigners have fled Libya at war (source: OIM).

The UN Refugee Agency (UNHCR) estimates that 2,000 people have drowned in the Mediterranean Sea in the past five months.

Death of Libyan dictator Qadafi.

Nearly 764,150 foreigners have fled Libya at war.

Source: Report on the "Left-To-Die Boat" by Charles Heller, Lorenzo Pezzani and Situ Studio, Part of the European Research Council project "Forensic Architecture" Centre for Research Architecture, Goldsmiths, University of London. www.forensic-architecture.org.

...but do not care to rescue. Drifting to hell under the eyes of the military (March-April 2011)

Counting migrant deaths

hy should one embark upon a macabre accounting exercise, by trying, in the absence of official data, to gather together figures that NGOs have difficulty collecting? Because it is vital to throw light on a situation which is too often considered either inevitable or trivial.

There is no official data concerning the number of migrant deaths at European borders, but according to the NGOs which attempt to document this phenomenon, the number rose from dozens at the beginning of the 1990s, to hundreds or even thousands per year at the outset of the 2000s. Of course, such calculations are partial: first, because the attention given to this issue by organizations that protect the rights of migrants significantly increased over the same period. Likewise, media coverage of "migration dramas" has intensified: there have been countless reports and documentaries on this issue over the last few years. It can thus be considered that, as much as a true increase in numbers of deaths, the development of (admittedly

imperfect) measuring tools, combined with the magnifying effects of the media, have contributed to the explosion of these figures. On the other hand, several factors have an opposite effect, including the invisibility of a likely significant but unknown proportion of deaths along migratory routes, in particular deaths at sea or in the middle of the desert[1], and the intentional concealment of certain deadly episodes in the "war on migrants" by police or political authorities. The authorities also know how to manipulate dramatic events in order to justify tightening controls. In such a scientifically unreliable context, why try to count migrant deaths? Because the victims of this war are today an inseparable part of the migration policy implemented by Europe at its borders and beyond. And because the lack of reliable data is itself a shocking reflection of a reality which must be confronted.

The organization United was the first to gather data on these deadly risks of migration. On its site there are no aisles

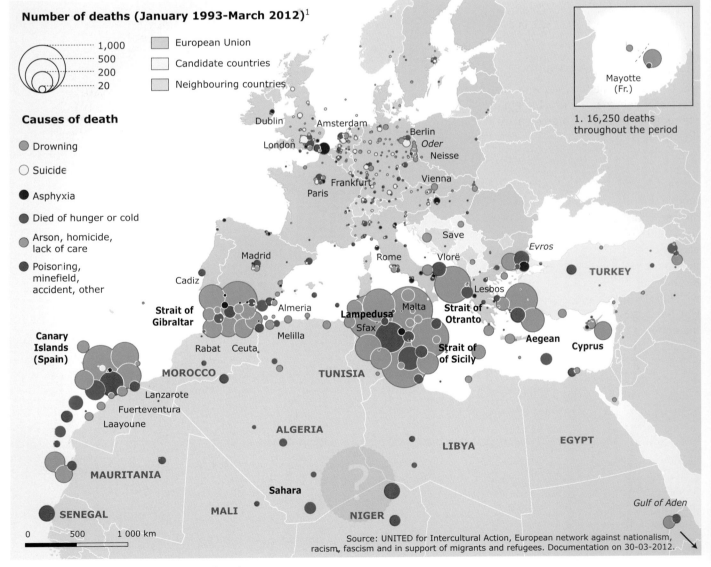

Number of deaths (January 1993-March 2012)[1]

1,000
500
200
20

European Union
Candidate countries
Neighbouring countries

Causes of death

Drowning
Suicide
Asphyxia
Died of hunger or cold
Arson, homicide, lack of care
Poisoning, minefield, accident, other

1. 16,250 deaths throughout the period

Mayotte (Fr.)

Dublin
Amsterdam
London
Berlin
Oder
Neisse
Frankfurt
Vienna
Paris
Save
Rome
Vlorë
Evros
Madrid
TURKEY
Lesbos
Cadiz
Almeria
Malta
Strait of Gibraltar
Lampedusa
Strait of Otranto
Sfax
Aegean
Cyprus
Melilla
Canary Islands (Spain)
Rabat Ceuta
Strait of of Sicily
Lanzarote
MOROCCO
TUNISIA
Fuerteventura
Laayoune
ALGERIA
LIBYA
EGYPT
MAURITANIA
Sahara
Gulf of Aden
SENEGAL
MALI
NIGER

0   500   1 000 km

Source: UNITED for Intercultural Action, European network against nationalism, racism, fascism and in support of migrants and refugees. Documentation on 30-03-2012.

Deaths per thousand on Europe's borders

or commemorative stones marking this silent slaughter, only rows and columns of numbers... The organization estimates the number of deaths over a 20-year period (1993-2012) to be more than 16,000. In relation to those who have drowned, for example, the calculation is based on the number of bodies found on beaches and estimates made by survivors. But the majority of accidents happen far out at sea.

In just the first semester of 2011, the UNCHR registered nearly 1,500 deaths off the shores of Malta, Libya, Tunisia and Sicily. Yet, during this period, the area was under intensive surveillance by Frontex patrols and ships operating under NATO command. In March 2011, 63 migrants fleeing Libya died while their vessel drifted at sea, despite a French military plane flying over them and alerts sent every 4 hours for 10 days. When the boat washed up on the Libyan coast, there were only 11 survivors, two of whom died soon after (see the map on page 139 "Drifting to hell under the eyes of the military"). Since the criminal prosecution launched against Tunisian fisherfolk in 2007, seafarers often prefer to change their route when they come across migrant vessels in distress, rather than rendering assistance to those on board.

Migreurop considers that, "these deaths without name or number say a lot about the process of dehumanization of migrants, who are reduced to surplus individuals who can disappear without trace"[2]. This conclusion was confirmed by the UNHCR spokesperson in Rome: "There are areas in the Mediterranean which are becoming lawless zones, where human life has no value"[3]. As evidence, to date no charges have been brought against the agents of the Royal Moroccan Marines accused by three boat people of causing their inflatable vessel to sink in the high seas, at dawn on 28 April 2008, by puncturing it with knives. The nine-metre-long *Zodiac* was was heading for Spain and carrying approximately 80 passengers from Nigeria, Ghana, Cameroon and Mali, 36 of whom drowned.

The "green border" separating Ukraine and Poland through forestland, is another deadly axis across which thousands of people transit every year, in particular those who, having fled conflict, as in Chechnya, seek protection in Europe. In September 2007, the deaths of three Chechen girls who were lost in the Polish mountains after illegally crossing the border in an attempt to reach Slovakia[4], drew the attention of European public opinion to a reality that Poland's EU membership in 2004 did nothing to change: not only has the strengthening of border controls failed to curb irregular immigration flows, but it

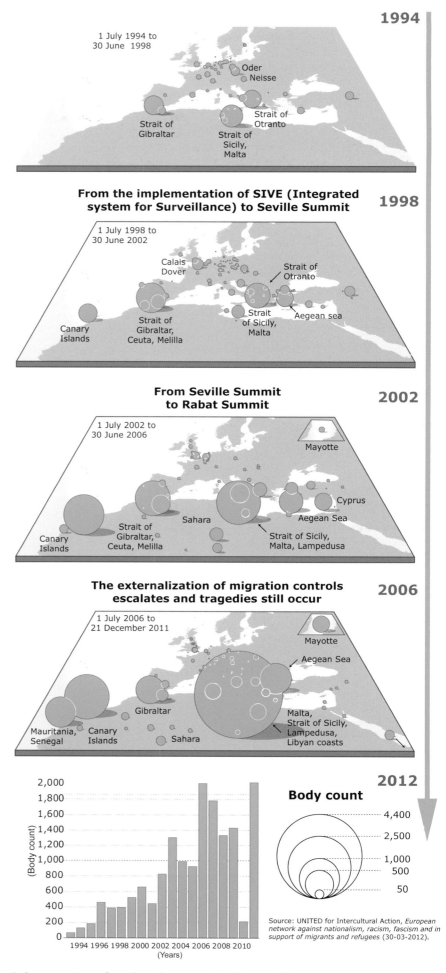

Source: UNITED for Intercultural Action, *European network against nationalism, racism, fascism and in support of migrants and refugees* (30-03-2012).

Schengen Area frontiers become terrible realities

has also multiplied the risks, for which there are, however, no precise records. The atlas of deaths at the borders, victims of restrictive migration policies, should include several chapters for which documentation remains sparse and incomplete: from the Mexico-United-States border to the Australian territorial waters, from the Gulf of Aden to the northern borders of South Africa and the relics of former colonial empires (in the Caribbean, for example), there are numerous frontlines where thousands of migrants fall each year, sometimes killed directly by border guards, but most often locked out of safe routes and forced to confront the "elements", which become guarantors of the house arrest of the poorest people.

Bearing this in mind, one could question why activists, associations and researchers seem to be obsessed with numbers, throwing about figures that are as imprecise as they are inconsistent. These mathematical illustrations are certainly a means of provoking the interest of journalists and other communication practitioners, whose expectations must be taken into account to have a chance of being heard. More fundamentally, it would seem that estimating the number of persons who have died while trying to reach Europe at several tens of thousands over 10 years, reveals a reality known to all historians and demographers: the difficulty of counting victims is inherent in situations of serious crisis or war and estimates are inevitably subject to debate and political manipulation. Even when they are imprecise, figures make a situation easier to grasp. The war on migrants passes from the domain of metaphors to a concrete reality, the consequences of which must be documented. The impossible census is ancillary to necessary exposure and analysis. It is also a question of moral imperative and of homage to the victims. To restore the personal nature of their journeys and their motives would of course be the best response to policies that aim to deny individual rights, but this is a limited exercise. Thus it becomes necessary to find other means of revealing the stories behind these often deadly journeys. Adding up the numbers of lives sacrificed on the altar of "migratory risk" is another means of giving an existence to these deaths without name.

Emmanuel BLANCHARD, Olivier CLOCHARD and Claire RODIER[5] ▣

1 In the middle of the Sahara, at the border between Mali and Algeria, the "village of migrants" of Tinzaouatine, a sort of no-man's land where those who have been deported from Algeria and those who are preparing to embark on the adventure for the first time gather, has a cemetery with anonymous graves of the victims of migration.

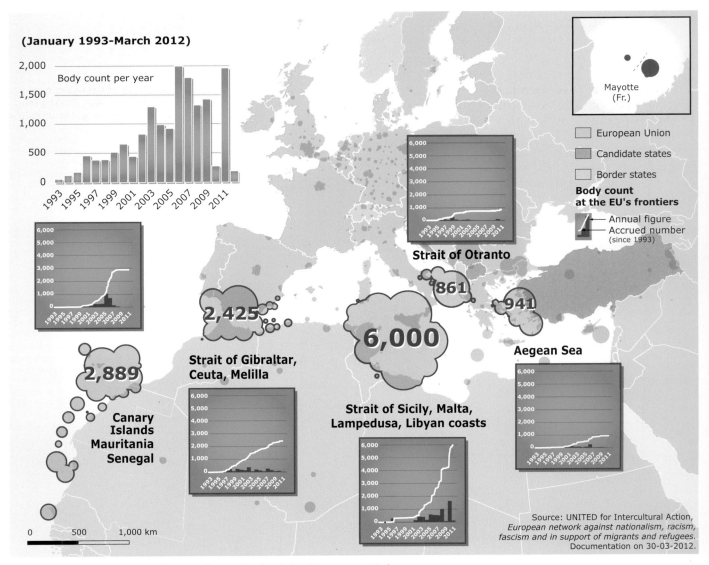

Dangerous crossings on the southern flank of the European Union

Source: UNITED for Intercultural Action, *European network against nationalism, racism, fascism and in support of migrants and refugees.* Documentation on 30-03-2012.

2 Emmanuel Blanchard and Anne-Sophie Wender (2007), *War on migrants: the black book of Ceuta and Melilla* (in French), (*Guerre aux migrants, le livre noir de Ceuta et Melilla*), ed. Syllepse.
3 UNHCR, *Migration of boat people to Europe*, 9 October 2007.
4 Cécile Chauffour, "Poland shaken by the death of three Chechen irregular immigrant girls", ("La mort de trois fillettes tchétchènes, immigrées clandestines, bouleverse la Pologne"), *Le Monde*, 19 September 2007.
5 This article is an updated summary of an article published in 2008 in the journal *Plein Droit*, No.76, entitled "Counting deaths"("Compter les morts"), www.gisti.or

ABUSES RESULTING FROM LEGALIZED VIOLENCE

Since the beginning of the 2000s, Europe has been waging a merciless fight against foreigners considered to be "undesirable". Security-based fantasies have little by little legitimized the closure of borders and violence against undocumented migrants, committed with impunity. Violence against asylum seekers, immigrants and their supporters has been trivialized to the point of becoming a genuine European tool for the "management of migratory flows".

Ill-treatment inflicted on departing migrants by security forces has been documented in numerous reports published by various organizations, which in the course of one year (2008) recorded almost 300 allegations of assault, resulting in injuries including punctured lungs, dislocated knees and the obstruction of respiratory passages[1]. Since 1991, the Institute of Race Relations (IRR) has registered 14 deaths of migrants by suffocation or cardiac arrest during deportation procedures[2]. More broadly, according to the Institute, the policy of forced return (deportation and detention) caused the deaths of 38 migrants on European territory, between January 2009 and June 2010[3].

Many of these deaths can be directly attributed to "security" forces using ill-adapted, dangerous, or even illegal methods. For example, some agents responsible for escorting migrants – from one detention centre to another, or from a centre onto a plane – regularly use offensive language or even racist insults as well as unjustified and excessive physical force. Deportation procedures are scenes of almost institutionalized brutality. Several EU countries have thus fine-tuned various methods of coercion which can be used during forced returns: shoulder, arm or leg- wrenches, knee in the back of the neck, use of handcuffs (even when a person is lying on the ground), attaching wrists and ankles while boarding a plane...

These forms of ill-treatment, symptoms of the normalization of violence inflicted on migrants, also reveal the ongoing privatization of forced return procedures. The implementation of such measures is often contracted out to private companies over which States choose to exert limited control. But sub-contracting this illegitimate violence in no way relieves States of their international obligations. European States remain fully responsible for such human rights violations.

In reality, despite reports of inhuman and degrading treatment suffered by migrants during deportation processes, despite the deaths, such practices continue and criminal sanctions for perpetrators are exceptional. It is as if, within the framework of the European fight against illegal immigration, the death of a migrant is just an unfortunate malfunction of the deportation machine...

Brigitte ESPUCHE ○

1 "Outsourcing Abuse – The use and misuse of state-sanctioned force during the detention and removal of asylum seekers", Birnberg Peirce & Partners, Medical Justice and the National Coalition of Anti-Deportation Campaigns, July 2008.
2 "Full list of deaths during deportations from Europe", Institute of Race Relations European News Team, October 2010.
3 "Accelerated removals: a study of the human cost of EU deportation policies", Institute of Race Relations, 2009-2010.

Migrants waiting in Calais, France, August 2010
Photo: Sara Prestianni

Maps

Part 4
Impact on departure and transit areas

Authors

Michel Agier (p.16) anthropologist, Ird, Ehess (France)

Peio Aierbe (p.82 et 118) editor, Mugak-Sos Racismo (Spain), Migreurop

Jean-Pierre Alaux (p.132), Research Officer, Gisti, Collectif des exilés (Paris)

Chloé Altwegg Boussac (p.20) lawyer

Carlos Arce (p.118) lawyer, Apdha (Spain), Migreurop.

Françoise Bahoken (p.56 & 120) cartographer, IFSTTAR (France)

Sophie Baylac (p.82) lawyer, Doctors of the world, Migreurop

Emmanuel Blanchard (p.140) teacher-researcher, Gisti (France), Migreurop

Pauline Brücker (p.22) political scientist, Iddri - Sciences Po (France)

Alessandra Capodanno (p.116) Arci (Italy), Migreurop

Sara Casella Colombeau (p.44 & 52) politist, Cee-Sciences Po (France), Migreurop

Violaine Carrère (p.126) Research Officer, Gisti (France), Migreurop

Pascaline Chappart (p.95 & 103) sociologist, Migrinter, cnrs, Gisti (France)

Claudia Charles (p.95 & 136) lawyer, Gisti (France), Migreurop

Marie Charles (p.86) lawyer, League of Human Rights (Belgium), Migreurop

Olivier Clochard (p.44, 69 & 140) geographer, cnrs, Migrinter, University of Poitiers (France), Migreurop

Benoît De Boeck (p.107) lawyer, Ciré (Belgium), Migreurop

Marie Duflo, (p.73) secretary of Gisti Administrative Council and co-ordinator of Migrants Outre-mer (France)

Brigitte Espuche (p.143) lawyer, Anafé (France)

Agathe Etienne (p.80) Migreurop

Liz Fekete (p.91) director of Institute of Race Relations (London)

François Gemenne (p.22) politics specialist, Cedem – University of Liège (Belgium), Iddri - Sciences Po

Emmanuelle Hellio (p.29 et 120) sociologist, University of Nice, Urmis (France)

Thomas Honoré, cartographer, Pôle Carto et InCittà (Marseille, France)

Chris Jones (p.65) Statewatch (United Kingdom)

David Lagarde (p.80) cartographer, Migreurop

Nicolas Lambert, cartographer, Riate, cnrs (France)

Alexandre Le Clève (p.36 & 96) Migreurop

Régina Mantanika (p.114) anthropologist, Csprp (France, Greece)

Nicole Mayer, Migreurop

Bénédicte Michalon (p.48) geographer, Ades, cnrs (France)

Alain Morice (p.12 et 29) anthropologist, Urmis, cnrs (France), Migreurop

Paulina Nikiel (p.40 & 112) anthropologist, University Jagiellonski of Krakow (Poland), Migreurop

Konstantinos Papantoniou (p.114) lawyer in detention centre, La Cimade (France)

Antoine Pécoud (p.78) sociologist, Unesco

Nicolas Pernet (p.130) lawyer in detention centre, La Cimade (France)

Pierre-Arnaud Perrouty (p.86) lawyer, League of Human Rights (Belgium), Migreurop

Jerome Phelps (p.109) Detention Action (London)

Frédéric Piantoni (p.72) geographer, University of Reims Champagne-Ardenne (France)

Julie Pierson (p.36) cartographer, Ades, cnrs (France)

Laurence Pillant (p.108) geographer, Telemme, Université d'Aix-Marseille (France)

Sara Prestianni (p.126) photographer, Migreurop

Hicham Rachidi (p.122) lawyer, Gadem (Morocco)

Claire Rodier (p.56, 69, 104 & 140) lawyer, Gisti (France), Migreurop

Gérard Sadik (p.61) national co-ordinator of asylum commission, La Cimade (France)

Isabelle Saint-Saëns, Migreurop

Lola Schulmann (p.36 & 95), Migreurop

Daniel Senovilla Hernández (p.26), lawyer, Migrinter, University of Poitiers (France).

Louise Tassin (p.80) sociologist, Urmis (France), Migreurop.

Elisabeth Vallet (p.24) Associate professor in the Department of Geography, UQAM, Montréal

Anne-Sophie Wender (p.126) co-ordinator, Pôle des solidarités internationales, La Cimade (Morocco)

Migrant camp near abandoned wagons in Patras,
Greece, January 2011.
Photo: Gabriel Pécot